TX
823
.Y68
1993

Young, Kay,
  1931-

Wild seasons.

$40.00

DATE			
7/94			

Wild Seasons

Kay Young

Wild Seasons

Gathering
and Cooking
Wild Plants of
the Great Plains

Illustrated by

Mark E. Marcuson

University of Nebraska Press
Lincoln and London

© 1993 by the University
of Nebraska Press
All rights reserved
Manufactured in the
United States of America
The paper in this
book meets the minimum
requirements
of American National
Standard for
Information Sciences –
Permanence of
Paper for Printed Library
Materials,
ANSI Z39.48-1984.
Library of
Congress Cataloging-
in-Publication
Data. Young, Kay, 1931–
Wild Seasons:
gathering and cooking
wild plants of
the Great Plains / Kay
Young; illustrated
by Mark E. Marcuson.
p.   cm. Includes
bibliographical refer-
ences and index.
ISBN 0-8032-4906-3
(alk. paper)
ISBN 0-8032-9904-4
(pbk.)
1. Cookery (Wild foods)
2. Wild plants,
Edible—Great Plains.
I. Title.
TX823.Y68   1993
641.6—dc20
92-39105   CIP

For the generation of grandchildren

Contents

Acknowledgments ix
Introduction xi
Glossary of Botanical Terms xvii
Glossary of Cooking Terms xxiii
Watercress 1
Stinging Nettles 6
Wood Nettles 13
Dandelions 16
Dock 23
Wild Violets 30
Asparagus 36
Catnip 41
Pokeweed 44
Lambs-quarters 49
Milkweed Shoots 53
Yellow Wood Sorrel 58
Pineapple-weed 60
Wild Roses 63
Wild Strawberries 68
Missouri Gooseberries 75
Prickly-pear Cactus Pads 81
Cattails 86
Mint 95
Day-lilies 100
Elderberry Flowers 104
Horehound 109
Milkweed Buds and Flowers 113
Wild Onions 117
Mulberries 121
Purslane 133
Buffalo Currants 137
Sandcherries 142
Juneberries 150
Milkweed Pods 157
Raspberries 161
Blackberries 168

Chokecherries and
Wild Blackcherries 175
May-apple 186
Leadplant 190
Wild Plums 194
Wild Grapes 201
Rose Hips 207
Prickly-pear Cactus Fruits 211
Smooth Sumac 215
Highbush Cranberries 219
Elderberry Fruit 223
Groundcherries 229
Hazelnuts 237
Hickory Nuts 242
Black Walnuts 248
Pecans 258
Pawpaws 269
Buffaloberries 273
Wild Persimmons 277
Jerusalem Artichokes 282
APPENDIX A: Canning,
Freezing, and Drying 289
APPENDIX B: Basic
Recipes 299
Additional Sources of
Information 303
List of Contributors 305
Index of Plants 307
Index of Recipes by Plant 310
Index of Recipes by Food Category 315

Acknowledgments

Many persons contributed to the making of this book, and it is a pleasure to acknowledge their assistance. It is not possible to list the names of all family members and friends who gave encouragement and other support, but their contributions are greatly appreciated.

I wish to thank the following persons especially, for without their assistance this work could not have been completed: my parents, Julius and Myrtle Young, who initially taught me about plants; folklorist Roger Welsch, who was the first to give support to the idea of this book; botanist Dr. Margaret Bolick, who assisted with botany questions along the way; botanist Eileen Schofield, who not only read the completed manuscript and made suggestions, but contributed a family recipe as well; ecologist Dr. A. Tyrone Harrison, who gave support and information, and with his wife Judy, contributed several recipes; Suzi Sybouts, who typed parts of the manuscript before I had my own computer; Gary and Debra Hinkley and Cheryl Leigh, who read the manuscript and offered suggestions; Jan Mowry and Richard Littleton, who helped me learn word processing; and prairie friends William Brandenburg, Jan Burch, Ruth Green, Kent and Ginger Haruf, Elaine Poland, Curtis Twedt, Michael and Julie Van Stappen, Norma Wagner, and Carl Wolfe, each of whom has had a special relationship to this book. In addition, I wish to thank the Nebraska Cooperative Extension in Lancaster

County and the NDSU Extension Service, North Dakota State University, Fargo, North Dakota, for their assistance.

Mark E. Marcuson, the artist who made the drawings, completed his work long before my part was finished. I will forever be grateful for his patience and support.

I have not met some of the persons who contributed recipes, but through their recipes, each of them has come to seem like a friend. Their names and contributions are listed at the back of the book. I wish to thank all of these persons most sincerely.

Introduction

Years ago, when using wild plants was part of everyday life, information and recipes were handed down through families and shared between friends. Today, information about wild plants is more often sought through books, and although much has been written about the edible wild plants of the eastern and western United States, considerably less has been published for the Great Plains.

This represents a serious lack, for across the fields and prairies and along the roadsides and wooded streams of the American heartland grow wild plants whose products rival the gourmet fare of any place in the world. Nettle noodles, dandelion quiche, cattail pollen pancakes, chokecherry syrup, and black walnut toffee are but a few of the delectable foods created from wild plants of the Great Plains.

When I was growing up in Nebraska, many families still used wild plants on a regular basis, and as a child, I helped my mother gather greens in spring and make wild fruit jams and jellies in autumn. When I had my own family, I carried on these traditions. It was great fun, and for most of my life I intended to write a wild plant cookbook. Even though my work was in the fields of folklore and botany, not until my children were grown did I find time to collect the recipes and write the accompanying botanical information. Now as I look back, I believe that gathering and consuming wild plants may have far more significance in a person's life than I had understood as a child or young mother.

Not only are certain wild plants nutritious and tasty, the gathering of them involves the important processes of exploration, discovery, and learning. Persons who explore and come to know the natural world around them develop a sense of how the earth works and a feeling of being connected to it. Even if the natural world that they explore and gather from is as limited as a backyard, what happens there each season is important in their learning. And even if they leave that particular place and never return, they carry with them an abiding concern for the earth and its many forms of life.

Perhaps because wild plants live and reproduce without the intentional aid of humans, they reveal more about the natural order and innate characteristics of an area than do domestic plants. Although we need domestic plants to feed the human populations of the world, we need an awareness and understanding of wild things in order to make choices that sustain, rather than impede, the natural systems of the earth. And just as we can never go back to subsisting wholly on wild things, neither can we wholly exclude wild things from our lives. The key is to integrate domestic and wild things wisely. In keeping with that concept, the recipes in this book combine wild plants with ordinary grocery store products, and readers are encouraged to grow wild plants in their yards along with domestic ones.

I have come to believe that it is important for us to know both the social and natural history of the area where we live. Just as the stories about persons who shaped our social and political history are important, so are the stories about the plants, animals, rivers, rocks, and soil that came before us. It is important to know the players and their roles, whether they are people or the animate and inanimate things of nature. Otherwise, it is like coming in at the middle of a play or film—if you don't know what has already taken place, you are less apt to get involved in what is currently happening or to care about how things turn out.

Beginning in the 1960s and continuing over a period of about twenty years, I interviewed many older persons who had lived in the Great Plains when large expanses of the land were still unplowed. Some had lived in dugouts or sod houses and many remembered that gathering wild plants was necessary for their family's survival. Overall, theirs had been a good life, these persons told me. Most described having to struggle and work very hard, but looking back, they said they wouldn't have traded places with anyone.

Yet, in detail, their stories included some of the most painful of human experiences. No one ever gets over the death of twin babies or even the barn that burned or the herd that perished in a sudden storm, but in spite of extreme misfortune, these people held a positive view of life and of each other.

The contrast between such tragic events and such positive spirit seemed remarkable, and I found myself thinking about this a great deal. Although it would be simplistic to propose a single explanation, a common thread that ran through the lives of these people is worth considering: their lives were intimately involved with the natural environment around them. Again and again, I heard reference to wild things or to a natural event that was soon to happen—the cranes would be back, the asparagus would be up, the plums would be ripe, the walnuts would fall—each event anticipated in a particular season and sequence. Weather, of course, could delay or preclude an expected event, but such odds were understood and accepted as part of the natural pattern.

Perhaps with a world view where natural cycles are a vital part of everyday living, people develop a framework in which to place their own lives. When a great loss or setback happens, they are still connected to something stable, a scheme or system that continues to work as it should. Certainly, garnering part of one's living from wild things creates a keen awareness and appreciation of the natural world and its cycles.

These thoughts and convictions were with me as I wrote this book. On a more basic level, the book is a guide for identifying and learning about selected wild plants and a collection of outstanding recipes for preparing them. It is not a survival book—only those plants whose flavor and availability warrant the time and effort required to collect or grow them are included. Wild mushrooms are omitted because learning about them solely from a book is too risky. Also, no uncommon or rare plants are included, and I implore readers to be mindful of the welfare of all wild plant and animal species.

For the purposes of this book, the Great Plains are considered to be the region extending from the Texas panhandle north into Canada, and from the Rocky Mountains on the west to the beginnings of the deciduous forest on the east. It includes the states of North Dakota, South Dakota, Nebraska, and Kansas, as well as much of Montana and parts of Wyoming, Colorado, New Mexico, Minnesota, Iowa, Missouri, Oklahoma, and Texas. Except for the Black Hills of South Dakota, the land of the Great Plains is mostly flat or gently rolling, and much of it was once covered with grasses and broad-leaved plants that do well in open sun; trees and shade-tolerant plants occurred mainly along streams and rivers. Today, the landscape of the Great Plains is greatly changed. Crop and lawn plants, trees, and introduced "weeds"—many from other parts of the world—have replaced much of the native flora. In addition, throughout the United States, plants have been moved from one region to another. Although some edible wild plants are still unique to the Great Plains, many of the plants in this book can be found in other regions of the United States and Canada.

Except for certain common names of plants, the *Flora of the Great Plains,* written by the Great Plains Flora Association and published by the University Press of Kansas in 1986, served as the authority for the botanical information, including botanical names. The *Flora* did not document or establish a standardized system for spelling common names, so where I felt a common name or its spelling in the *Flora* did not agree with common usage, I used names or spellings from other sources.

Plant names are no small matter. They are important in determining a plant's identity and for looking up additional information. Most plants have three kinds of names: botanical names, ordinary or colloquial common names, and official common names.

Botanical names are logical and consistent. Because standardization is a major goal, a plant will have at any given time only one correct botanical name, which is assigned in accordance with rules set by an international congress and is used throughout the world. Botanical names consist of the following: the genus and species (these are Latin and are normally italicized in print), the initials or name (often abbreviated) of the person who identified and classified the plant, and, if the plant if a subspecies or variety of a species, the subspecies or variety designation (also in italics). This system works so well for botanists, particularly those engaged in academic work, that they use botanical names almost exclusively.

The situation is different for county extension agents, agronomists, and botanists working in the public sector—although they may use botanical names among themselves, they must use common names when working with the public. But knowing which common name to use can be difficult because plants often have more than one, and a name used for a particular plant in one place may refer to an entirely different plant somewhere else. This situation led some botanists, agronomists, and others to seek a standardized system of common names similar to the one used for botanical names. So, over a number of years, committees (usually regional) have worked to select an official common name for each wild plant in that region and to develop a standardized system for spelling the names. Therefore, *colloquial* common names are the ordinary names by which plants are known in any particular group or community—and a single species may have many colloquial names. *Official* common names are those selected by an official committee as the preferred common names for the plants in that particular area. In some instances the official common name selected for a plant by one committee differs from that selected by another committee.

For the plants in this book, I have given the botanical name, one or more colloquial common names, and the official common name from the list compiled by the Nebraska Statewide Arboretum, except that where the Arboretum's official spelling resulted in a long, difficult-to-pronounce name, I have used a more traditional spelling.

The book is organized chronologically: beginning with spring, plants are presented in the order in which their edible parts become available for harvest. Because milkweeds, wild roses, prickly-pear cacti, and elderberries have more than one edible part, the general information about these plants appears with the description of the first product to be harvestable; their later products are discussed in proper sequence of harvest.

For each plant, information is given on identification, geographical distribution, habitat, which parts are edible, when to collect, and what cautions (if any) to observe. Additional pertinent information and the recipes follow. Because certain words have a different meaning in botany than they do in common usage, and because some words may not be familiar to readers, a glossary of botanical terms is included. The definitions in the glossary of cooking terms and the detailed directions given in some of the recipes will already be known by experienced cooks, but novices may need these aids.

The recipes came from various sources. Some are traditional recipes from my family and community, some I made up, and some were contributed by persons who responded to a letter I mailed to one hundred small-town newspapers scattered across the Great Plains. All of the recipes for jam, jelly, and syrup have been altered to comply with the new canning guidelines of the United States Department of Agriculture, but changes in contributed recipes for whatever reason, were made with the consent of the contributors.

Over the years I often adapted conventional recipes to accommodate wild fruits and vegetables, and no doubt readers will further alter these recipes to meet their own needs. Salt can be omitted, skim milk can be used in place of whole, and vegetarians can substitute vegetable products for the animal-based counterparts—for example, vegetable for chicken broth, or agar for gelatin.

Before getting started with edible wild plants, it is extremely important to know that although many wild plants are delicious and safe to eat, others are poisonous—and some of the poisonous ones taste good too. People often believe that if something is "natural," it must be wholesome, or at least harmless, but that is not always true. Death, as well as life, is a natural process and in the Great Plains, as in most areas of the world, there are wild plants so poisonous that eating only a small portion could be fatal. The rules that follow cannot be emphasized too strongly. Do not hesitate to call your county agent if you are unsure about the identity of any plant. Also ask your county agent for help if you do not know the hazardous plants and animals of your area.

Guidelines for the Safe and Sustainable Use of Edible Wild Plants:

1. Check information about wild plants with more than one good authority. (Books, your county agent, or a local botanist.)

2. Be certain that you have the right plant. Common names can be misleading because two or more plants may have the same common name. As much as possible, learn the botanical names of the plants you use.

3. Be certain that you have the right *part* of the right plant. On the same plant, the chemistry of one part may be different from the chemistry of another part. For example, the leaves may be safe to eat, but the fruit may be poisonous—or the other way around.

4. Use plants and plant parts at the right stage of maturity. Some leaves may be eaten only when immature, some fruits may be eaten only when fully ripe, etc.

5. Never sample a plant to see if it is safe to eat.

6. Don't overeat of any plant—be especially cautious the first time.

7. Collect from areas that have not been sprayed—better yet, grow the plants in your own yard and don't use sprays.

8. Be careful when you pick or cut. Do not gather large amounts of any plant that is not common in your area. Only abundant plants (such as dandelions) should be dug and, if you do dig, replace the soil and tamp it back in place.

9. In years when wild fruits and nuts are scarce, pass them by so that birds and other wild animals will have sufficient food.

10. Respect the rights of other persons; be considerate. Always obtain permission to gather from someone else's property or from the adjacent roadside.

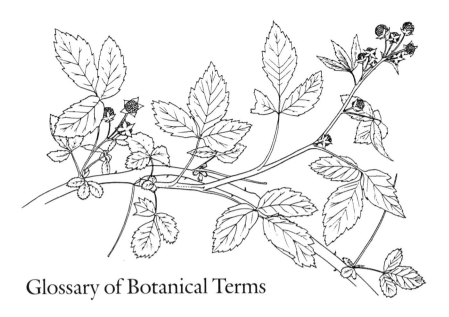

Glossary of Botanical Terms

Achene: a small, dry, thin-walled, one-seeded fruit that does not open when ripe.

Alternate leaf arrangement: a leaf arrangement in which only one leaf occurs at a node, causing an alternate pattern of leaves along a stem, branch, or twig. See diagram.

Annual plant: a plant that sprouts from seed, then grows, flowers, fruits, and dies all within one growing season.

Axil: the angle formed between a stem and the upper side of a leaf or petiole. See diagram.

Basal rosette: a circular cluster of leaves at the base of a plant.

Biennial plant: a plant that sprouts from seed and grows during one growing season, then flowers, fruits, and dies during the second growing season.

Blade: the expanded, flat part of a leaf. See diagram.

Bulb: a swollen underground bud with thick, fleshy scales. See diagram.

Catkin: a spikelike, usually hanging cluster of flowers having small leaflike structures but no petals.

Compound leaf: a leaf that is divided into leaflets. The leaflets of a pinnately compound leaf are arranged on two sides of an extended leaf stalk (petiole). See diagram.

Entire (leaf or margin): continuous, without lobes or teeth. See diagram.

Floret: a small flower, especially one of the small flowers in a dense head of flowers.

Fruit: the seed-bearing organ of a flowering plant. It may be large or small and juicy, dry, soft, hard, or papery.

Germination: the sprouting of a seed.

Habitat: the kind of place in which a plant naturally grows.

Herb: a plant that is not woody aboveground.

Husk: an outer covering of some fruits.

Hybrid plant: an offspring from plants of different varieties or species.

Introduced plant: a species that came or was brought into an area where it did not originally occur.

Leaf: a single blade or a compound (divided) blade, with or without a stalk, but attached to a stem, branch, or twig, at the site of a node. See diagram.

Leaflet: one of the divisions of a compound leaf. See diagram.

Lobed (leaf or margin): partially divided, the projections and indentations pointed or rounded. See diagram.

Midvein (midrib): the middle vein of a leaf, usually more prominent than the other veins. See diagram.

Native plant: as used in this book, a plant species that was present in the Great Plains before that region was explored or settled by Europeans and other immigrants.

Naturalized plant: as used in this book, a plant species that was not present in the Great Plains before the arrival of non-Native people but, when introduced, became well established and now continues to live and reproduce naturally.

Node: the place on a stem, branch, or twig where a leaf or leaves are attached (although some nodes are without leaves). Typically, a bud or branch is present at a node. See diagram.

Opposite leaf arrangement: a leaf arrangement in which two leaves occur at a node, making a pattern of opposite pairs along a stem, branch, or twig. See diagram.

Pedicel: the stalk of a flower.

Perennial: a plant that ordinarily lives through three or more years. Many perennials do not flower until their second or third year.

Petiole: the stalk of a leaf. See diagram.

Prickle: a small, sharp outgrowth of the skin of a plant.

Rhizome (rootstock): an underground stem, usually horizontal, rooting at the nodes and sending up shoots. See diagram.

Scalloped (leaf or margin): having blunt or rounded teeth. See diagram.

Serrate (leaf or margin): having sharp teeth pointed forward. See diagram. (Double serrate: serrate with the teeth appearing to be in pairs.)

Shoot: new growth of a plant, usually appearing in spring.

Spine: a rigid, very sharp outgrowth from a stem; tips of spines may be straight or barbed.

Stalk: the main aboveground organ or stem of an herb. Also a slender structure that supports a leaf, a flower, or a fruit.

Stem: the main organ of a plant (usually aboveground but sometimes belowground) that supports other plant parts and transports water and nutrients.

Taproot: a stout, vertical main root of a plant. See diagram.

Tuber: a short, thickened underground branch or stem. See diagram.

Wild plant: a native or introduced plant that can live and reproduce on its own without human assistance.

Leaf margins

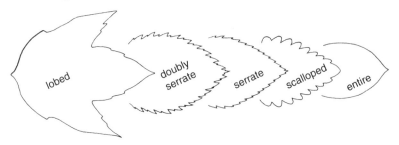

Underground Parts

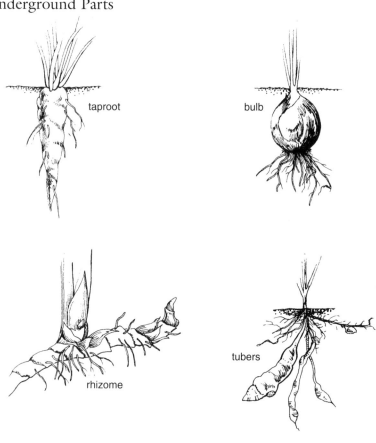

Simple and pinnately compound leaves

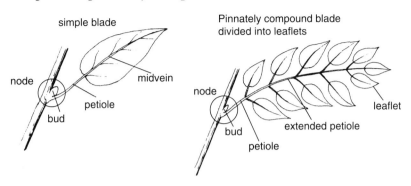

simple blade

Pinnately compound blade
divided into leaflets

node

midvein

petiole

bud

node

bud

extended petiole

leaflet

petiole

Leaf arrangements

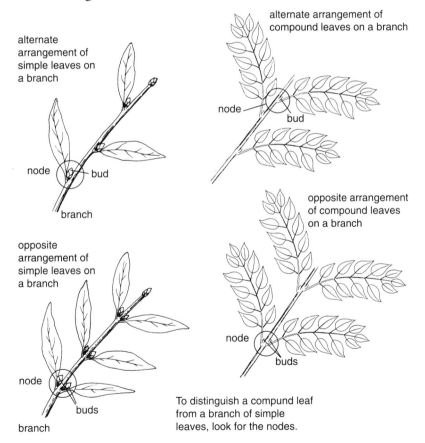

alternate arrangement of
compound leaves on a branch

alternate
arrangement of
simple leaves on
a branch

node

bud

node   bud

branch

opposite arrangement
of compound leaves
on a branch

opposite
arrangement of
simple leaves on
a branch

node

buds

node

buds

branch

To distinguish a compund leaf
from a branch of simple
leaves, look for the nodes.

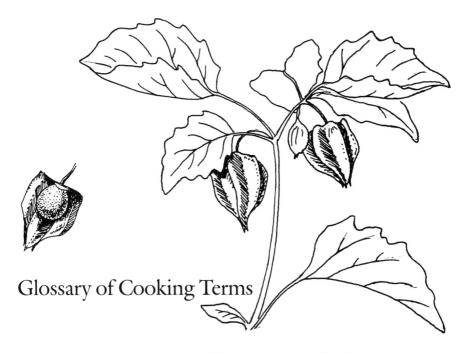

Glossary of Cooking Terms

Agar: a seaweed product that is used like gelatin to cause liquid to jell.

Bundt pan: a deep cake pan with a hole in the center, something like an angel-food cake pan, but slightly smaller and usually fluted.

Blanch: to heat quickly and for a very short time in boiling water.

Colander: a perforated bowl, usually metal or plastic, used for washing and draining fruits and vegetables.

Cone-shaped colander: a perforated metal cone with a stand, used with a pestle for extracting juice and pulp from fruits and vegetables.

Cream: to beat vigorously with a spoon or an electric mixer until the ingredients are smooth and blended.

Dash: a very small amount—approximately what would come out with one shake of a salt shaker.

Double boiler: a set of two cooking pots that fit together, one over the other. Water is brought to boil in the lower pot, then the second pot fitted into place above it. Food cooks in the upper pot above the boiling water. Double boilers are used for cooking tender ingredients that might be ruined by high temperatures.

Fold: to mix ingredients by gently turning the top layer over and bringing up the bottom layer. A rubber spatula is commonly used for this procedure.

Headspace: in jars and other containers, the empty space between the food and the lid.

Kettle: as used in this book, a deep cooking pan with a capacity of 4 or more quarts.

Kitchen towel: a cotton towel with little or no lint, heavier and more closely woven than a dish towel.

Pot: as used in this book, a deep, medium-sized cooking pan with a capacity of about 2½ quarts.

Saucepan: a small but deep cooking pan.

Scald: to treat with boiling water for a short time.

Simmer: to cook gently just below the boiling point.

Steep: to soak in water that is nearly boiling.

Stir-fry: to cook small pieces of food quickly in cooking oil in a shallow pan while stirring constantly.

Whisk: a tool made of several wire loops, used for beating eggs or other light ingredients into a froth.

Wild Seasons

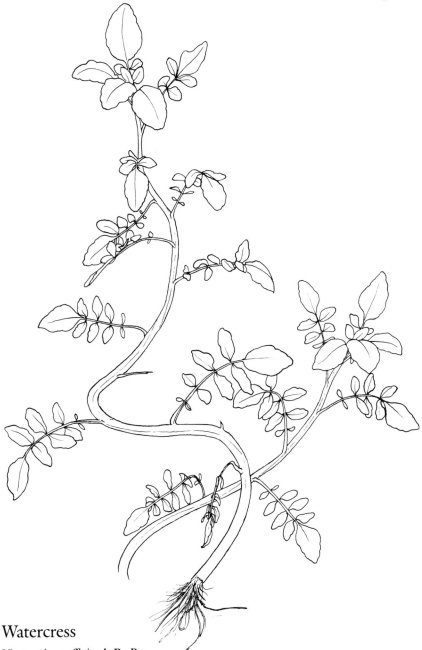

Watercress
Nasturtium officinale R. Br.

Mustard family: Brassicaceae

Description: Watercress is an introduced perennial aquatic plant. It forms floating mats on water or creeps along banks where it attaches to the mud by threadlike roots. The leaves are smooth and compound, each leaf made up of from one to several opposite pairs of leaflets and a single, terminal leaflet usually larger than the others. The flowers are white with 4 petals and occur in clusters. The fruits are slender pods with two rows of seeds.

Distribution: Widely naturalized throughout much of the United States and into Canada; in scattered areas of the Great Plains.

Habitat: Quiet to moderately fast-moving, clear water.

Edible parts: Tender leaves and stems, either cooked or uncooked.

Seasons to collect: Any time of year plants can be found.

Cautions: Being able to recognize watercress is rarely a problem. Unfortunately, however, many of the streams and wet areas where watercress grows are polluted, and thus the plants and animals that live there become contaminated. Do not use watercress or any plant from areas that might be polluted. Even in wilderness areas away from chemical contaminants where the water looks clean and clear, it is necessary to take precautions against bacteria or parasites such as giardia. This can be done by washing the plants in water that has been treated with purifying tablets (available at camping stores and some pharmacies). Also, it is possible to grow your own watercress.

Additional information and recipes: Watercress gathered in the wild is the same as that available in grocery stores, except the wild plants may be fresher. And freshness counts with watercress, for once it is picked, it does not keep well.

Should you wish to grow watercress in your own yard, collect or buy a few sprigs and place them in water. When roots develop, plant the sprigs in a spot where they will receive some shade and some sunlight each day and where the soil can be kept fairly moist. Such plants may not survive over winter, not because of the cold but because of the drier environment. However, watercress roots so easily that it is a simple matter to replace the plants each spring.

Tolerant of cold temperatures as well as hot (if it has water), watercress may be used throughout much of the year. Often it is the first edible green plant of spring, as well as the last wild treat before wetlands freeze over in winter.

Look for plants not yet in bloom and collect the upper leaves and stems only—the lower parts of the plant are coarse and stringy. Scissors work well to snip the tender tops without stirring up mud or sand below.

Once home, prepare the water for washing the watercress by using purifying tablets according to the directions on the package. Wash the watercress well, swishing the branches to remove sand and dirt. This procedure, followed by a light saltwater rinse (¼ cup salt to a gallon of water), will usually dislodge anything that might be clinging, but to be certain, inspect your harvest carefully, especially the underside of the leaves—even very small snails make an unpleasant crunch.

After it has been washed, watercress may be used raw or in cooking. Chopped or pureed, it can be frozen in water for up to a month and used in soups and stews.

To freeze watercress

2 cups loosely packed watercress

2 cups water

Read about freezing, Appendix A.

Finely chop the watercress and stir it into the water, or process the watercress and water at medium speed in a blender. Freeze the mixture in ice cube trays and store the frozen cubes in a plastic bag in a freezer.

Cream of watercress soup

1 cup chopped watercress or 5 to 6 frozen watercress cubes

2 cups chicken broth

1 cup light cream or milk

1 tablespoon margarine or butter

salt and freshly ground black pepper to taste

In a saucepan, heat the watercress and broth and let simmer about 7 minutes or until the watercress is tender and dark green. Do not overcook. Add the cream or milk, margarine or butter, salt, and pepper. Heat again but do not boil. Serve hot with croutons. A light sprinkling of paprika or nutmeg, as well as a floating sprig of fresh watercress, make nice additions to each bowl of soup. Makes 3 to 4 servings. (For a nondairy soup, substitute 1 cup of liquid nondairy coffee creamer or an additional cup of broth for the cream or milk.)

The following recipe is especially good served with buttered toast for dunking. It makes a satisfying meal for Sunday evening when no one feels much like cooking. Make this soup just before serving, because it will curdle if reheated.

Watercress-tomato soup
For each serving:
2 tablespoons heavy cream
1 cup tomato juice
1 to 2 tablespoons chopped, fresh watercress or 1 cube frozen watercress (see above)
salt and freshly ground black pepper to taste
small dab of butter or margarine
   Put the cream into the soup bowls and set them aside. Heat the tomato juice and watercress in a pot over medium heat. Simmer gently for about 7 minutes, then increase the heat. When the juice mixture reaches a full boil, immediately pour it into the soup bowls and stir quickly to blend it with the cream. Add salt, pepper, and butter to each bowl—and if desired, a sprig of fresh watercress. Serve at once. (Do not reheat.)

Watercress sandwiches
Spread thin slices of bread first with margarine or butter, then with softened cream cheese. Add a layer of coarsely chopped watercress. Close the sandwiches, cover with a damp cloth, and refrigerate for at least 1 hour before serving. Wholewheat or pumpernickel breads are especially good with watercress.

Spring greens with leftover potatoes
Often when gathering watercress in early spring, you will find other young plants such as dandelions, docks, or lambs-quarters along the way. There may not be enough of any one of these plants to use but when they are tossed with watercress, then heated in a little margarine or butter with slices of leftover potatoes, the combination of flavors is delicious.

Spring medley salad
Collect tender young leaves from such plants such as watercress, wild onion, dandelion, violet, and lambs-quarters. Simply wash the leaves well, pat them dry, then cut or tear them into pieces. Use whatever dressing you prefer.

Rowena's Salad Dressing (below) is superb, but make it within half an hour of serving—it seems to lose flavor when made too far in advance.

Rowena's salad dressing
1 or 2 cloves of garlic, peeled
1 teaspoon granulated sugar
½ to 1 teaspoon salt
3 tablespoons vegetable oil (olive oil gives a good flavor)
1 tablespoon lemon juice
dash of grated nutmeg and freshly ground black pepper

Chill the greens. In a wooden salad bowl crush the garlic, then grind it into a paste with the sugar and salt. Stir in the oil, then the lemon juice, nutmeg, and pepper. Mix well; toss with the chilled greens.

mature plant

edible young plants

Stinging nettle, burn nettle, nettle

Urtica dioica L. subsp. *gracilis* (Ait.) Seland.

Nettle family: Urticaceae

Description: Stinging nettle is a native perennial herb that may grow to a height of 6 feet or more, but commonly stands no more than 4 feet at maturity. Plants spread by underground stems and by seed. The leaves are opposite and dark green with serrate margins. Often in very young plants, the underside of the leaves is tinged a dark reddish purple. Both stems and leaves are armed with scattered stinging hairs. The flowers are small and greenish white and hang in clusters from the axils of the leaves. Similarly, the clusters of small dry fruits are inconspicuous. Note that young nettle plants will not yet have developed flowers or fruits.

Distribution: Throughout much of the Great Plains except the southwest; into Canada. (A similar subspecies, probably introduced from Europe, has naturalized widely in the eastern United States, with scattered populations elsewhere.)

Habitat: Rich, moist soil in woods and along fence rows, ditches, and streams; in full sun or in partial shade.

Edible parts: Leaves and stems of tender young plants up to about 6 inches tall (more mature plants are coarse and strongly flavored), cooked fresh or dried and cooked later.

Seasons to collect: End of winter, early spring. Stinging nettle is one of the first plants to emerge in spring. Sometimes young plants can be found again in late summer or autumn, especially from around the base of older clumps that have been cut.

Cautions: Although cooking renders the stinging nettle harmless, touching fresh plants or even brushing against their leaves can result in painful stings. Plant cutters and a pail work well for collecting, but some persons use leather gloves and pick by hand, and some pick bare-handed, having become adept at touching the plant with the less sensitive underside of their fingers, and not touching the leaves with the top of their fingers or hands. If you get stung—and most persons do—remember that the sting does not last long. (A common practice for hastening relief is to apply the juice from crushed leaves of one of the large-leaved docks that are often found growing nearby.) Drying greatly reduces the stinging property of the nettle, but some persons may want to use gloves when stripping the leaves from dried plants. Never attempt to eat uncooked stinging nettles.

Additional information and recipes: Persons who have been stung may be more than a little skeptical when they hear the stinging nettle acclaimed as one of the mildest and most delicious of all greens, wild or domestic. The explanation for the nettle being fierce in the wild yet tame on the table is that the stinging sensation is caused not by sharpness of the hairs, but by an acid contained in them. Because this chemical is quickly broken down by heat, cooking renders nettles safe to eat.

Just how it was discovered that cooking transformed the nettle into delectable table fare is lost in time, but its long history of use in many parts of the world is well documented. In Europe, the nettle was commonly used for greens, added to soups and stews, or made into a kind of vegetable pudding. A seventeenth-century English cookbook recommended that cheeses be mellowed between layers of fresh nettle leaves.

Gardeners have long composted nettle to enrich soil and watered plants with nettle "tea," the latter made by soaking dried nettle plants for several days in water. And whether food for plants or for people, the stinging nettle is credited with being highly nutritious.

Perhaps most intriguing of all is a mystery involving the notion that nettle juice, in combination with a certain proportion of salt, will coagulate milk. Euell Gibbons and several other authors of wild plant books have described this phenomenon, but I have never been able to make it happen. Once, feeling particularly curious, I decided to give the matter several days' attention. I tried pasteurized, raw, powdered, and canned milk and both boiled and freshly extracted nettle juice with various amounts of salt—all without the slightest sign of success. I would have set the matter aside permanently had I not found the following account in *A Modern Herbal,* by M. Grieve: "The juice of the nettle, or a decoction formed by boiling the green herb in a strong solution of salt, will curdle milk, providing the cheese-maker with a good substitute for rennet. The same juice, if rubbed liberally into small seams in leaky wooden tubs coagulates and will render them once more watertight."

Now, even more determined, I picked a bucket of fresh nettles and with the Grieve book under my arm, knocked at the back door of a local dairy. Two chemists listened patiently and kindly agreed to run the appropriate tests. Later, they reported that they could find nothing in the juice of the plants I brought them that would cause milk to congeal—the pH was about neutral and no enzyme or other chemical could be isolated that might explain the nettle's curious reputation for being a coagulant.

Maybe this characteristic is absent in the subspecies of stinging nettle native to the Great Plains but present in the European subspecies now found throughout the eastern United States and that likely served as the basis for Euell Gibbons's Nettle Junket dessert, which he claimed would jell when chilled. Maybe soil or time of year make a difference. Maybe it really doesn't work. Anyway, I have not given up researching this intriguing matter.

More easily demonstrated is the stinging nettle's unique ability to retain quality—flavor, color, and nutrition—after being dried. I know of no other leafy plant, wild or domestic, that has this wonderful property. Not even the woodnettle (described in the next section) dries well for food.

In winter, a handful of dried stinging nettle leaves added to boiling soup broth, or a bagful cooked for greens, will reconstitute bright green and delicious, much like fresh nettle plants in spring. Crumbled leaves are especially good in cream-of-potato soup or vegetable stew and, when ground into a powder, constitute the critical ingredient for nettle noodles (a recipe that appears below).

Inasmuch as the nutritional value of the nettle had long been recognized in Europe, it is not surprising that the practice of feeding dried or fresh nettles to livestock was something that settlers brought with them to the Plains. Descendants in eastern Nebraska remember that dried nettles were mixed with hay to make horses' coats sleek, and that in spring, freshly chopped nettles were fed to fowl to keep them healthy and to promote egg laying.

Today, nettles—fresh or dried—are more often eaten by people than by livestock. Although some persons freeze or can young nettle plants, drying still seems the easiest and least expensive method of preservation.

It may be helpful to know that about ½ pound of fresh nettles makes one serving of cooked greens. Usually, a grocery sack half full of loosely packed nettles will weigh about 2 pounds and amply serve four persons. Drying greatly reduces the bulk and weight: a full grocery sack (4 pounds) will dry out to about ¾ pound.

Before using nettles, wash the plants well in several rinses of water, and rather than draining the water from the last two rinses, lift the plants out of the water before pouring it out. In this way, sediment that may have settled to the bottom of the washing vessel will not be redeposited on the plants.

To dry stinging nettles
Select plants no more than 6 inches tall. After washing the plants, shake off as much water as possible and hang them upside down in a shady place away from dust and sun until thoroughly dry. I string a clothesline back and forth inside my garage and hang them with clip clothespins, leaving the garage

door up to allow circulation of air, but I have seen them laid out to dry on clean window screens held up by sawhorses. Sometimes a screen is placed in the back of a station wagon or van. No doubt other methods work as well, as long as the plants are placed in a shady, dry area with good circulation of air.

It is important that nettles be *brittle* dry before being stored or they will mold just as grass clippings or any moist plant material will do in a closed space. Often leaves *appear* to be dry but actually contain enough moisture to cause them to spoil. One way to test for dryness is to place a few leaves in a mortar and try grinding them into powder with the pestle. If they seem leathery and don't grind up well, they are not yet dry enough. Once truly dry, nettles must be stored in tightly covered jars in a cool place away from light. If your harvest is large, you may double-bag the dried plants for a few days in heavy paper grocery sacks (tightly closed) until you can find appropriate containers. But remember that paper bags absorb moisture and are therefore unsuitable for storage where there is even the slightest bit of dampness. Dried nettles are best if used within 9 months.

You might consider keeping a quart jar of crumbled leaves handy in the refrigerator. That amount will flavor a lot of soup and does not take up much space.

To make nettle powder

After the nettle plants have dried, remove the leaves and discard the stems. Pulverize the dried leaves into a powder with a mortar and pestle, then sift the material through a fine sieve to remove coarse particles. Flavor is more easily lost from nettle powder than from the whole leaves, so if not to be used right away, refrigerate the powder in a tightly covered container and use it within a few weeks. Better still, pulverize the leaves as you need them.

Nettle noodles

2 egg yolks
1 teaspoon soft margarine or butter
2 tablespoons light cream or evaporated milk
2 tablespoons nettle powder (see directions above)
½ teaspoon baking powder
¼ teaspoon salt
½ to ⅔ cup all-purpose flour

Using a fork, combine the egg yolks with the margarine or butter. Add the cream or milk, the nettle powder, baking powder, and salt. Stir until well mixed. Using a large spoon, work in enough flour to make a firm but pliable dough that doesn't stick to your hands. Begin with ½ cup of flour and add more if necessary. (The amount of flour needed will vary because the size of egg yolks varies.)

With your hands, knead the dough only until it holds together well. Divide the dough in half and, using a rolling pin, roll each half on a lightly floured surface until very thin. Carefully roll the dough up into loose scrolls and then transfer these to a cutting board (in order not to damage your pastry cloth or other surface when cutting the noodles). With a sharp knife, cut the rolled dough diagonally into strips ½ inch wide—or whatever width you prefer. Toss the noodles gently with a little flour so they won't stick together (the diagonal cut also helps prevent sticking). Cook the noodles as directed below or freeze them in a tightly covered container for later use. Makes 4 servings. The recipe may be doubled, tripled, or more.

Not only are nettle noodles good in soup, they may be served alone with a little seasoning or baked as an accompaniment for roast meat. But however they are used, they must be cooked in boiling broth or water first, and to ensure tenderness, it is important that the liquid be boiling *before* the noodles are added. To prevent boiling over, use a large pot and drop the noodles into it a handful at a time. When all have been added, boil uncovered for about 10 minutes, then reduce the heat, cover with a lid, and allow to simmer for another 5 to 10 minutes, stirring several times to prevent the noodles from sticking to the bottom of the pan.

To make soup, use 4 cups water or broth for each recipe of noodles. Season to taste. Herbs such as green onion, basil, parsley, or simply a handful of dried nettle leaves, make good additions.

For baked noodles, reduce the liquid to 3 cups and when the noodles have cooked, pour them into a greased baking dish, add meat drippings or butter, and season to taste. Cover with a lid and bake for about 40 minutes at 350 degrees. These noodles seem to go especially well with wild game.

To serve noodles as a side dish without baking, use the 3 cups of liquid, but after the noodles have cooked, simply turn off the heat, cover with a lid, and allow them to remain in the pot for about 15 minutes or until most of the liquid has been taken up. Add butter, sesame oil, or other seasonings.

Hot nettle greens

Use a steamer, or place the young nettle plants in a pot with approximately 1 cup of water for each 2 cups of nettles. Bring the water to a boil, then stir so that all of the nettle leaves wilt. Reduce the heat to medium, cover with a lid, and cook for 10 to 15 minutes or until the greens are tender and bright green.

Remove the greens from the heat and drain. (The cooking water will be brown or greenish brown—reserve it for a healthful drink or use it for watering plants.) Nettle greens require little or no salt and may be served plain or with butter, toasted sunflower seeds, crumbled bacon, or a sprinkling of vinegar.

To freeze nettle greens

Read about freezing, Appendix A.

Wash and sort the young plants, then place them in a wire basket in a large kettle of boiling water. Cover with a lid and boil for 3 minutes. Remove the kettle from the heat, then remove the basket of greens and immerse it in ice water. When cooled, drain the greens and ladle them into small containers, leaving 1 inch headspace; freeze.

When ready to use the frozen greens, place them in a small amount of boiling water and cook, covered, for about 5 minutes or until piping hot throughout. (Use a fork to stir the greens several times while cooking.) Drain and serve as instructed for hot nettle greens above.

Potato and nettle casserole

350 degree oven

3 large potatoes

1 cup heavy cream, such as whipping cream

½ cup cooked, drained, and chopped nettle leaves

salt and freshly ground black pepper to taste

1 teaspoon thinly sliced green onion (optional)

Peel the potatoes, slice them about ¼ inch thick, and arrange the slices in a well-greased casserole. Combine the other ingredients, stir to mix, and pour this over the potatoes. Place the uncovered casserole in the oven. Several times during baking, spoon some of the cream up over the top layer of potato slices. Bake until the potatoes are tender and the cream has cooked down into a thick sauce—about 1 hour. Makes 4 to 6 servings.

To use this recipe over a campfire—where it seems to taste better than anywhere else—use a heavy skillet with a good lid. Prepare the ingredients as described above and place them in the skillet, but cover the skillet with the lid and cook over a medium fire for about 40 minutes, then remove the lid so that the steam can escape. Allow to cook for another 20 minutes or so. Spoon the cream up over the top layer of potato slices several times during the latter period of cooking.

Wood nettle

Laportea canadensis (L.) Wedd.

Nettle family: Urticaceae

Description: The wood nettle is a native perennial herb, which, under good growing conditions, may attain a height of 3 feet or more. The leaves are medium green, serrately toothed, and alternate. (Note that leaves of the stinging nettle are opposite, making it easy to distinguish the two plants even when they are young.) Stinging hairs occur on various parts of the plant, particularly on the stems and on the midveins of the leaves. The flowers are small, greenish white, and borne in clusters in the axils of the upper leaves with female flowers above the male flowers. Thus the seeds, which are enclosed in small, flat, disklike fruits, develop at the top of the plant. In spring, when the wood nettle is tender and good to eat, neither flowers nor fruits will have yet formed.

Distribution: Scattered areas of the eastern United States; throughout much of the eastern Great Plains and into Canada.

Habitat: Rich, moist soil in woods or along shaded streams.

Edible parts: Cooked leaves and stems of tender, young plants up to 8 inches tall—more mature plants are coarse and unpalatable. Unlike stinging nettle, wood nettle plants do not dry well.

Season to collect: Spring. Wood nettle shoots usually emerge less than a month after those of stinging nettle.

Cautions: Touching fresh wood nettle plants can result in a painful sting, but once cooked, the young plants are mild tasting and safe to eat. Cautions and instructions for picking wood nettle are the same as for stinging nettle. Never attempt to eat uncooked wood nettle.

Additional information and recipes: Unlike stinging nettle, the wood nettle does not produce additional crops of young plants in autumn, so cooking with wood nettle must be done in spring when the plants are young and tender.

Wood nettle and stinging nettle are similar in flavor and each may be substituted for the other in most recipes. (An exception would be recipes calling for *dried* nettle, because only the stinging nettle dries well.) Of the two, wood nettle is the more tender and is thus preferred for the following salad, adapted from a Korean recipe.

Cooked wood nettle salad

6 cups (⅓ grocery sack) of fresh wood nettles
8 cups of water
4 or 5 green onions, including tops
1 medium carrot, peeled
2 cloves garlic, peeled
2 tablespoons sesame oil or other vegetable oil (do not use solid shortening)
2 tablespoons sesame seeds
salt and freshly ground black pepper to taste

In a large pot, heat the water to boiling. Wash the wood nettles well, then drop them into the boiling water. Using a long-handled spoon to avoid being burned by steam, push the wood nettles down into the water—they will wilt quickly. Allow the wood nettles to remain in the boiling water for about 2 minutes. Remove the pot from the heat; drain and discard the water (or drink it or use it, cooled, to water plants). Cover the pot with a lid and set it aside until the wood nettles have cooled.

Meanwhile, put the sesame seeds into a small skillet over medium heat. Stir constantly until the seeds become light brown, then remove them from the skillet. When the seeds have cooled, use a mortar and pestle to crush them, then set them aside. (Once toasted, sesame seeds require refrigerated storage.)

Slice the onions and carrot into thin diagonal strips. Mince or crush the garlic. Place the onions, carrot, garlic, and oil into a small skillet and stir-fry only until the carrot strips have turned bright orange. Do not overcook—the carrot should remain firm and flavorful.

Add the onion-carrot-garlic mixture to the wood nettle greens, then sprinkle with the toasted sesame seed and season with salt and pepper. Stir gently until combined. Place the salad in a covered bowl and allow the flavors to mingle for at least 2 hours before serving. This salad may be served cold or at room temperature, but if it is to be served more than 2 hours after mixing, it should be refrigerated. Makes 4 servings.

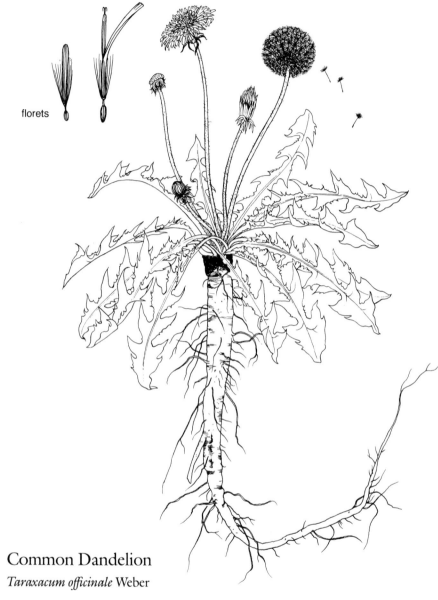

florets

Common Dandelion
Taraxacum officinale Weber

Red-seeded Dandelion
Taraxacum laevigatum (Willd.) DC.

Sunflower family: Asteraceae

Description: Dandelions are introduced perennial herbs with a fleshy tap-root. The fresh root, as well as the leaves and flower stalk, will exude a milky juice when cut or broken. The leaves occur in a basal rosette and are lance-shaped with pointed teeth or shallow to deep lobes. The flower stalks are leafless and hollow and vary in height from less than 1 inch to more than 12 inches. Leaves and flower stalks may be smooth or have short hairs. The flowers are yellow, but what looks like one flower having many petals, is actually many small flowers, called florets, held together at the base to form a crowded head. Each floret will mature into a single achene with an umbrella-like tuft of soft bristles to carry it aloft in the wind. (Red-seeded dandelion can be distinguished by its reddish achenes.)

Distribution: Throughout much of the United States and into Canada; widely distributed in all states of the Great Plains.

Habitat: Lawns, gardens, open areas, roadsides, meadows, and stream banks.

Edible parts: Young leaves, cooked or uncooked; older leaves, cooked; buds and flowers, cooked; roots, roasted and brewed for a hot drink.

Seasons to collect: Roots, anytime of year; young leaves, most abundant in spring but good anytime they can be found; older leaves, throughout the growing season; buds and flower heads, most abundant in spring and late autumn but good anytime they can be found.

Cautions: Do not use dandelions from lawns or other areas that may have been treated with insecticides or herbicides or that are frequented by neighborhood dogs.

Some researchers have warned that drinks containing high levels of tannin may be harmful. Ordinary tea and many herb teas, including that made with dandelion root, contain tannin.

Additional information and recipes: Likely it will surprise persons who work endlessly to rid their yards of dandelions to learn that those little yellow flowers are not native to the Great Plains. And not only that. Although dandelion seeds no doubt came into the Great Plains by accident with settlers, seeds were brought intentionally as well. Some settlers, once they realized the Plains were devoid of dandelions, wrote back to Europe for seeds and carefully planted dandelions in their yards and gardens.

As greens, dandelion leaves were not only relished for their slightly bitter taste, but highly regarded as a spring tonic as well. Many persons remember mothers or grandmothers engaging in an age-old rite of early spring—the searching out and picking of dandelion greens. Even now, in spite of the battle waged against it, the dandelion remains the best known wild edible plant across the Great Plains.

My first taste of dandelion was when I was a child and a neighbor invited me over to share some "spring greens." We sat in her porch swing, each of us with a small bowl. I remember how very good the greens tasted and how wonderfully secure I felt to realize that if I were ever lost and without food there were plants, all around me, that could be eaten. I don't suppose that children today would think about such things, but it was the Depression then and even young children were aware of the hard times. I have long since forgotten the name of that kind and interesting woman, but often I have wished I could thank her for helping me begin a lifetime of enjoying wild plants and their uses.

Years later I learned that, to avoid bitterness, dandelion leaves are best if picked before the heat of the day and from plants that have not yet produced flowers that season. Leaves from plants in bloom or from those that have finished blooming are not harmful, simply more bitter, and much of the bitterness can be removed by boiling and draining off the cooking water. (Don't discard the cooking water—drink it as a nutritious tonic or use it to water plants.) Also, choose light-colored leaves; the darker green ones are more bitter.

Dandelion leaves are good added to soups, stews, scrambled eggs, omelets, and quiche. Often, when prepared alone as greens, they are garnished with slices of hard-cooked egg and served with vinegar on the side to be added at the table. Tender young leaves need not be cooked and make a good addition to tossed salad. Ordinarily, the unopened flower heads ("buds") are best cooked but may be used uncooked if blanched as described below.

To blanch dandelion plants and delay their blooming, simply cover them with a board or an overturned pail. In about a week, they will have blanched to a pale greenish white and be exceptionally mild and tender. Sometimes dandelions are covered naturally with loose soil thrown up by pocket gophers. Often, by gently digging into these mounds, enough tender leaves and unopened flower heads can be found to add an interesting touch to fresh salad or to flavor soup or scrambled eggs.

Dandelion florets are edible, too, and are particularly good in scrambled eggs, casseroles, and quiche. They are usually removed from the disklike base, which is bitter. For years I *cut* the florets from their bases, then a friend showed me that *twisting* them off was easier and more efficient. To do this, simply hold the base with one hand, and with the other, twist the head of florets as though you were unscrewing it. If this seems awkward, or if you object to having your fingernails temporarily stained, use a knife or scissors.

Florets should be removed from their bases soon after picking—otherwise they continue to mature and become tough and unpalatable. Once free of the bases, florets will keep for several days if refrigerated in a covered container.

One more thing about dandelions: sometimes, especially in spring, you may discover that along with the flower heads you have harvested a whole army of tiny insects. Don't panic and don't discard your harvest. These very minute insects are harmless and will leave on their own if you simply put the flower heads into a shallow bowl and strike the side sharply with your hand. Repeat this several times, but wait long enough between strikes to allow the insects time to move out. Do all this outdoors, of course, then proceed to use the flower heads as usual.

When roasted, ground, and brewed, the root of the dandelion makes a delicious drink, which is usually served hot. It tastes more robust than tea but not as strong as coffee, and does not contain caffeine.

Traditional dandelion greens
4 cups dandelion leaves (other greens may be included)
2 strips of bacon, cut into pieces
salt, freshly ground black pepper, sugar to taste
1 hard-cooked egg, sliced
vinegar to taste

Place the leaves in a pot with enough water to cover, then bring to a boil over medium heat, cover with a lid, and allow to cook for about 4 minutes. Remove the pot from the heat and drain off the excess water.

Fry the bacon over medium heat until crisp. To avoid being burned by steam, turn off the heat and allow the grease to cool slightly before adding the cooked leaves (which will have retained some water). Add the leaves, turn on the heat, and stir until the water has mostly cooked away and the flavors are well blended—about 1 minute. Season with salt, pepper, and sugar. Remove from the heat. Transfer the greens to a serving bowl and garnish with egg slices. Serve hot. A sprinkling of vinegar may be added at the table. Makes 2 servings.

Dandelion greens and new potatoes

16 to 20 walnut-size new potatoes
4 cups young dandelion leaves
1 egg
¾ cup water
2 tablespoons vinegar
salt, freshly ground pepper, sugar to taste
3 strips of bacon, cut into pieces
1 tablespoon all-purpose flour

Wash, but do not peel the potatoes, then boil or steam them until tender. In a bowl, combine the egg, water, vinegar, salt, pepper, and sugar. Beat with a whisk or fork until well mixed. Set aside. Fry the bacon over medium heat until crisp, then move it to the side of the skillet. Add the flour and stir until lightly browned. Add the egg-water-vinegar mixture all at once and stir until thickened. Add the dandelion leaves and continue to stir until they are wilted and tender. Season with salt, pepper, and sugar—stir until well blended. Remove from the heat and ladle immediately over the hot potatoes. Makes 6 to 8 servings.

Scrambled eggs with dandelion

1 cup coarsely cut dandelion leaves
(or substitute buds for up to ¼ cup of the leaves)
2 green onions, including tops, sliced diagonally
2 tablespoons cooking oil
8 eggs, slightly beaten
salt and freshly ground black pepper to taste
crisply fried bacon or bits of ham (optional)

Place the leaves (and buds if you are using them) in a saucepan with enough water to cover. Bring to a boil, cover with a lid, and allow to boil gently for about 4 minutes. Remove from the heat, drain, and set aside. In a skillet, stir-fry the onion slices in oil until tender but not browned. Add the cooked dandelion and stir until well mixed with the onion. Add the eggs, salt, and pepper (and cooked bacon or ham, if desired); stir to mix. Reduce the heat to low. Stir again, cover, and allow to cook until the eggs have set. Serve immediately. Makes 4 servings.

Dandelion quiche

350 degree oven
9-inch single pie crust, baked

1 cup grated cheese such as Swiss, sharp Cheddar, or Gruyere
1 cup coarsely cut dandelion leaves
1 ½ cups milk, half-and-half, or light cream
¼ cup thinly sliced green onion tops
½ cup dandelion florets
salt and freshly ground black pepper to taste
3 eggs, beaten

Before assembling the quiche, make certain that the oven is hot and that all ingredients have been prepared as shown: pie crust baked and cooled, cheese grated, dandelion and onions cut, and florets removed from their bases. Sprinkle the grated cheese over the bottom of the pie crust and set it aside.

Place the dandelion leaves in a saucepan with enough water to cover. Bring to a boil and allow to cook for 4 minutes. Remove from the heat and drain away the liquid. Add the milk or cream, and stirring constantly, heat to the point of boiling, but do not allow to boil. Remove from the heat. Stir in the onion, florets, salt, and pepper; set this aside also.

Beat the eggs in a large mixing bowl. Pour the hot milk mixture into the beaten eggs and immediately stir well to combine. Pour this over the cheese in the pie crust. Bake for 20 to 25 minutes or until the quiche is somewhat puffed and the surface lightly browned. Remove from the oven and allow to cool for at least 15 minutes before cutting. Makes 6 to 8 servings.

Small pieces of cooked bacon or ham, bits of sauteed mushrooms, or cooked diced vegetables make interesting variations. Such additions should be in small pieces, because large chunks make cutting the quiche difficult.

Dandelion brew
350 degree oven
For each cup of beverage you will need to dig one medium-sized root.

Wash the roots and scrub them with a vegetable brush to remove any soil, but do not peel them or remove root hairs. Split very large roots lengthwise so they will bake in the same amount of time as the smaller ones. Pat the roots dry with a paper towel and place them on a cookie sheet. Bake for about 1 hour and 15 minutes—about the same time and temperature required to bake potatoes. Check for doneness by breaking a root in two—when done, the root should be very dry and brittle and smell a little like chocolate. Small roots should be brown most of the way through, but larger roots will have a lighter-colored core.

The right amount of baking is important because if not baked enough, the roots will have little flavor; if baked too long, they will taste burned. You may need to experiment a few times to determine the correct amount of baking time for your particular oven. When the roots are done, remove them from the oven, allow them to cool, then crush them with a mortar and pestle. Store in a covered container in a cool place. Use the coarse particles like ground coffee; use the powder like instant coffee. Serve plain or with milk and sugar—either way, a drop of vanilla extract for each cup makes a nice addition.

Curly dock, sour dock, yellow dock
Rumex crispus L.

Patience dock, spinach dock, yellow dock
Rumex patientia L.

Buckwheat family: Polygonaceae

Description: Both curly dock and patience dock are introduced perennial herbs growing from a fleshy taproot. In spring, the leaves emerge in a rosette and grow rapidly, sometimes measuring 1 foot or more in only a few weeks. Leaves of both species are smooth, lance-shaped, and light to medium green with a prominent midvein. Typically, the margins of the leaves are uneven, with the leaves of patience dock ranging from flat to slightly wavy and the leaves of curly dock being quite wavy. A few weeks after the leaves appear, a flower stalk emerges and grows rapidly, eventually reaching a height of 2 to 3½ feet. Leaves on this stalk are alternate and considerably smaller than those at the base. A thin, papery sheath called an ocrea (plural, ocreae) covers the place where each leaf is attached to the stalk. Typically light green, moist ocreae are present early in the growing season but dry and fall away in summer or autumn. The flowering portion of the stalk is branched and bears numerous clusters of small greenish-white flowers, which soon develop into small, flat, rusty-brown fruits. (From the illustration, readers may recognize docks as the plants that produce the tall rusty-brown stalks so often gathered along roadsides for dried arrangements.)

Distribution: Curly dock: throughout much of the United States and into Canada; widely naturalized in the Great Plains. Patience dock: throughout much of the northern and eastern United States and into Canada; scattered throughout much of the central and eastern Great Plains.

Habitat: Moderately moist soil along ditches, streams, fence rows, and roadsides; common in open areas such as fields, yards, and gardens where soil has been disturbed; often found in full sun but will tolerate some shade.

Edible parts: Tender leaves, cooked. Note that the young leaves at the center of the rosette are most commonly sought, but if tender, more mature leaves may be used as well.

Seasons to collect: Most plentiful in spring, but tender leaves may be used at any time of year they can be found.

Cautions: Numerous species of dock are found in the Great Plains, but with the exception of curly and patience dock, all are too bitter to be edible. Although not poisonous, the bitter docks can be irritating to the mouth and throat and can cause indigestion. In general, dock species having smaller, narrow leaves are bitter. Such plants will be easy to recognize, but several of the large-leaved species are also bitter and may be difficult to distinguish from the edible docks. Once a large-leaved dock is found, the only easy way to tell if it is one of the edible species is to sample a small portion of a leaf. Leaves of curly dock have a sour, pleasant flavor; those of patience dock are mild or only slightly sour. Neither is bitter.

Note that this is the only instance in this book where tasting is recommended as a means of identification. I stand by the rule never to put a part of any plant into your mouth unless you know what that plant is and that it is safe to eat. However, if you are *certain that the plant you are about to sample is one of the large-leaved docks,* then the worst you're in for is an unpleasant taste.

Remember that dock is generally considered a weed. Do not collect from areas where plants may have been sprayed. Docks transplant easily and growing them in your own yard will ensure a safe source. (To prevent their spreading by seed, remove flower stalks as soon as they form.)

Additional information and recipes: When hiking, camping, or just generally being outdoors, people often come into contact with stinging nettle. A folk remedy for nettle sting is to crush the stems and leaves of one of the large-leaved docks and apply the juice directly to the painful area. When bruised, these docks exude a clear juice that feels slick and soothing, somewhat like lotion. Dock juice does seem to bring relief and where nettles occur, dock plants can often be found nearby. Also, a cool dock leaf applied to a mosquito bite tends to relieve the itching.

To use dock for food, pick tender leaves and wash them in several rinses of water, then instead of pouring off the last rinse, gently reach in under the leaves and lift them out of the water. This avoids stirring up sediment that may have accumulated at the bottom of the container. Shake the leaves and lay them out to drain. Leaves up to 6 inches in length may be used with the midvein intact. The midvein of larger leaves is best removed—simply fold a leaf lengthwise and with scissors or a sharp knife cut along the midvein through both thicknesses of leaf.

Note that no matter how carefully dock leaves are cooked, they will fade to a dull khaki color.

Dock greens
Steam the dock leaves or cook them in a small amount of water until tender (5 to 10 minutes). Season with salt, freshly ground pepper, and butter or margarine.

To freeze dock greens

Read about freezing, Appendix A.

Dock is too tender to treat like most garden greens. Use small (1 cup) glass or plastic containers so that the greens may be frozen and reheated quickly. Prepare a shallow pan of ice water.

Remove the midveins from the leaves and cut or tear large leaves into pieces. For each quart (4 cups) of loosely packed dock, use about 1 cup water. Put the water into a kettle over high heat, add the dock, bring to a boil, then cover with a lid. Cook until the dock is thoroughly wilted—about 3 minutes. Lift the lid and stir the dock several times while it is cooking.

Remove the kettle from the heat and ladle the dock into the containers, leaving 1 inch headspace. Place the containers in the pan of ice water, being careful not to get ice water in the containers. Gently stir the cooked greens with a fork so they will cool evenly. When the greens are cold, tightly close the containers, then freeze. A quart of coarsely cut fresh leaves, fairly well packed, will make about 1 cup of greens.

When ready to use, steam or boil the frozen dock in a small covered pot for about 7 minutes. (If necessary, add a little water.)

Crockpot pork and dock

2 pounds lean ground pork
½ cup water
1 tablespoon cornstarch
¼ cup soy sauce
1 teaspoon brown sugar or honey
½ to 1 teaspoon salt
½ teaspoon freshly ground black pepper
½ cup cornstarch
¼ cup water
2 tablespoons cooking oil
8 cups coarsely chopped dock leaves

Place the pork in a large bowl. In a small bowl, stir together the first amount of water, the first amount of cornstarch, the soy sauce, sugar or honey, salt, and pepper. Pour this over the pork and work it in until well blended, then set this mixture aside for about 15 minutes.

Meanwhile, mix the second amount of cornstarch with the second amount of water to make a paste, then spoon this out onto a plate. Divide the meat mixture into from 8 to 12 portions and form these into balls. Pour the oil into a large skillet and place it over medium heat. You are now ready to begin browning the meatballs, which are somewhat fragile and best handled individually. Roll each meatball in the cornstarch paste until it is well coated, then carefully place it into the hot oil. After all the meatballs are in the skillet, begin loosening and turning them with a spoon or spatula so that they brown evenly. When well browned, carefully transfer the meatballs to the crockpot. Add ½ cup water, cover with the lid, and cook 2½ to 3 hours at a low setting.

Don't clean up the skillet after browning the meatballs. Later, the pork drippings and small amount of remaining oil will add flavor to the cooked dock leaves. (Inasmuch as the dock will not be cooked until close to serving time, you may want to find a place in the refrigerator for the skillet.)

A half hour or so before serving, put the dock leaves into the skillet with about ¼ cup of water. Cover with a lid and allow the dock to cook until wilted, then uncover and stir until the drippings have been taken up by the leaves. Open the crockpot and carefully spoon the dock leaves over the meatballs. Put the lid on the crockpot and allow the leaves to cook for another 5 to 10 minutes. Makes from 4 to 6 servings. This is especially good served with boiled potatoes or rice.

Dock roll-ups
small sausage links, large sausage links such as Italian or Polish sausage, or wieners
dock leaves

For breakfast or to serve as an hors d'oeuvre, use small sausage links; for a main part of the meal, use large sausage links or wieners. Allow 1 medium or 2 small dock leaves for each small sausage; allow 2 to 4 medium dock leaves for each large sausage or wiener.

Wash the dock leaves and pat them dry with a kitchen towel, then to make them roll up easily, remove the midvein from each leaf, large or small. Set the leaves aside.

Place a small amount of water in a pot (about ½ cup, more or less, depending on the size of the pot). If you have a steamer basket, place it inside the pot. Set the pot aside also.

In a skillet, brown the sausages or wieners on all sides. Reduce the heat, cover with a lid, and cook until *thoroughly* done, then allow the meat to cool until comfortable to handle. For large sausages or wieners you may want to make a lengthwise slit in each link (being careful not to cut through the ends or through the backside) and stuff each one with cheese or mustard.

Lay out the dock leaves according to the number and size of the sausages or wieners. If the leaves are small or if you are using large links, you may need to overlap 2, 3, or 4 leaves for each link. To make a roll-up, place a sausage link or wiener across the end of a leaf (or overlapped leaves) and simply roll it up. Carefully place each roll-up, seam side down, into the pot or steamer basket. Cover with a lid, place over medium-high heat, and cook only until the leaves are tender—no more than 2 or 3 minutes. Carefully remove the roll-ups (tongs help) and serve them hot.

Dock roll-ups can be made in advance and reheated in a microwave or conventional oven. For serving breakfast to a large group, make the roll-ups the day before, cover and refrigerate them, then reheat, batch by batch, as needed the following morning.

Roast pork with dock dressing
350 degree oven
2 pounds lean pork roast
2 tablespoons cooking oil (for browning roast)
8 slices bread (choose bread that isn't soft and gummy)
2 eggs
1 cup water
2 tablespoons minced onion
½ teaspoon salt
½ teaspoon freshly ground black pepper
2 cups coarsely chopped dock leaves

The baking time required for a pork roast of this size, with or without bone, is from 40 to 45 minutes per pound. The dressing requires less baking, so it should be added about 45 minutes before the roast will be done. However, the addition of dressing cools the roast slightly, so the overall baking time must be extended by 15 or so minutes. Larger roasts may be used or the recipe for dressing doubled, but baking times will need adjustment. If in doubt, simply bake the roast and dressing separately, allowing the proper amount of time per pound for the meat and allowing 45 or more minutes for the dressing, which is done when it is puffed and browned.

For this recipe (roast and dressing baked together), use a covered roaster or other container having a capacity of about 3 quarts. Brown the roast in cooking oil over medium-high heat. Cover and bake for 1 hour. While the roast is baking, make the dressing.

Toast the bread by laying it on the racks in the oven, turning each slice at least once so that both sides are lightly browned. (This won't interfere with the roast.) Tear the toasted bread into approximately 1-inch pieces and put these into a large mixing bowl. Combine the eggs, water, onion, salt, and pepper in a small bowl and mix well with a fork, then pour this mixture over the toasted bread chunks. Add the dock leaves and stir with a fork until well combined. Cover and refrigerate until ready to bake.

After the roast has baked for 1 hour (longer for a larger roast), remove it from the oven and from the roaster. If necessary, skim off and discard excess fat, but reserve the browned meat drippings and any meat juice. Add enough water to the drippings and juice to make ½ cup liquid and stir until the meat drippings are well dissolved in the water. Slowly pour this liquid over the dressing, moistening as many pieces of bread as possible, then stir until the moisture is evenly distributed throughout.

Return the roast to the roaster. Spoon the dressing loosely around the roast, cover, and return the roaster to the oven for another 45 minutes or until the roast is done and the dressing is puffed and steaming. If you prefer dressing browned and with a slight crust, remove the cover for the last 10 to 15 minutes of baking. Makes 4 to 6 servings.

Blue prairie violet, meadow violet, wild violet
Viola pratincola Greene

Downy blue violet, wild violet
Viola sororia Willd.

Violet family: Violaceae

Description: These violets are short native perennial herbs spreading by seed. The leaves are heart-shaped; those of blue prairie violet are smooth and have scalloped to toothed margins; those of downy blue violet are usually hairy and have scalloped margins. The showy flowers of both species have 5 petals and are usually bluish purple to purple but may be white. In addition, inconspicuous flowers, borne closer to the ground, are produced. Not opening, these flowers self-pollinate and often produce an abundance of seed. Both kinds of flowers develop capsules that when dry, split suddenly along three seams, casting out their tiny seeds in something akin to a small explosion.

Distribution: Throughout much of the eastern Great Plains with scattered populations west.

Habitat: Yards, lawns, open woods, stream banks, prairie borders, and roadsides.

Edible parts: Flowers, cooked or uncooked; leaves, cooked or uncooked.

Seasons to collect: Flowers, in spring; leaves, any time they can be found.

Cautions: The wild violets used for food are those having heart-shaped leaves and flowers that are white or shades of purple or blue. Other species besides the two described above occur elsewhere and are edible, but violets having yellow flowers or divided leaves are reported to cause stomach upset and, therefore, are not recommended. Do not use violets from lawns or yards that may have been sprayed with chemicals.

Additional information and recipes: Violet leaves have a mild flavor and retain their deep green color even when cooked. For salads, the leaves are best used in spring, but for cooking as greens or in soup or stew, leaves may be used throughout the growing season.

Unlike the flowers of the fragrant sweet violet of Europe, which has now naturalized in parts of the eastern United States, the flowers of violets native to the Great Plains have little, if any, fragrance or flavor. However, whether purple, lavender, blue, or white, the flowers of these native violets make an exceptionally attractive garnish for salads, soups, and desserts. When crystallized with sugar, violet flowers are often used on cakes or frosted cookies.

Purple, lavender, or bluish flowers impart a beautiful color to jelly and syrup, but deep as the color may be at first, it tends to fade, even when the jelly or syrup is stored away from light. Thus, it is best to use violet products within a few months after they are made. Freezing the jelly or syrup slows the process of fading.

When making violet syrup or jelly, select the deepest-colored violets you can find. Pick the flowers but leave the stems. Each batch of syrup or jelly will require a full quart of flowers and shaking the container from time to time while picking will settle the flowers and give a more accurate measurement. Once home, remove any flower stems or foreign particles. It is necessary to use boiling water to extract the color from the flowers. The resulting liquid will be blue but will turn lavender or lavender rose with the addition of acid such as is present in rhubarb or lemon juice.

To make violet liquid

Fill a quart canning jar with flowers (again shaking the jar several times as you fill). Add enough boiling water to cover the flowers (2½ to 3 cups) and allow this to steep for about 8 hours. Drain the liquid, pressing the flowers with the back of a spoon—pressing is important because much of the color will have remained in the flowers. Discard the flowers. Measure the liquid. There should be at least 2 cups—if less, add water to make that amount.

For instructions about how to make the rhubarb juice for the recipes that follow, see Appendix B, and for important instructions about preserving jelly and syrup, see Appendix A.

Wild violet syrup

2 cups violet liquid
½ cup rhubarb juice (or 2 tablespoons lemon juice plus ½ cup water)
2 cups granulated sugar
½ cup light corn syrup
Few grains of salt

Read about syrup making, Appendix A.

Combine all of the ingredients in a large, heavy kettle and stir well. Place over medium-high heat and bring to a boil. Allow to boil gently for 15 minutes. Quickly skim off the foam, and pour the syrup into hot scalded jars, leaving ½ inch headspace. Cap the jars with two-piece screwband lids and process for 10 minutes in a boiling water bath. Makes about 2 cups of syrup.

Wild violet jelly

2 cups violet liquid
1 cup rhubarb juice (or ¼ cup lemon juice plus ¾ cup water)
1 box powdered pectin
4 cups granulated sugar
  Read about jelly making, Appendix A.
  Measure the sugar and set it aside. Stir the violet liquid, rhubarb juice (or lemon juice and water), and the pectin together in a large, heavy kettle. Place over high heat and stirring constantly, allow the liquid to come to a full boil. Add the sugar all at once and stir until it is dissolved. When the liquid again reaches a full boil, begin timing. Stirring constantly, allow it to boil hard for 1 minute. Remove from the heat and quickly skim off the foam. Pour jelly into hot, sterile jars, leaving ¼ inch headspace. Cap the jars with two-piece screwband lids and process for 5 minutes in a boiling water bath. Makes about 4½ cups of jelly.

Crystallized wild violet flowers

fresh violet flowers
1 egg white
granulated sugar
  Choose a warm sunny day—damp weather prevents proper drying. Wash and drain the flowers and gently pat them dry with a paper towel. Remove the stems, being careful not to tear the petals apart.
  Beat the egg white until slightly foamy. Using tweezers, dip each flower into the egg white and let the excess drain off. Still holding the flower with the tweezers, sprinkle it with sugar, turning it so that it will be evenly coated. Place the flowers on waxed paper. If needed, add sugar to the centers of the flowers. Straighten and separate the petals with a fresh toothpick. Place the sugared flowers on a rack or screen in a warm, dry room until they are thoroughly dry.
  Crystallized flowers may be kept for up to a month if stored in a single layer in a tightly covered container in a cool place. Do not freeze.

  The following recipe calls for a loose-leaf type of lettuce. If homegrown lettuce is not yet ready at the time the violets in your area are in bloom, leaf lettuce (not iceberg) from a grocery may be used, but the recipe for cream dressing is a very old one that was developed for use with the tender, light-green leaf lettuces usually grown in home gardens.

Wild violet and lettuce salad with cream dressing
1 cup loosely packed young violet leaves, stems removed
2 cups loosely packed leaf lettuce leaves
20 or more fresh violet flowers
CREAM DRESSING
2 tablespoons cider vinegar
2 tablespoons granulated sugar
⅔ cup heavy cream
salt and freshly ground black pepper to taste

Wash the violet and lettuce leaves. Remove as much water as possible, cover, and refrigerate until well chilled.

Meanwhile, combine the vinegar and sugar, stirring until the sugar is mostly dissolved. Add the cream, salt, and pepper and stir well. Chill until ready to use. Just before serving, toss the violet leaves, lettuce, and dressing together. Strew violet flowers over the top.

Note that the salad may be made using all violet leaves and no lettuce, but the contrast of flavors and textures as well as the light and dark shades of green make a more interesting salad. Makes 3 to 4 servings.

Chicken dumplings with wild violets
CHICKEN AND BROTH
one 2- to 3-pound frying chicken, whole or cut into pieces
8 cups water
Salt and freshly ground black pepper to taste

Use a large, heavy kettle having a 4- to 5-quart capacity. Place the chicken and water in the kettle and heat to boiling. Reduce the heat to medium-low, cover, and simmer until the chicken is tender—about 50 minutes.

Remove the chicken from the heat and allow it to cool. Pour off the broth, and when the chicken is cool enough to handle, remove and discard the bones and skin. Cut the meat into bite-sized pieces and set these aside. Skim the fat from the broth, then pour the broth back into the kettle and add salt and pepper to taste.

If possible, use a domed lid to cover the kettle when cooking the dumplings—the water that condenses inside the lid will follow the curvature and run down the sides instead of dripping onto the dumplings.
DUMPLINGS
⅔ cup milk
2 tablespoons cooking oil
1 ⅓ cups all-purpose flour

2 teaspoons baking powder
½ teaspoon salt
1 cup loosely packed violet leaves

Stir the milk and oil together in a medium bowl. Sift the flour, baking powder, and salt together into the milk-oil mixture and stir only until it holds together in a moist dough. Let stand for 5 minutes. Meanwhile, heat the broth to a gentle boil.

For each dumpling, scoop up a rounded teaspoonful of dough and carefully put it into the boiling broth in such a way that it floats freely. To be light and fluffy, dumplings must cook at the surface of the broth where they can expand. (When dough is *dropped* into broth, it often sinks and sticks to the bottom of the kettle—such dumplings will be gummy.)

When all of the dumplings have been placed in the broth, adjust the heat so that the broth simmers without boiling over them. Allow the dumplings to cook, uncovered, for 3 minutes, then cover and cook for 12 minutes without lifting the lid.

At the end of the cooking time, carefully push some of the dumplings aside and add the violet leaves and cut-up chicken, stirring them gently into the broth. Replace the lid and cook for 3 to 4 minutes more. Dumplings are best served immediately—rewarmed they are less tender. Fresh violet flowers make an attractive garnish. Makes 4 to 6 servings.

Wild violet and noodle soup
2 to 3 cups of noodle soup
1 cup fresh violet leaves, loosely packed
½ cup light cream or milk
salt and freshly ground black pepper to taste
about 20 fresh violet flowers

Use homemade noodles or prepare canned or dried noodles according to the directions on the container. Add the violet leaves to the soup and cook over medium heat until the leaves are tender—about 4 minutes. Add salt and pepper. Stir in the cream or milk and pour the soup into the serving bowls. Carefully place several violet flowers in each bowl so that they float on the surface. Serve immediately. Makes 4 servings.

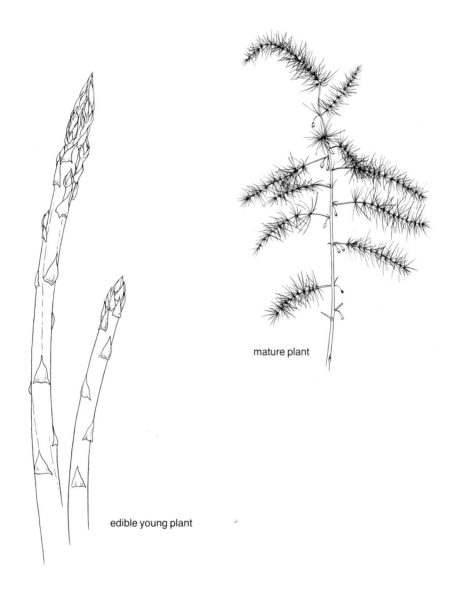

mature plant

edible young plant

Asparagus
Asparagus officinalis L.

Lily family: Liliaceae

Description: Wild asparagus is an introduced perennial herb that has escaped from cultivation. The roots are much branched, forming a tangled mat, which in a mature plant may extend out a considerable distance. In spring when asparagus first emerges from the soil, the shoot is light green and tender with small, scalelike leaves folded up against the thick stem. The shoots rapidly grow into tall, slender plants. Often mistaken for ferns at this stage, the plants are much branched with many small branchlets resembling thin leaves, but the true leaves are scalelike and even smaller. The flowers are small, greenish white, and bell-shaped, some developing into bright red berries later in summer. Although relished by birds, these berries are not considered edible for humans.

Distribution: Throughout much of the eastern and northern United States and into Canada; common in the eastern and north-central Great Plains, less common in the western part.

Habitat: Rich, moist soil in wooded areas, fields, and yards; along fence rows where plants sprout from seeds dropped by birds; often found in partial shade, but will grow well in full sun if the roots are protected from heat.

Edible parts: Young, tender shoots, cooked or uncooked.

Season to collect: Spring.

Cautions: Eat young tender shoots only. Other parts of the plant may contain toxins.

Additional information and recipes: Wild asparagus is a delicious treat— so delicious that it is considered bad manners to ask other persons where they find wild asparagus. Once spotted, it can easily be identified because it looks like the asparagus sold in grocery stores. The spotting, however, can be a bit tricky. Newly emerging shoots are often obscured by dry grass and leaves, and even when a shoot has grown clear of ground debris, its green color and simple shape may make it difficult to see. From a fellow wild-plant enthusiast I learned how to focus selectively on asparagus even where it is growing amid other vegetation.

Begin by locating a clump of asparagus in the wild, but instead of immediately picking it, stand back and look it over. Walk around, examining it from various angles and distances. Notice how it looks against other plants and colors. Observe it from both a standing and a sitting position. Bend over and look at it upside-down. After awhile, cut a shoot, sit back, and eat it right there, still examining the clump from which it came. Somehow this works to make finding asparagus easier.

In addition, it may be helpful to know that being a perennial, asparagus comes up each spring from the same root mass as it did the year before, so wherever you see dried asparagus stalks, new shoots are likely to grow at the base in spring. For additional help in learning to spot the dried stalks, read the section on asparagus in Euell Gibbons's *Stalking the Wild Asparagus* (available at most libraries). Gibbons's description of asparagus is a classic and one on which I cannot improve.

After finding a clump of asparagus, it is tempting to return to the same plant for subsequent pickings. Shoots may be taken from a clump twice during a season, but then the shoots should be allowed to grow and mature so that the plant can store food for the following year. (Also, be aware that the shoots produced by very young plants will be thin and spindly—pass these by for a year or two until they develop stems of at least ½ inch diameter.)

Don't abandon your asparagus clumps once the harvesting period is over. Continue to watch the stubby shoots change during summer into tall, delicate plants, then scout the surrounding area and take note of other asparagus clumps that you may have missed earlier. Some persons even make asparagus maps.

For those areas where only a few shoots can be found, asparagus may be enjoyed simply as a nibble. Even a single raw shoot cut diagonally into thin slices will add flavor to a tossed salad. Where asparagus is plentiful, it is often cooked in a variety of ways. Whole shoots are usually boiled or steamed. Sliced shoots may be boiled, steamed, cooked in cream, or stir-fried in a little oil. However you fix asparagus, cook it only until tender—the flavor is drastically harmed by overcooking.

Preparation of the shoots is simple: wash them under running water to dislodge any dirt or sand trapped under the flaplike leaves and trim away the bottom ends if they seem tough—but keep those trimmings for making soup.

Cooked asparagus
1 pound asparagus shoots, trimmed
½ to 1 cup water
salt and freshly ground black pepper to taste
   Tie the shoots into a bundle with white string. Pour the water into a tall

pot (such as a stove-top coffeepot) and bring it to a boil. Stand the asparagus bundle in the boiling water, cover with a lid, and cook for about 12 minutes. The bottom portions will cook in the water, the tips will cook in the steam. (Drain the cooking water and reserve it for soup.) Carefully remove the shoots. Serve plain with salt and pepper or with butter, sour cream, or other dressings. Makes 4 servings.

Stir-fried asparagus slices

1 pound asparagus, trimmed
3 tablespoons vegetable oil
salt and freshly ground black pepper to taste

With a sharp knife cut the asparagus diagonally into thin slices (about ¼ inch thick). In a skillet, heat the oil slightly, then add the asparagus slices. Season with salt and pepper. Turn the heat to medium-high and cook, stirring constantly, until the slices are bright green and tender but not browned. The cooking time will be only a few minutes. Makes 4 servings.

Variations of this recipe are numerous. Try adding stir-fried mushrooms and onions or season the slices with garlic powder while they are cooking, then sprinkle with toasted, crushed sesame seeds. (Directions for toasting sesame seeds appear in the section about woodnettle.) A topping of sour cream or yogurt just before serving is simple, but very good.

Cream of asparagus soup

1 pound asparagus
3 cups chicken broth or water
¼ cup butter or margarine (½ stick)
¼ cup all-purpose flour
1 cup milk or light cream
salt and freshly ground black pepper to taste
dash of ground or grated nutmeg

Trim the asparagus and set the tender portions aside. In a large pot combine the liquid and the parts that were trimmed away. Simmer for about 10 minutes to extract the flavor from the trimmings. Meanwhile, slice the tender portions diagonally into pieces about ½ inch thick. Remove the trimmings from the liquid, then save the liquid, but discard the trimmings. Add the tender slices to the liquid and again simmer about 10 minutes.

While the slices cook, melt the butter or margarine in a small skillet. Add the flour and stir, allowing the mixture to bubble for less than a minute—do not let it brown. Add the milk or cream all at one time and stir with a fork or whisk. When the mixture is thick and well blended, add it and the seasonings to the pot of hot liquid and asparagus. Stir well to combine. Serve hot with croutons or buttered toast. The soup may be reheated just before serving, but for best flavor, do not allow it to simmer very long. Makes about 6 servings.

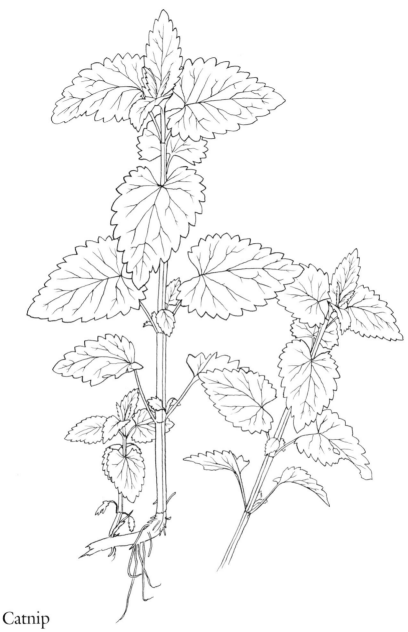

Catnip
Nepeta cataria L.

Mint family: Lamiaceae

Description: Catnip is an introduced, widely naturalized perennial herb, usually much branched and attaining a height of up to 3 feet at maturity. The leaves are opposite with blunt teeth along the margins; the upper surface is smooth to slightly hairy, the lower surface has more hairs, making the leaves soft to the touch. The flowers are pale lavender and born in clusters at the tip of the stem and branches. The fruits (which look like seeds) are numerous and very small. When cut or bruised, the plant emits a strong mintlike odor.

Distribution: Scattered throughout the United States and into Canada; common throughout the Great Plains.

Habitat: Yards, wooded areas, and along ditches, fence rows, and roadsides.

Edible parts: The fresh or dried leaves for tea.

Seasons to collect: Any time of year that live plants can be found—usually from spring until frost.

Cautions: In spring, the young shoots of stinging nettle may be mistaken for shoots of catnip. An easy way to tell them apart is to notice the teeth along the margins of the leaves. The teeth on stinging nettle leaves are sharply pointed; those on catnip are blunt to rounded.

Although often sold as an herb, catnip is sometimes considered a weed. Collect from areas that have not been sprayed with herbicide.

Additional information and recipes: Opinions differ about catnip tea, but many persons consider its mintlike flavor pleasant and find it a soothing and calming drink, particularly at bedtime. Cats, too, exhibit individual preferences—some are much attracted to this plant, while others are indifferent.

Brought to this continent by settlers, catnip soon escaped from cultivation and became so widespread that it is often believed to be a native plant. Catnip can be transplanted or started from seed, and because it has a short taproot, it is easily controlled by hoeing.

Although catnip is better known for hot tea, iced catnip tea is good, too. Unlike most herbal teas, catnip is more often brewed from fresh leaves than from dried, and although good either way, the flavors are quite different.

It seems not to matter what time of day catnip is picked or whether young or mature parts are selected. However, I recommend choosing the young, upper leaves and stems because they are apt to be cleaner than the lower portions of the plant. I prefer tea made from fresh leaves picked just before brewing, so I grow a clump of catnip just outside the back door where it can be easily reached even when the ground is muddy. In winter, of course, I do use dried leaves.

To dry catnip

Pick catnip branches and wash them well. Shake off as much water as possible, then pat dry with a towel or hang the branches up until no water remains. Remove the leaves from the stems and discard the stems because they take considerably longer to dry.

For large amounts, spread the leaves in a single layer on kitchen towels in a large pan with sides. Protect from dust by covering the pan with cheesecloth or a single kitchen towel. Set the pan in a light, dry place away from direct sunlight. For small amounts, place the leaves in a single layer between tissues in a large book. Either way, allow the leaves to remain until brittle dry, then store them in a tightly covered container in a cool place.

Catnip tea

To use fresh catnip, pick a handful of upper branches and wash them well. (If making iced tea, pick a large handful.) Stems and leaves may remain attached.

To use dried catnip, allow 1 tablespoon crumbled leaves for each cup of hot tea and 2 tablespoons for each cup of iced tea.

In a pot, heat a quart of water to boiling. Then turn off the heat, stir in the catnip, and cover with a lid. Allow the catnip to steep about 5 minutes.

To serve hot, pour the tea directly into cups or into a heated teapot. (Heat the teapot by filling it with hot water, letting it stand at least a minute, then pouring out the water.) Add honey, sugar, or lemon if desired.

To serve cold, simply pour the hot tea over ice to cool it. Honey, sugar, or lemon makes a good addition, but honey will dissolve better if added before the tea is cooled.

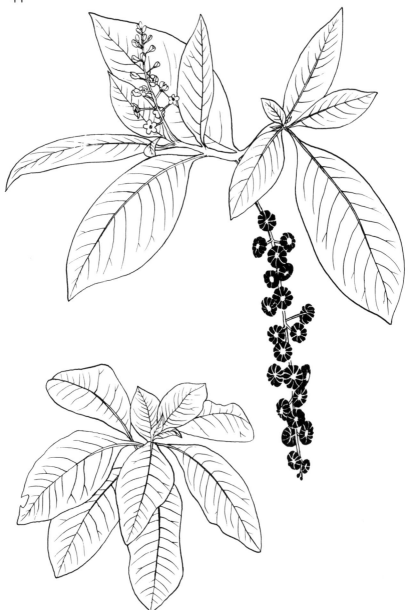

Pokeweed, pokeberry, poke, inkberry

Phytolacca americana L.

Pokeweed family: Phytolaccaceae

Description: Pokeweed is a tall perennial herb native to the eastern United States but introduced and naturalized in the southeastern Great Plains. Fast growing, pokeweed may attain a height of 10 feet or more in a single summer. Plants die back with the first hard freeze, but come up the following spring to begin their remarkable growth all over again. In spring, when the shoot first emerges, it is light green and smooth with opposite or alternate leaves folded up against the rather thick stem. In a few days, the leaves open outward. As the plant grows, the stem and older branches remain smooth but may become tinged with purple or deep red. The leaves become quite large, up to 15 inches long. The flowers have 5 petals and are small and white, often with tinges of pink or green. They hang in long drooping clusters. The ripe berries, which look something like miniature round pillows tacked in the middle, are deep purple, quite juicy, and contain numerous small seeds.

Distribution: Throughout much of the eastern United States, especially the southeast, with scattered populations wherever introduced; common throughout the southeastern Great Plains.

Habitat: Rich, moist soil along fence rows, ditches, and streams. Often in wooded areas and in places where the soil has been disturbed, such as in fields, gardens, and yards.

Edible parts: Properly cooked young shoots 8 inches or less in height, with leaves folded up against the stem or relaxed outward. (Some persons eat the specially prepared immature leaves from the tips of branches, as well as the specially prepared stems, but read the cautions and other information below.)

Seasons to collect: Shoots in spring. (In the southeastern United States, certain parts are collected throughout the summer.)

Cautions: Any discussion of pokeweed must contain a strong warning that much of the plant contains a harmful compound that can be absorbed through the skin, particularly through abrasions. This compound (a mitogen) can cause serious changes in the blood, so don't handle uncooked pokeweed if you have cuts or skinned places on your hands. Also, wear gloves for yard work involving pokeweed, especially when handling mature plants or when moving roots. If you grow your own pokeweed, surround the plants with tall wire or otherwise isolate them from human traffic and from pets such as dogs and cats. (Don't be alarmed if you see birds eating the ripe berries—birds can eat many things that humans and other mammals cannot.)

Although some persons use the stems and immature leaves from older plants, I recommend that if you try pokeweed, you use only the young shoots, 8 inches or less tall, and that you cut them off at least an inch above the ground to avoid any contact with the root. Cook the shoots as directed; never eat uncooked pokeweed.

Additional information and recipes: If ever a plant was a paradox, pokeweed is that plant. Probably posing more hazards than any other edible wild plant, it is also one of the best known and most commonly eaten. In the southeastern United States, pokeweed serves as a vegetable staple for many rural families and is available, commercially canned, to urban residents as well.

A long tradition has taught southerners how to use this plant safely, but in other areas where pokeweed has spread, important details about its use are often lacking. Pokeweed is certainly good tasting and is included here with the hope that the information presented will help readers use the plant safely.

My own experience with pokeweed began years ago. Each spring I would glean a few shoots here and there along a nearby roadside, being careful to select only very young shoots. But then one year, friends who did likewise became extremely ill. From what they said later, I suspected they had used "too tall" shoots, but the whole affair scared me enough that I stopped using pokeweed altogether.

Then, a few years later, I heard that women in southeastern Kentucky not only gathered pokeweed in midsummer, but picked leaves from plants that towered above their heads. Again I became interested in the edibility of pokeweed and more than a little curious. That is how I came to be in Harlan County, Kentucky, one spring for the annual Poke Sallet Festival, a celebration which, according to advertisements, served up *bushels* of pokeweed in the form of "poke sallet."

In hopes of being able to observe the picking, I had arrived a few days early, but the collecting was already underway in nearby mountains and locating the picking crew would have been impossible. However, I was directed to the home of a family everyone felt sure could provide the information I'd come so far to find. That family immediately took me in. The woman, who was born in the area and had lived there all her life, was well versed in the art of collecting and cooking pokeweed, having been taught by her mother and grandmother.

Poke leaves, she said, could indeed be gathered from tall plants in summer, but it was only the *very young* leaves from the *tips* of branches that were picked. These were prepared in much the same way as the shoots of spring: boiled in two waters, drained, then fried in pork grease—usually from salt pork or bacon. Shoots or leaves or a combination of both cooked in this manner were what was known as poke sallet.

I told her about my friends who had eaten pokeweed shoots and become ill. She said this could happen, but that it was because the shoots were too mature or had not been cooked properly.

To my surprise, she described cooking the *branches* of pokeweed as well. She explained that the harmful compound in the branches is found in the skin, and she set about to demonstrate. First she peeled away every bit of skin, then split the branches and cut them into chunks. She boiled these chunks in the same manner as the leaves and shoots, but she then rolled them in cornmeal and fried them in grease. It seemed that bacon or some kind of pork figured into nearly every method of preparing poke.

This kind couple not only offered to show me how to pick and prepare the various offerings of pokeweed, they generously invited me to spend the night in their home so that we could get an early start the following day.

The next morning was busy: not only did we pick a bushel of poke, we butchered the hog as well. Other members of the family came to help, and by noon all of us sat down to heaping plates of poke sallet, fried poke chunks, cornbread, baked beans, and very fresh pork chops. I have never tasted a better meal.

Back home in Nebraska, I planted a patch of pokeweed in my backyard, but behind a tall wire fence to prevent children from getting into it. In spite of having eaten both the fried branches and the cooked leaves from the tips of the branches without ill effect, I stick to the young shoots of spring. Skinning those branches can be difficult: every bit of skin must be peeled away. And getting just the right leaves at the tips of the branches can be tricky, too. Cooks in the South have been taught first-hand by mothers and grandmothers who knew the pokeweed plant well, having been taught in the same way by their mothers and grandmothers. Freshly cooked, canned, or frozen, pokeweed is an important part of the traditional foodways of the South.

Poke sallet

Pick 1 gallon (about one-half bucketful) of pokeweed shoots. Wash them well. Put the shoots into a large kettle and pour in enough boiling water to cover. Let boil for about 10 minutes. Drain and add more water, boil again for about 10 minutes, then drain once more. In a skillet, fry some bacon or salt pork until well done, then add the poke. Stir and cook for about 5 minutes. Serve hot. Makes about 6 servings.

To freeze pokeweed shoots
Read about freezing, Appendix A.

Gather young shoots about 3 to 4 inches tall. Wash, then drain them well. Place the shoots in a wire basket and plunge them into boiling water for 2 minutes, then drain. Place the wire basket with poke shoots into ice water to cool. Drain again, then pack enough for individual meals in heavy plastic bags. Freeze. (To reheat, place the frozen shoots into a pot with a small amount of water and cook for about 10 minutes. Discard the water. Fry the shoots in bacon grease until tender.)

To can pokeweed shoots
Use a pressure canner and follow the manufacturer's directions. Also see general comments about canning, Appendix A.

Wash the shoots well and remove any large or tough stems. In a large kettle, cover the shoots with boiling water and allow them to cook for 10 minutes, then drain and discard the water. Cut through the shoots several times with a sharp knife. Pack the shoots into hot jars leaving 1 inch headspace. Add ¼ teaspoon salt to pints, ½ teaspoon salt to quarts. Add boiling water to just cover the shoots (still leaving 1 inch at the top). Cap the jars with two-piece screwband lids and process in a pressure canner. For altitudes of 1,000 feet or less, use 10 pounds of pressure; for altitudes of more than 1,000 feet, use 15 pounds of pressure. With either pressure, process pints for 1 hour and 10 minutes, quarts for 1 hour and 30 minutes. Carefully remove the jars from the canner and allow them to cool away from drafts.

edible young plant

mature plant

Lambs-quarters, wild spinach, pigweed
Chenopodium album L.

Pitseed goosefoot, lambs-quarters, wild spinach, pigweed
Chenopodium berlandieri Moq.

Goosefoot family: Chenopodiaceae

Description: The lambs-quarters are annual herbs reproducing by seed. The leaves are alternate and somewhat diamond-shaped to triangular. Typically, the underside is covered with a white mealy substance, as is the upper surface of newly formed leaves at the top of young plants. The stem of the young plant is smooth, green, and tender. Later, as the plant matures, the stem toughens, becomes grooved, and may be tinged with red. Mature plants are branched and commonly reach a height of 4 feet or more. The flowers are small and pale green and occur in dense, irregularly shaped clusters in the axils near the tips of the branches. Although inconspicuous, these flowers put out a great deal of pollen, much to the discomfort of hay fever sufferers. The fruits (which look like seeds) are small and occur in clusters.

Distribution: Scattered across the United States and into Canada; throughout the Great Plains.

Habitat: Common in yards, gardens, and barnyards and along ditches, fence rows, and roadsides.

Edible parts: Cooked leaves and stems of young plants up to about 8 inches tall; very young leaves may be used uncooked in salads.

Seasons to collect: Spring, early summer—sometimes a new crop of young plants can be found in late summer or early autumn.

Cautions: Many persons consider lambs-quarters a weed to be eradicated, so be aware that plants along roadsides and in vacant lots may have been sprayed with herbicides. To avoid sprays, allow lambs-quarters to grow in a selected spot in your own yard, but cut or mow these plants before they mature and produce pollen.

Collect only the *Chenopodium* species that fit the description above. Some species have a strong, unpleasant odor and little is known about their edibility.

Additional information and recipes: Next to the dandelion, lambs-quarters seems to be the wild plant most commonly gathered for greens in the Great Plains. In the past, the young lambs-quarters commonly gathered for greens in the Great Plains was considered to be *Chenopodium album,* a plant introduced from Eurasia. However, it is now generally recognized that some native species, particularly *Chenopodium berlandieri,* also have been used.

Mild flavored and easy to prepare, it remains a spring tradition with families from both rural and urban areas. Although not as early as dandelion and stinging nettle, young lambs-quarters plants (stems as well as leaves) are ready to eat long before garden greens and are an exceptionally good source of vitamin A.

Because the stems of young lambs-quarters are tender, it is possible to harvest large quantities by hand in a relatively short time. This may be one of the reasons that lambs-quarters was so often the plant canned for winter greens in the Great Plains. A retired meter reader told me that in Kansas City during the Depression of the 1930s, he frequently saw large quantities of lambs-quarters—often bathtubsful—being washed in preparation for canning. Other persons have recalled that lambs-quarters was one of the few edible wild plants that could be found in urban areas during the Depression. Today, lambs-quarters is more often frozen than canned, because freezing results in better retention of flavor and color.

With the exception of the very young leaves, lambs-quarters is usually not eaten raw. It is much like spinach and may be substituted for spinach in most recipes. Lambs-quarters is good in soup, stew, scrambled eggs, quiche, and omelet and can be used to make the cold salad described in the section on woodnettle or any of the stinging nettle recipes except those requiring dried plants—the leaves of lambs-quarters do not dry well.

By far, the most common way to serve lambs-quarters is as greens—boiled or steamed until tender, heated in bacon grease, and served with a sprinkling of vinegar and perhaps slices of hard-cooked eggs. A letter from a Nebraska woman describes the lambs-quarters tradition so well it will serve as a recipe:

Lambs-quarters greens

I often helped mother gather plants to cook and eat. We called it "gathering greens." We cooked (boiled) the greens and the prepared product looked like canned spinach. Mother looked over the gathered greens, sorted, and washed them, then put them on the stove with a small amount of water, boiled the greens until tender, then drained off the excess water. She had a skillet ready with hot bacon grease; into this she added the cooked greens, and stirred them until heated through. She then brought the greens to the table with seasoning of salt and pepper—the vinegar was optional. Some people preferred it with just bits of crisp bacon and salt and pepper, nothing else. I liked the vinegar (just a small amount). If it was spring, I'd ask you to come out to Gresham and I would fix you a "mess of greens." (I use that expression because that was Mama's words.)

Aretta Doremus, Gresham, Nebraska

To freeze lambs-quarters greens

Read about freezing, Appendix A.

Wash and sort the young plants, then place them in a wire basket in a large kettle of boiling water. Cover with a lid and boil for 2 minutes. Remove the kettle from the heat, then remove the basket of greens and immerse it in ice water. When cooled, drain the greens and ladle them into small containers, leaving 1 inch headspace; freeze.

To use later, put the frozen greens into a pot with about ½ cup boiling water, cover with a lid, and cook over medium-high heat for about 5 minutes or until the greens are piping hot all the way through.

Creamed lambs-quarters with mushrooms

4 tablespoons margarine or butter

½ cup thinly sliced onion

½ cup sliced mushrooms

2 cups lambs-quarters leaves and stems, coarsely chopped

¼ cup water

2 tablespoons all-purpose flour

1 cup milk

salt and freshly ground black pepper to taste

½ cup dairy sour cream (optional)

Place the onion, mushrooms, and margarine in a skillet and cook over medium heat until tender, but not browned. Add the lambs-quarters and water; cover with a lid and cook until the leaves are tender and bright green—about 4 or 5 minutes. Remove the lid. With a fork, pull the ingredients to one side and tilt the skillet so that the melted margarine drains away from the onions and mushrooms. (Usually the water will have cooked away, but if water still remains, cook with the lid off until only melted margarine remains.) Add the flour to the melted margarine; stir and cook until the flour-margarine mixture bubbles. Add the milk all at once and stir everything together until the liquid has thickened. Season with salt and pepper. Makes about 3 servings. Good served over toast, potatoes, or rice.

Sour cream makes an interesting variation. Add it to the other ingredients just before serving, stirring over low heat only until heated through —do not allow to boil.

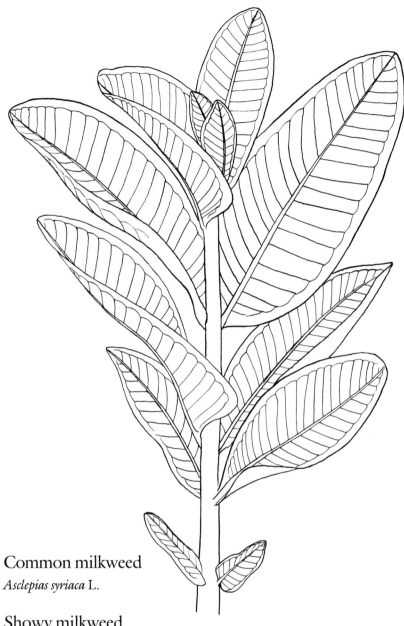

Common milkweed
Asclepias syriaca L.

Showy milkweed
Asclepias speciosa Torr.

Milkweed family: Asclepiadaceae

Description: Common milkweed and showy milkweed are hardy native perennial herbs having milky juice. They reproduce from seed and from deep underground stems. The plants are usually unbranched, with common milkweed typically reaching a height of 2½ to 4 feet at maturity, and showy milkweed usually no more than 3½ feet. The leaves are opposite and entire with a prominent midvein. In spring when the young plants first emerge from the soil, the leaves are folded up against the thick stem of the shoot, but soon afterward relax outward. As the plant grows, the leaves become fairly large and quite leathery, but retain a covering of fine hairs on the underside. The flower buds are borne in tight green clusters that develop into loose, rounded clusters of flowers varying from pale pink to deep rose and occasionally lavender. Each flower has 5 petals bent downward and a crown of 5 lobes. Though similar, the flowers of showy milkweed are larger than those of common milkweed and have thicker pedicels. Only a few flowers from each cluster will develop seed pods (technically, follicles), which taper to a slightly curved tip and are covered with small hornlike appendages. Immature pods are firm and dull green with very soft appendages. As the pods mature, they become fibrous and spongy, then dry and brittle and gray, finally splitting open along their seams to release tufted seeds into the wind.

Distribution: Throughout the eastern and north-central United States and into Canada, with scattered populations west and south; in the Great Plains, common milkweed is more prevalent in the east, showy milkweed in the west, with both occurring in the north-central portion.

Habitat: Open areas, fields, yards, fence rows, roadsides, and ditches; usually in full sun.

Edible parts: Cooked young shoots up to about 7 inches tall (with leaves folded up against the stem or relaxed outward); flower buds and flowers (see page 114); and immature pods (see page 158).

Seasons to collect: Young shoots in spring; flower buds and flowers in early summer; flowers and immature pods from middle to late summer.

Cautions: Not all milkweed species are edible. Use only those species and plant parts specified as edible and cook them according to the directions given for each part. Until they are cooked, even the edible species of milkweed contain chemicals toxic to people and other mammals—never eat any part of milkweed raw and do not allow plants to remain where they might be grazed by livestock. Furthermore, milkweed juice can irritate the skin; wear gloves for picking or wash hands thoroughly.

Make certain that you have the right plant—some poisonous plants, such as the dogbanes (*Apocynum* species), closely resemble the edible milkweeds, especially at the shoot stage. Unless confident that you can tell these plants apart, you must ask an expert for help. Your county extension service or local weed board can provide information about the specific plants in your area. Note that not all plants having milky juice are milkweeds, and not all species of milkweed have milky juice.

Take care not to disturb monarch butterfly caterpillars that may be feeding on the milkweed leaves. In recent years the number of these butterflies has greatly decreased due to the destruction of wilderness areas in Mexico where they overwinter—it would be a shame to cause them harm in their summer range as well.

Additional information and recipes: Well known as a threat to grazing animals and stubbornly hardy in fields and gardens, milkweeds are mainly viewed as plants to be eradicated. Given this information, it may be surprising to learn that if properly cooked, parts of both the common and showy milkweeds are not only edible, but exceptionally good tasting. Years ago, milkweed served as an important vegetable in the diets of Plains Indian people, who often added the shoots and pods to soups and boiled the flowers to obtain a kind of syrup. Beginning in spring and continuing until late summer, both of these milkweeds offer one edible treat after another.

In spring the young shoots may be boiled and served like asparagus; in early summer the cooked clusters of flower buds resemble broccoli; in midsummer, when these clusters open, the flowers can be dipped into batter to make delicious deep-fried fritters; and by late summer the tender young seed pods are good boiled and stuffed with fillings. Because of this bountiful succession, it may be helpful to plant an "indicator" clump of milkweed in your backyard so that by observing it you will know when each part is ready to harvest in the wild. Hoeing will keep the clump from spreading, and you can eat the pods before seeds mature and spread to neighbors' yards.

When the young shoots first appear, they look something like asparagus and a lot like dogbane (which not only is toxic but, fortunately, tastes awful even when cooked). Once you are certain you have found the right plants, select shoots up to about 7 inches tall and, if possible, harvest them not more than an hour before cooking.

In order for shoots to be edible, the milky juice must be removed by boiling them and discarding the water. Milkweed enthusiasts differ on the number of minutes and the number of boilings needed, but they agree that heating the water to boiling before pouring it over the shoots is more effective for removing the milky juice than placing the shoots in water and allowing them to warm gradually as the water heats. The following method seems to be the most common.

Milkweed shoots
Use two pots. Place the shoots in one pot and heat water in the other. When the water boils, pour enough over the shoots to cover them well, then place the pot over medium heat and allow the shoots to boil gently for 4 minutes. Drain and discard the water. Again heat and pour in enough boiling water to cover the shoots, boil for 4 minutes, and discard the water. Repeat a third time.

Once cooked, shoots may be served plain with simple seasonings or incorporated into other recipes. A can of chicken-gumbo soup (undiluted) makes a good seasoning—simply add it to the shoots after they have been drained, then heat and serve.

Milkweed shoots are good in casseroles, and because the flavor is something like that of green beans, they may be substituted wherever green beans might be used—but do remember that the shoots must first be cooked according to the directions above.

Hearty milkweed sandwich
To make 2 sandwiches, have ready:
8 milkweed shoots, cooked according to the directions above
2 slices of bread
margarine or butter
½ cup toasted sunflower seeds or 4 slices of crisply fried bacon
4 thin slices of tomato (optional)
CHEESE SAUCE
½ cup cream or undiluted evaporated milk
1 teaspoon cornstarch
½ teaspoon Worcestershire sauce
¼ teaspoon dry mustard
¼ teaspoon freshly ground black pepper
1 cup grated cheese such as sharp cheddar, Gruyere, or a processed cheese
    In a heavy medium-sized pot over low heat or in the top of a double boiler

over boiling water, stir together the milk, cornstarch, Worcestershire sauce, dry mustard, and black pepper. Stirring constantly, cook until the sauce thickens. Add the cheese and stir only until it melts. Turn off the heat, cover with a lid, and allow the sauce to remain in the pot or in the top of the double boiler so that it will stay hot until ready to be used.

TO ASSEMBLE THE SANDWICH

Cut each cooked milkweed shoot diagonally into slices about ½ inch thick. Toast the bread and spread it with margarine or butter. Arrange the milkweed slices on the toasted bread; add the sunflower seeds or bacon, and tomato if desired. Ladle the hot cheese sauce over each sandwich and serve immediately. Makes 2 open-faced sandwiches. Recipe may be doubled, tripled, or more.

Variations include spreading the toast with mayonnaise, substituting nuts for the sunflower seeds, and adding 1 to 2 tablespoons of white wine with the cheese. A Pinot chardonnay is just right for this, but any dry white wine would do. (Note that wine, even when cooked or in combination with other ingredients, can pose a serious problem for anyone sensitive to alcohol. Never serve food containing alcohol without informing guests.)

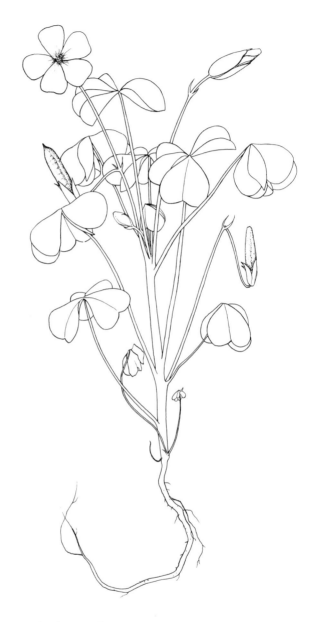

Yellow wood sorrel, sheep shower

Oxalis stricta L.

Wood sorrel family: Oxalidaceae

Description: Yellow wood sorrel is a delicate native perennial herb growing to a height of up to 12 inches. Stems may be smooth or covered with downy hairs. Leaves are cloverlike, divided into three inverted heart-shaped leaflets, and may be green or purplish. The flowers, which bloom throughout the growing season, are yellow with 5 petals and develop into small, green capsules having rows of small, round seeds.

Distribution: Scattered throughout the United States; common throughout the Great Plains.

Habitat: Wooded areas, yards, and gardens; in full sun or partial shade.

Edible parts: Uncooked leaves, flowers, fruits. (Heat destroys the sour flavor.)

Seasons to collect: From early spring to late autumn.

Cautions: Wood sorrel contains oxalic acid, which in large amounts can be harmful. However, the amount in yellow wood sorrel eaten as a nibble or as a garnish for a salad is not a problem.

Do not gather plants from lawns or other areas that may have been sprayed with chemicals or may be frequented by dogs.

Additional information and recipes: Growing abundantly in lawns and gardens, yellow wood sorrel is unpopular with grass enthusiasts but much liked by children who eat its flowers, leaves, and seed capsules, calling the plant among themselves "sour clover," "sauerkraut," "pickles," and "sour bananas"—the latter because of the shape of the seed capsules. By whatever name, it is one of the best known of all edible wild plants throughout the United States.

Uses for yellow wood sorrel

Strewn over potato salad or scrambled eggs, the flowers and leaves of yellow wood sorrel make an attractive garnish. Leaves, flowers, and seed capsules make interesting additions to vinegar-and-oil dressing and are good in tossed salad or on chilled asparagus tips.

Pineapple-weed, wild chamomile
Matricaria matricarioides (Less.) Porter

Sunflower family: Asteraceae

Description: Pineapple-weed is a short, erect annual herb that spreads by seed. It is introduced and has naturalized widely. Under good growing conditions, pineapple-weed may reach a height of 10 or more inches but commonly stands no more than 6 inches at maturity. The plants are usually branched, especially near the top. The leaves are medium green, smooth, and finely divided. The flowers have a fragrance and flavor reminiscent of pineapple, but what appears to be a single flower is really a head of very small green or yellow-green florets crowded together. As the seeds ripen, the heads take on shades of tan or gray. (Note that what appear to be seeds are actually small, dry fruits called achenes, each containing a single tiny seed. In the information that follows, I will refer to the achenes as seeds.)

Distribution: Scattered throughout much of the northern United States; in the Great Plains, throughout much of North Dakota, scattered populations south to southern Nebraska.

Habitat: Dry soil, in open areas such as railroad yards, often along roads and driveways.

Edible parts: Immature flower heads, fresh or dried for tea.

Seasons to collect: Anytime flower heads can be found, usually late spring to late summer.

Cautions: The flowers of pineapple-weed produce pollen which, although inconspicuous, is present in the tea. Persons who are allergic to ragweed pollen may find that they are sensitive to the pollen of pineapple-weed as well. If you have allergies, it is better to begin with only a small amount of this tea, and even if all goes well, don't make it your main drink. In general, persons who tend to develop pollen allergies would do well to drink teas brewed from leaves rather than those made with flowers.

Additional information and recipes: Pineapple-weed grows so easily from seed, it is no wonder settlers were successful in getting it started in so many places. It is not known just when pineapple-weed was brought to the Plains, but years ago I interviewed several older women who remembered picking it when they were children in the late 1800s. One woman had lived near Yankton, South Dakota, and the other women had lived in southeastern Nebraska. From their descriptions, it would seem that pineapple-weed was already well established in those areas at that time.

If you want to grow pineapple-weed in your yard, remember that although immature flower heads are best for tea, mature (ripe) seed heads must be collected for planting. (Seed heads are not desirable for tea because they shatter.) Although flower heads and seed heads are similar in appearance and are often present on the same plant at the same time, they are easy to tell apart. Flower heads are compact and green and feel slightly moist when crushed between the fingers; seed heads are dry and readily fall apart when crushed. Remember also that the color of the mature seed heads is grayish or slightly tan. When crushed, both flower heads and seed heads exude a wonderful fragrance—and the flavor of the tea will be much like that. I consider tea made from pineapple-weed flowers to be superior to the chamomile teas available commercially.

To dry pineapple-weed

Collect the flower heads and shake them out onto a kitchen towel on a cookie sheet. Put this in a light, airy place out of direct sunlight until the heads are thoroughly dry. Store the heads in tightly covered containers in a cool place.

Pineapple-weed tea

For each cup of tea:

2 to 4 tablespoons pineapple-weed flower heads, fresh or dried

1 cup boiling water

Heat water in a saucepan, and when it reaches the boiling point, turn off the heat and stir in the flower heads. Cover the pan with a lid and steep for about 7 minutes. Meanwhile, heat a teapot or cup by filling it with boiling water. When the tea has steeped, discard the water in the teapot or cup and fill it with tea, pouring the tea through a strainer and pressing the flower heads with the back of a spoon against the side of the strainer to extract more flavor. Serve the tea immediately, adding honey, sugar, or lemon, if desired.

Wild roses

Rosa species

Rose family: Rosaceae

Description: Most of the several native species of wild rose are upright or sprawling shrubs, although two climbing roses, one native and one introduced, occur in the Great Plains. All reproduce by underground stems or roots and by seeds. The leaves are alternate and divided into from 3 to several leaflets arranged as opposite pairs with a terminal leaflet. Leaflets of some species are rounded, others are pointed; the margins are toothed. Most species are more or less armed with sharp prickles on stems and branches, but at least two may have few or no prickles. The flowers have 5 petals (double forms are rare) with color ranging from white to pink to deep rose. Fruits, commonly called hips, are red to red orange at maturity and contain numerous seeds.

Distribution: Scattered across much of the United States, except the arid southwest, and into Canada; scattered throughout the Great Plains, but less common to absent in the southwest, climbing species only in the southeast.

Habitat: Varies with the species of wild rose; some found in moist soils, some in drier soils; often on hillsides, rocky ledges, open woods or prairies, and along roadsides and fence rows.

Edible parts: Flower petals, cooked or uncooked; ripe fruits (hips), fresh or dried, cooked or uncooked (see page 208).

Seasons to collect: Flower petals in late spring or early summer; hips in late summer, throughout autumn, and into winter.

Cautions: Petals and hips of all wild roses are considered to be edible, but do not collect from plants that have been sprayed or pick from frequently used roadsides where plants may be contaminated by dust or exhaust fumes. Garden roses may be used if you can determine that the plants have not been sprayed or treated with systemic insecticides. Be aware that many plant nurseries use systemic chemicals on roses and that such poisons remain in the plant for a long time.

Rose flowers are a favorite with bees. When picking petals be patient and let a bee finish its work in a flower. Bees are easily annoyed by shooing or other acts meant to hurry them on.

Additional information and recipes: Due to their relatively short stature and the fact that they often grow amid grasses, wild roses may go unnoticed except when they are in bloom, but at that time they are a beautiful sight along roadsides and fences.

Rose petals

Like those of many other wild plants, flowers from individual rose bushes vary greatly in eating quality. Sampling a petal is no help in selecting good-tasting flowers because a single raw petal will have little or no taste. Fortunately, with roses fragrance and flavor go together, so how the petals will *taste* when cooked can be determined by checking the *fragrance* of the fresh petals. The deeper shades of pink are usually best, but it is important to pick any rose petals before the heat of the day—for example, before 11:00 A.M. By afternoon, both fragrance and flavor are greatly diminished.

For collecting, you will need a small pair of scissors and a container that can be hung over your arm, such as a basket or light pail. A pail with a lid is ideal because the flavor is better retained if the petals are covered soon after they have been picked.

If you gently remove a petal from a rose you will see that the base where it was attached to the center of the flower is lighter in color. This part of the petal is bitter and must be removed. Fortunately, that can be easily accomplished as you pick. Simply bring your hand up around a flower, grasping all of the petals together, then pull them off with a gentle tug. While still holding the petals in one hand, snip off all the base parts with the scissors you are holding in the other hand, then deposit the petals in the container. In this way the picking proceeds rapidly and in a short time you will have a pint or more of petals.

There is a second reason to recommend this method of collection. By taking petals only, you leave the center portion of the flower (which contains the male and female parts) to mature into a hip. As a result, two crops may be harvested from a single flower.

Once home with your harvest, refrigerate the petals until they are to be used. But don't wait long. Rose petals deteriorate quickly and are best used within a day after picking. Fresh rose petals make an attractive addition to salads, desserts, and drinks. When petals are used in cooking, the flavor is best preserved by recipes that require minimal heat, because the flavor is contained in volatile oils that are easily carried off by steam. This principle is the basis for distillation, a process whereby the flavor and fragrance of a plant can be extracted by boiling it in water, then collecting and quickly cooling the steam so that it condenses into a liquid again. When rose petals are processed in this manner, the resulting product is rose water, a marvelous es-

sence used both as a flavoring and as a fragrance. Because distillation requires equipment not usually found in an ordinary kitchen, it is a bit tricky
for the average cook. However, should you wish to pursue the subject, refer-
ences can be found in most public libraries. For instructions using rather
simple equipment, see *Stalking the Healthful Herbs* by Euell Gibbons.

Rose petal syrup is easy to make and although the flavor is slightly diluted
by the sugar, this syrup can be used in much the same way as rose water. In a
recipe calling for 2 tablespoons of rose water, use 6 tablespoons of rose petal
syrup, then decrease the amount of sugar in the recipe by 6 tablespoons.

One of nature's most delectable treats, rose petal syrup has innumerable
uses. It is delicious on hot biscuits, pancakes, sopaipillas, pound cake, ice
cream, yogurt, and fresh fruit. It is also good as a glaze for baked ham, duck,
squash, yams, and sweet potatoes. In order that as little flavor be lost as possible, add rose petal syrup about 15 minutes before removing the baked food
from the oven and cover the food with a lid. After removing the food from
the oven, allow the lid to remain in place for about 10 minutes before
serving.

The following recipe for rose petal syrup calls for rhubarb juice. If that is
not available, an equal amount of lemon juice may be substituted, but lemon
tends to overpower the delicate rose flavor, whereas rhubarb complements
it. Instructions for making rhubarb juice are in Appendix B.

Wild rose syrup
⅓ cup rhubarb juice
2 cups fresh rose petals
1 ½ cups water
2 ½ cups granulated sugar
a very few grains of salt
¾ cup water
1 package powdered pectin

Using an electric blender set on low, blend the rhubarb juice, petals, and
the first amount of water. With the blender still running, slowly add the
sugar and salt. Continue blending until the sugar has dissolved. Turn off the
blender but allow the mixture to remain.

In a medium pot combine the second amount of water and the pectin. Stir
well. Heat, stirring constantly, until the mixture reaches a full boil. Begin
watching a clock and allow the mixture to boil hard for 1 minute, continuing
to stir to prevent burning. Remove from the heat.

With the blender again set on low, slowly pour the hot pectin into the rose petal mixture and continue blending until smooth. Turn off the blender and wait a few minutes to allow the foam to rise to the surface. Skim off the foam, pour the syrup into hot, sterile jars, and screw on the lids. Allow the syrup to cool for at least 6 hours and not more than 12 hours at room temperature before refrigerating or freezing it. Makes about 4½ cups of syrup.

Wild strawberry

Fragaria virginiana Duchn.

Woodland strawberry, wild strawberry

Fragaria vesca L.

Rose family: Rosaceae

Description: Like most other strawberries, these native species are perennial herbs that spread by horizontal stems (runners). The leaves are borne on stalks rising from the base of the plant and are divided into 3 leaflets having toothed margins. For *F. virginiana,* the tooth at the tip of the leaflet will usually be shorter and more narrow than the teeth on either side of it, whereas for *F. vesca* it will usually be longer and wider than the teeth on either side. Leaflets and leaf stalks may be more or less hairy. Flowers are white with 5 petals and occur in clusters of from 2 to several. Fruits are red, juicy, and smaller than cultivated strawberries but similar or superior in flavor. Note that technically the fruit is called a receptacle, and that what appear to be seeds are actually small, dry fruits called achenes, each containing a single seed. The achenes of *F. virginiana* are imbedded in small, shallow dimples, whereas those of *F. vesca* are set on a smooth, undimpled surface.

Distribution: Wild strawberry (*F. virginiana*): scattered throughout much the United States (except arid regions) and into Canada; fairly common in the northern and eastern portions of the Great Plains and adjacent eastern states. Woodland strawberry (*F. vesca*): northern and eastern United States and into Canada; scattered populations in North Dakota, South Dakota, Nebraska, and adjacent eastern states.

Habitat: Roadsides, prairies, and open woods; in full sun or partial shade.

Edible parts: Ripe fruits, cooked or uncooked; leaflets, dried and brewed for tea.

Seasons to collect: Fruits in late spring to early summer; leaflets, throughout the summer.

Cautions: For the sake of the plants, harvest leaflets after the plant has made its main growth for that season. Also, take leaflets here and there from numerous plants rather than picking many leaflets from any one plant.

Additional information and recipes: The journals of early explorers and the letters of settlers tell us that wild strawberries were once abundant in the eastern prairies of the Great Plains. In the early 1900s the botanist Melvin Gilmore noted their use by native peoples along the Missouri River and wrote that the people "luxuriated in them in their season."

When I interviewed older persons about their memories of wild plants, descendants of settlers mentioned wild strawberries as an important and plentiful fruit. One man recalled that as a child, he sometimes gathered several quarts of them in a single day. Preservation, he said, was accomplished by layering the strawberries alternately with sugar in a crock, covering them with a lid, and storing them in an outdoor cellar that was extremely cold. He said this was the most delicious fruit he had ever tasted.

Today, wild strawberries are far from plentiful but occur here and there along ditches and streams. They transplant well and make an attractive, low-maintenance ground cover, but if you try this, start with more than one plant and select plants from different places in the patch or from different patches. Although a single strawberry plant will spread and soon cover a sizable area, if all of the plants originate from one parent plant, the blossoms will not develop fruit. If you already have such a patch, simply transplant a few wild strawberry plants from other sites into your patch. The following year, your patch should bear fruit.

Wild strawberries are easy to pick, and preparation simply involves a thorough washing and the removal of the green hulls attached to the stem end of each fruit. They are so good fresh, just as they are, that it seems a shame to alter them by cooking or freezing, but in winter when fresh fruits are not available, strawberry jam or strawberry shortcake made with the frozen fruits will seem a very special treat.

Though not widely known, the dried leaflets of wild strawberry make a good tea. Because the flavor is mild and has something of a mellowing effect, they are best used in combination with more strongly flavored ingredients, such as mint leaves or rose hips.

Wild strawberry leaf tea

To dry the leaflets, first wash them well, then pat them dry with a paper towel. Lay a kitchen towel in the bottom of a large pan with sides, then arrange the leaflets in a single layer on the towel. Cover the pan with a light cloth (to allow circulation of air but protect the leaflets from dust), then place the pan in a light, airy place out of direct sunlight. After several days, when the leaflets are brittle dry, put them into a container having a tightly fitting lid and store in a cool place.

To brew the tea, use about 1 to 2 teaspoonsful of crumbled leaves and 1 cup of boiling water for each cup of tea desired. Brew as for mint tea, page 98.

Wild strawberry jam

7 cups wild strawberries

1 package powdered pectin
7 cups granulated sugar
  Read about making jam, Appendix A.
  Measure the sugar and set it aside. Crush the strawberries in a large, heavy
kettle. Add the pectin and stir well. Place the kettle over high heat and bring
the mixture to a full boil. Add the sugar all at once and continue stirring until
the mixture again reaches a boil. Begin timing and, stirring constantly, allow
to boil hard for 1 minute. Remove from the heat, quickly skim off the foam,
and pour the jam into hot, sterile jars, leaving ¼–inch headspace. Cap the
jars with two-piece metal lids and process them for 5 minutes in a boiling water bath. Makes about 8 cups of jam.

Wild strawberry and rhubarb jam

4 cups rhubarb stalk cut into ½-inch pieces
2 cups granulated sugar
2 cups wild strawberries
1 envelope unflavored gelatin or 1 teaspoon powdered (not flaked) agar
  Read about making jam, Appendix A.
  Combine the rhubarb and sugar in a large bowl and stir well. Cover the
bowl and set it aside at room temperature for 3 to 4 hours. At the end of that
time, the juice from the rhubarb will have combined with the sugar. Measure
out 1/4 cup of this juice and combine it with the gelatin or agar, stir well, and
set it aside.
  Put the rest of the rhubarb and juice, as well as the strawberries, into a
large, heavy kettle. Stir gently and bring to a boil over medium-high heat.
Reduce the heat, but do not cover the kettle.
  If using gelatin, allow the mixture to boil gently for 11 minutes. Stir constantly toward the end of the cooking time. Remove the kettle from the heat
and add the softened gelatin, stirring until well mixed.
  If using agar, allow the mixture to boil gently for 10 minutes, then add the
softened agar. Continue to stir and cook for another 2 minutes.
  Pour the jam into hot, scalded jars, put lids in place but do not screw them
on tightly. Allow the jam to cool to room temperature, then tighten the lids
and store the jars in a refrigerator or freezer. Makes 3 ½ to 4 cups of jam.
  This jam is wonderful on fresh bread or yogurt and is a good way to
stretch the wild strawberry flavor when you have a limited amount of fruit.

Wild strawberry syrup

wild strawberries, water, and granulated sugar

Measure the strawberries. For each cup of strawberries, you will need ¼ cup of water.

Place the strawberries in a heavy kettle and crush them with a potato masher. Add the water and stir well. Place the kettle over high heat only until the liquid begins to boil. Reduce the heat to low, cover the kettle with a lid, and allow the strawberries to simmer only until tender—about 8 minutes. (Longer cooking results in loss of flavor.)

Remove the kettle from the heat and allow the strawberries to cool until comfortable to handle. Strain the mixture through a jelly cloth. Discard the mashed fruit; save and measure the juice.

Return the juice to the kettle and add an equal amount of sugar. Stir well and place over medium heat. Stir constantly until the sugar is dissolved and the mixture reaches the boiling point. Begin timing and allow to boil gently for 2 minutes. Remove the kettle from the heat and skim off the foam. Pour the syrup into hot, scalded jars, put lids in place but do not screw them on tightly. Allow the syrup to cool to room temperature, then tighten the lids and refrigerate or freeze the jars to store. Yield: about half as much syrup as there were strawberries to begin with.

Wild strawberry sunshine topping

1 cup granulated sugar

2 tablespoons water

2 cups strawberries

Have ready a shallow heat-resistant container, such as an 8 x 8–inch glass or enamel baking pan (do not use aluminum).

In a heavy saucepan, work the sugar and water together with a spoon— the result will be a thick, grainy mixture. Place this over high heat and, stirring constantly, bring it to a boil. Continue stirring and allow the mixture to cook for 3 minutes—don't worry that it remains grainy.

Add the strawberries to the hot sugar in the saucepan, and stirring constantly, again bring the mixture to a boil. Stir and cook for 5 minutes. The mixture should now be smooth, rose-colored, and syrupy, with lumps of strawberries. Remove it from the heat and pour it into the heat-resistant pan. Cover the pan with a screen or netting to keep out insects, then place it outdoors where it will receive full sun throughout the day. Choose a location up off of the ground and check from time to time to make sure it has not been discovered by ants. Leave the strawberry syrup mixture in the sun for 3 days, but bring it in each night. (Choosing a different location each day for the sunning will help outwit ants.) After 3 days, pour the mixture into a jar, cover with a lid, and refrigerate. Makes ⅔ to 1 cup of topping. Sunshine topping is especially good spooned over yogurt and is excellent with butter on fresh bread.

Wild strawberry shortcake

Use 2 cups fresh strawberries or make the topping below. The topping is best when made a day ahead and allowed to chill thoroughly. The cream may be whipped ahead or just before serving. The biscuits are best made just before serving.

TOPPING FOR SHORTCAKE

½ cup granulated sugar

½ cup water

2 tablespoons lemon juice

2 cups strawberries

Stir the sugar and water together in a heavy saucepan over high heat. Bring to a boil and cook for 3 to 4 minutes to make a thin syrup. (Syrup should measure about ½ cup.) Remove the saucepan from the heat. Allow the syrup to cool, then place it in the refrigerator until thoroughly chilled. Put the strawberries into a bowl. Stir the cooled syrup and lemon juice together and pour this over the strawberries. Stir gently to mix. Makes 2 cups of topping.

If refrigerated in a covered container, this topping will keep for several days. For longer storage, it must be frozen, but it freezes exceptionally well and is outstanding on yogurt or ice cream and as a spread for breads.

WHIPPED CREAM

1 cup heavy cream, chilled

1 tablespoon granulated sugar

1 teaspoon vanilla extract

Using a wire whip, egg beater, or electric mixer, beat the cream, sugar, and vanilla together until thick. Cover with a lid and refrigerate until ready to use.

SHORTCAKE

450 degree oven

1 cup plus 2 tablespoons all-purpose flour

2 teaspoons baking powder

1 tablespoon granulated sugar

¼ teaspoon salt

3 tablespoons margarine or butter

1 egg

¼ cup milk

Grease a cookie sheet with margarine and set it aside.

Sift the flour, baking powder, sugar, and salt together into a large bowl.

Add the margarine or butter, then, using a pastry blender or two knives, cut it in only until coarsely blended.

Beat the egg and milk together with a whisk, then add this to the dry ingredients and stir gently only until combined—mix no more than is necessary to bind the dough together. Turn the dough onto a lightly floured surface and pat it out, using a pushing, rather than a pressing, motion. With a rolling pin lightly roll the dough to a thickness of about ½ inch, again pushing more than pressing. Using a circular cookie cutter or an empty 12-ounce frozen-juice can, cut out 6 biscuits (the number of biscuits may vary depending on the thickness of the dough). Place the biscuits on the cookie sheet, then bake until light brown—about 12 minutes. Remove the biscuits from the oven and from the cookie sheet—serve while still warm.

To serve, spoon fresh strawberries or strawberry topping over each biscuit. Place a dollop of whipped cream on top of each serving and add more strawberries or topping. Makes 6 servings. (Recipe may be doubled or more.)

Wild strawberry leather
140 degree oven
5 cups strawberries
¼ cup granulated sugar or honey

Line two 15 x 10–inch jelly roll pans with plastic wrap and secure the edges with tape. Set aside.

Put the strawberries, a few at a time, into an electric blender and puree until smooth. Add the sugar or honey and blend only until well combined. Spread the strawberry mixture evenly in the pans.

Strawberry leather may be dried in the sun or in an oven. If you choose to use sun, protect the leather from insects by covering it with a screen or netting and make sure the pans are placed where they will receive full sun throughout the day. Bring the pans inside at night and place them out again each morning. Selecting a new site each day will help in avoiding ants. If you prefer oven drying, place the pans in the oven with the door slightly open—a spool works well to hold the door ajar. Allow the leather to remain in the oven from 6 to 12 hours or until it is quite dry and no longer sticky to the touch.

Remove the leather from the oven and from the pans. Cut each leather into four pieces. Roll and wrap each in plastic wrap. Store in a tightly covered container in a cool place and use within 3 months, or freeze. Makes 8 generous servings.

Missouri gooseberry, gooseberry

Ribes missouriense Nutt.

Currant family: Grossulariaceae

Description: The Missouri gooseberry is a prickly native shrub growing to about 3½ feet tall. The leaves are alternate, light green, deeply lobed, and often as broad as they are long; the margins are scalloped. The flowers have 5 pale green to white petals and are borne below the branches, as are the fruits, which are smooth and round with lengthwise stripes. Pale green at first, the fruits turn brownish purple when ripe. The seeds are small and numerous.

Distribution: Eastern and central United States and into Canada with scattered populations west; eastern Great Plains.

Habitat: Dry to moist woods; often at the edges of woods or windbreaks, along stream banks, in ravines; sometimes along fence rows; often in shade or partial shade.

Edible parts: Nearly ripe and fully ripe fruits, cooked or uncooked.

Seasons to collect: Late spring to early summer.

Cautions: Pick carefully to avoid being stuck by the prickles on the branches.

Additional information and recipes: In flavor and cooking characteristics, the fruits of wild gooseberries and garden gooseberries are similar, but I prefer to grow the wild Missouri gooseberry because it seems more resistant to the mildews that commonly afflict ordinary garden gooseberries.

Gooseberry fruit may be used ripe or underripe or in combinations, but when using the underripe fruits choose those that are nearing ripeness—they will be large and light green. For jelly, the underripe fruits are often preferred because they contain enough pectin to jell on their own, whereas fully ripe gooseberries require the addition of commercial pectin.

To find gooseberry fruits, bend down and look up under the branches. Although the bushes are sharply armed, the fruit is fairly easy to pick. It's the preparation later that is more time-consuming. Washing and sorting are simple enough, but for most recipes, the stem and blossom ends of each gooseberry fruit must be removed. This takes time. The exception is gooseberry jelly, for which stems and blossom ends are simply strained out after cooking, making removal unnecessary. (For this reason I have made jelly more often than jam.)

To freeze gooseberries
Read about freezing, Appendix A.
Gooseberries freeze well just as they are. Simply wash them, remove the stems and the blossom ends, place them in containers with tightly fitting covers, and freeze. It is not necessary to add sugar.

Gooseberry custard pie
450 degree oven to start
pastry for an 8-inch single-crust pie
1 ¼ cups granulated sugar
⅓ cup all-purpose flour
2 tablespoons cold water
3 egg yolks
2 tablespoons melted margarine or butter
1 teaspoon vanilla extract
3 cups fresh or frozen underripe (green) gooseberries
boiling water
Roll out the pastry and arrange it in the pan, then set aside.
Put the egg yolks, cold water, margarine, and vanilla into a bowl and beat with an electric mixer until blended. In another bowl stir the flour and sugar together, then add this mixture to the yolk mixture, stirring well. Set aside also.
Pour enough boiling water over the gooseberries to cover, then wait no longer than 1 minute and drain well. Put the drained gooseberries into the pie crust. Pour the yolk mixture over the gooseberries, spreading it out with the back of a spoon. Place the pie in the 450 degree oven for 12 minutes, then reduce the heat to 350 degrees and bake until the custard is set—about 45 minutes.
Make the meringue about 15 minutes before the pie is to come out of the oven.
MERINGUE
3 tablespoons granulated sugar
2 tablespoons cornstarch
½ cup boiling water
3 egg whites at room temperature
3 tablespoons granulated sugar
Mix the first amount of sugar and the cornstarch together in a small saucepan; add the boiling water and cook over medium heat until thick and nearly clear. Remove the saucepan from the heat and set aside until the contents have cooled.

Put the egg whites into a deep glass or metal bowl. Do not use plastic, which tends to harbor oil, because if oil is present the whites will not become stiff. Also, it is important that no oil or fat be present on the beaters, so after beating the yolks for the custard, remove the beaters from the mixer and wash them thoroughly in hot, soapy water.

With the electric mixer, beat the whites until they are thick and foamy. Gradually add the second amount of sugar and continue beating until they are very stiff. Add the cooled cornstarch mixture and beat slowly only until blended.

When the pie is done, remove it from the oven and reset the temperature at 325 degrees. Spoon the meringue onto the pie, being careful to spread it to the crust so that it seals all the way around. Return the pie to the oven and bake until the peaks of the meringue are lightly browned—about 10 minutes. Makes 6 servings.

Traditional gooseberry pie

450 degree oven to start

pastry for a 2-crust 9-inch pie

3 cups underripe (green) gooseberries

1 ½ cups granulated sugar

3 tablespoons quick-cooking tapioca

½ teaspoon salt

2 tablespoons butter or margarine

Roll out the pastry and arrange the bottom crust in the pie pan; set aside.

In a medium pot, crush 1 cup of the gooseberries. Stir in the sugar, tapioca, and salt, then set this aside for about 5 minutes to allow the tapioca to soften in the gooseberry juice. Cook, stirring constantly, until the mixture thickens.

Put the remaining gooseberries into the pie shell and pour the thickened filling over them. Scatter pieces of margarine or butter over the surface, then place the top crust over all and seal the edges. Make a 2-inch slit in the top crust to allow steam to escape during baking. Bake at 450 degrees for 10 minutes, reduce the temperature to 350 degrees and bake about 30 minutes longer or until the crust is lightly browned. Makes 6 to 8 servings. If possible, serve slightly warm.

Underripe gooseberry jelly

TO EXTRACT THE JUICE

4 cups underripe (green) gooseberries

1 cup water

Place the gooseberries and water in a large, heavy kettle over medium-high heat, cover and allow to boil gently until tender—about 20 minutes. Remove the kettle from the heat and allow the mixture to cool until comfortable to handle, then strain it through a damp jelly cloth. Makes about 2 cups of juice.

TO MAKE THE JELLY

2 cups gooseberry juice

2 cups granulated sugar

Read about jelly making, Appendix A.

Combine the juice and sugar in a large, heavy kettle. Place over medium-high heat and stir well, then allow to boil until the jelling point is reached— usually about 5 minutes but sometimes longer, depending on the amount of pectin the fruit contains. Test for doneness with a thermometer or use the spoon or cold saucer methods. When the jelly is done, remove the kettle from the heat, quickly skim off the foam, and pour the jelly into hot, sterile jars, leaving ¼ inch headspace. Cap jars with two-piece screwband lids and process for 5 minutes in a boiling water bath. Makes about 2 cups of jelly.

Note that jelly made from green, unripe gooseberries is a delicate shade of rose.

Ripe gooseberry jelly

TO EXTRACT THE JUICE

10 cups ripe gooseberries

2½ cups water

Place the gooseberries and water in a large, heavy kettle over medium-high heat, cover and allow to boil gently until tender—about 20 minutes. Remove the kettle from the heat and allow the mixture to cool until comfortable to handle, then strain it through a damp jelly cloth. Makes about 5 cups of juice.

TO MAKE THE JELLY

5 cups gooseberry juice

1 box powdered pectin

7 cups granulated sugar

Read about jelly making, Appendix A.

Measure the sugar and set it aside. In a large, heavy kettle, combine the juice and pectin. Stir well. Place over high heat and, stirring constantly, bring to a hard boil. Add the sugar all at one time and continue stirring. Again bring to a boil, then begin timing and boil for 1 minute, still stirring constantly. Remove from the heat, quickly skim off the foam, and pour into hot, sterile jars. Cap the jars with two-piece screwband lids and process for 5 minutes in a boiling water bath. Makes about 8 cups of jelly.

Ripe gooseberry jam

8 cups ripe gooseberries
4 cups granulated sugar
⅓ cup lemon or rhubarb juice

Read about jam making, Appendix A. Instructions for making rhubarb juice are in Appendix B.

Thoroughly crush the gooseberries or process them in a blender. Place the gooseberries, sugar, and juice in a large, heavy kettle over medium-high heat and stir until the sugar is dissolved and the juice begins to boil. Reduce the heat and, stirring frequently, allow to boil gently until the jam is thick enough to hold a slightly rounded shape in a spoon—about 6 or 7 minutes. Or test for doneness with the cold saucer method. When done, remove from the heat and skim off the foam, then stir well and pour into hot, sterile jars. Cap the jars with two-piece screwband lids and process for 5 minutes in a boiling water bath. Makes 4 cups of jam.

Underripe gooseberry jam

Use the recipe for ripe gooseberry jam above, but increase the sugar to 5 cups and omit the lemon or rhubarb juice.

Plains prickly-pear cactus, bigroot prickly-pear, beaver-tail

Opuntia macrorhiza Engelm.

Cactus family: Cactaceae

Description: A perennial herb occurring in clumps, the plains prickly-pear reproduces both vegetatively and by seed. The stems are jointed, each being a flat segment called a pad. (Clumps spread vegetatively when roots develop on the underside of pads that touch soil.) Pads are armed with sharp spines that grow from dotlike places called areoles and that occur mostly on the upper portions and along the margins. The spines are surrounded at the base by tufts of barbed hairs called glochids. New pads, as well as flowers and eventually fruits, are produced on areoles located along the margins of older pads. The flowers appear in late spring or early summer and are especially attractive, with many large yellow petals surrounding an often reddish center. The ripe fruits are large oval berries varying from rose to purple and often tinged with green. Seeds are numerous. The fruits are spineless but are dotted with areoles, which may or may not be free of glochids.

Distribution: Throughout Kansas, with scattered populations south and north; not reported in North Dakota. (Other species of prickly-pear occur in North Dakota and in scattered dry areas throughout the Great Plains.)

Habitat: Dry open places, rocky areas, and prairies, usually in full sun.

Edible parts: Young pads, cooked; ripe fruits (including seeds), cooked or uncooked (see page 212).

Seasons to collect: Young pads in late spring to early summer; older pads throughout the summer; fruit from late summer through autumn.

Cautions: No prickly-pear cactus pads or ripe fruits are poisonous—it is the spines and glochids that pose a danger. Wear heavy shoes—spines easily pierce canvas and may even penetrate rubber soles. Gloves do not provide adequate protection. For picking, use a long-handled fork or tongs, as well as a knife or plant cutters, but be prepared to remove a few stickers anyway. Standard equipment for minor brushes with cacti includes an ordinary table fork to lift away pads that catch on shoes or clothing, and tweezers and a magnifying glass for removing spines and glochids. (Resist the temptation to pull glochids out with your teeth—glochids in the tongue are even worse than glochids in the fingers.) More serious encounters with glochids, such as grasping a pad or stepping into a cactus patch, may require medical attention. A first-aid measure for small areas of skin (a few fingers, the sole of a foot, etc.) is to coat the area with a white water-soluable glue such as Elmer's and then fan or blow the glue dry. More than an hour may be required before the glue has dried thoroughly, but when it has, gently peel it away—along with the glochids. Stubborn cases may require leaving the glue on overnight. (Never apply glue to large areas of skin.)

Additional information and recipes: More than one species of prickly-pear cactus occurs in the Great Plains, but because the plains prickly-pear is fairly common, is only moderately spiny, and has juicy fruit, it is the one recommended. Pads of other species occuring in the Great Plains may be good to eat, but their fruits are usually too dry to be palatable. Although prickly-pear fruits, known as tunas, and pads, called nopales, are readily available in food markets in the Southwest, usually the only way to acquire cactus fruit or pads in the Great Plains is to harvest them from the wild.

When searching for prickly-pears, look for plants having at least ½ inch between the patches of spines on the pads. Older pads may be used, but new pads are preferred because they are more tender and have fewer spines—or at least shorter ones. Note that the white fuzz often seen on the pads is a substance produced by a scale insect that feeds on cactus juice. Although it is probably not harmful, readers will probably want to pass up such pads.

When picking, grasp the pad securely with tongs or spear it with the long-handled fork, then cut it free at the joint. (Cut carefully in order not to injure the plant.) Use a metal pail for collecting because once spines or glochids become embedded in plastic, they can be difficult to remove. Another method is to layer the pads between crumpled newspapers in a disposable cardboard box. First-time cactus gatherers often bring home more pads than they need—6 to 8 pads are adequate for most recipes.

When washing and preparing the pads, handle them with tongs or pliers. Some persons singe the pads over a flame to remove spines and glochids before cooking. Others claim that spines and glochids are best removed after the pads have been boiled. I do singe older pads before cooking, but cook young pads just as they are, removing the stickers once the pads have cooled.

When cooked, the young pads of prickly-pear taste something like a combination of okra and green pepper. Older pads have a stronger flavor, but either is good chopped and added to scrambled eggs or omelets or any mixture with tomato and onion, such as chile or Spanish rice.

To prepare cactus pads

Wash the cactus pads under running water. Singe them or not, depending on your preference. Place the pads in a large pot with enough water to cover. Bring the water to a boil, then cover with a lid and cook over medium heat until the pads are tender—about 15 minutes for young pads, a few minutes more for older pads. At the end of the cooking period, drain and discard the liquid; allow the pads to cool until comfortable to handle.

Neither spines nor glochids are softened much by cooking, so for removing them, you will need to lay the pads on a hard surface that can't be penetrated—a kitchen counter top works well and is handy to the sink.

The first step is to get a good hold on the pad. Use pliers and grasp the pad securely by the joint end. Then using scissors, trim away about ¼ inch all around the upper edge of the pad (the part where spines and glochids are most numerous). Still holding the end of the pad in the pliers, rest the pad on the hard surface and remove the spines and glochids by scraping them off with a table knife. If you are not successful with the knife, try dislodging them with the end of a potato peeler.

When all of the glochids are removed from one side of the pad, rinse it, then turn it over and remove the spines and glochids on the other side. Rinse again, then check carefully for places you may have missed. A magnifying glass can be a great help at this point. Finally, trim away the fibrous part of the pad at the joint end. When the pads have been cleaned, dice them or cut them into thin strips. Place these in a bowl and pour boiling water over them, stir well, and drain off the water. This removes some of the slick, jellylike liquid so characteristic of cactus pads.

Pickled cactus relish

1 tablespoon pickling spices
1 ½ cups cooked, chopped cactus pad
¾ cup chopped onion
¾ cup apple cider vinegar
¼ cup water
½ cup granulated sugar
½ teaspoon salt
1 tablespoon mustard seed

Tie the pickling spices in a small cloth or put them into a tea ball. Place this and the remaining ingredients, including the mustard seed, in a pot over medium-low heat. Cook uncovered for 10 minutes, then remove the pot from the heat, cover with a lid, and allow the relish to cool and mellow for about 4 hours. Remove and discard the pickling spices. Stir the relish well and ladle it into containers having lids. Store in a refrigerator. Use within 2 months. Makes 2 cups of relish.

Cactus tartar sauce
½ cup cactus relish
½ cup salad dressing

Drain and discard the liquid from the relish. Stir the relish and salad dressing together in a small bowl, then cover and chill thoroughly. Serve cold with hot or cold fish. Store in a refrigerator. Use within 2 weeks. Makes about ¾ cup of sauce.

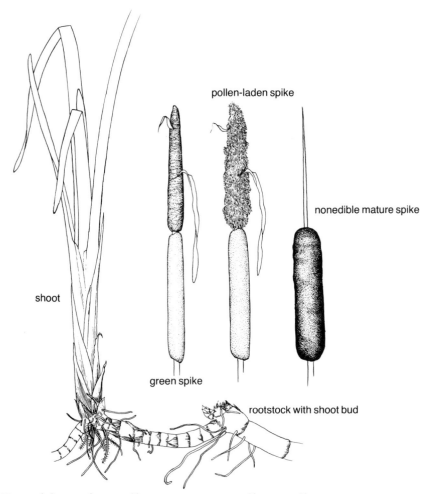

pollen-laden spike

nonedible mature spike

shoot

green spike

rootstock with shoot bud

Broad-leaved cattail, common cattail, cattail
Typha latifolia L.

Narrow-leaved cattail, cattail
Typha angustifolia L.

Cattail
Typha domingensis Pers.

Cattail family: Typhaceae

Description: These three species are native to the Great Plains and hybridization between them is common. Cattails are tall perennial marshland herbs having shallow creeping rootstocks and long, narrow swordlike leaves, which are smooth and have no midvein. Typically, mature plants have a central unbranched stalk with a terminal spike. The broad-leaved cattail has broader leaves and a thicker spike than the other two species. In spring, the leaves appear a few weeks before the central stalk, which, when it first emerges, is covered by a thin pale-green papery sheath. This sheath soon falls away to reveal a velvety green spike divided into two distinct sections. The green upper section is a cylindrical cluster of densely packed male flower buds that soon open to release a considerable amount of yellow dustlike pollen into the air. The pollen fertilizes the female flowers, which make up the green (sometimes brownish) densely packed lower section of the spike. In the broad-leaved cattail these two sections are adjacent, whereas they are separated by a short segment of stalk in the other two species. Soon after the pollen has been shed, the male flowers wither and fall away, leaving the cylinder of fertilized female flowers below to develop into minute tufted dry fruits containing seeds.

Distribution: Cattail species are common in wet areas throughout the United States and into Canada; in the Great Plains, broad-leaved and narrow-leaved cattails are widespread; *T. domingensis* is found mainly in the southern portion, but is reported from scattered sites as far north as the Platte River.

Habitat: Quiet or slow-moving water such as streams or marshes, also moist lowlands and ditches; usually in full sun.

Edible parts: Shoot buds on rootstocks, cooked or uncooked; rootstocks (as starch), specially prepared and cooked; young shoots, cooked or uncooked; upper section of the green spike (the cylinder of male flower buds), cooked; pollen, sifted and cooked. Spikes of the broad-leaved cattail are more succulent and produce more pollen than the other two species. (As survival food, any part of the cattail may be eaten cooked or uncooked, but mature leaves and spikes are tough and unpalatable.)

Seasons to collect: Rootstocks and buds on the rootstocks, anytime they can be found; young shoots, spring; green spikes and pollen, spring to midsummer, depending on latitude and altitude, with the period of pollination typically lasting *only a couple of weeks*. (Because this period is so short, it is important to keep a close tab on what is happening in a cattail marsh. Otherwise, you may miss one or both of these stages and have to wait an entire year. It may help to know that in southeastern Nebraska, cattails pollinate about the first or second week of June; pollination will occur earlier in areas south, later in areas north, and even later at high altitudes.)

Cautions: Cautions here have to do with the places where cattails are found. Take time to find out where the water comes from, and don't collect from places where water might be polluted. Even in wilderness areas, peel the buds and rootstocks. Turn to the section on watercress, page 2, and read about collecting from wet areas. Although exceptions might be found, cattail pollen seems not to cause hayfever, even for persons having other pollen allergies.

Additional information and recipes: The cattail has been called a wilderness grocery store because nearly every part of the plant is edible at some time during the year.

Once washed and peeled, the rootstocks of cattail may be crushed to extract a starchy material that can be added to the ingredients of baked goods or made into a soft, moist paste something like bean dip. These rootstocks may be used throughout the year but are best from late autumn through spring. However, to me, this product seems overrated. First, gathering the rootstocks is cold and messy work, and second, I've never been able to obtain nearly as much starch as is often claimed possible. If you want to try it, a method is given below.

Cattail root starch

Wash and peel the rootstocks, then crush them with a hammer. Put this material into water and using your hands, tear it apart and swish it back and forth to loosen as much of the starch from the fibers as possible, then pour the liquid through a strainer having rather fine mesh. Save the water-starch mixture and discard the fibers. Allow the water-starch mixture to sit undisturbed for at least an hour, then slowly pour off most of the water, being careful not to disturb the starch, which will have settled at the bottom. Pour the starch and remaining water into a tall container such as a glass canning jar so that what water is left may be more easily poured off the top. Finally, spoon the starch out into a large shallow pan, then place the pan in an oven set at a very low temperature (a gas pilot light is usually enough), and allow the starch to dry for an hour or so. At this point, its consistency will be somewhat like bean dip. I have not found cattail starch to be the kind that will thicken gravies or puddings. The flavor is good, but considering the time and effort, it seems the least rewarding of all the cattail products.

Cattail shoot buds

Easier to prepare, yet good tasting, are the shoot buds found at the ends of rootstocks or around the base of the plant. These can be washed thoroughly, peeled back to the center portion, and eaten raw or boiled like a vegetable. Again, I dislike fishing around in mud—I find the plant more interesting when the shoots come up in spring.

Cattail shoots

The tender pale base portion of the young leaves and shoots, sometimes called Cossack asparagus, can be eaten raw or cooked. Perhaps the Cossacks have a different species of cattail, for ours neither resemble nor taste like asparagus, but are more reminiscent of the tender base portion of grasses, which many of us nibbled as children. And cattail shoots are collected in much the same way: simply reach down—in this case to the surface of the mud or water—grasp the shoot, and give a sharp tug. Usually the shoot separates from the rootstock at the base and you get a clean, tender, blanched shoot. These may be nibbled raw, added to salads, or sliced diagonally and stir-fried with wild greens or other vegetables. I choose large shoots, peel away the outer leaves to eliminate any mud, then split the shoot lengthwise and open it up. This will make it possible to find the immature leaves at the center of the shoot—they are exceptionally tender and quite good tasting.

Green cattail spikes

From a distance, young cattail spikes are difficult to spot because they are nearly the same green color as the surrounding leaves. It is advisable to begin checking on them early and to examine the plants at close range.

Harvest the upper portion of the spike as early as it can be found. Use a knife or plant cutter for easy harvesting. Boiled in salted water for 15 to 20 minutes, the spikes may be eaten with butter much like corn on the cob, but expect them to be more firm and less juicy. When cooked, the flower buds may be scraped from the thin central core and added to soup or baked in a casserole like corn.

Cattail spike casserole

350 degree oven
2 cups cooked cattail flower buds, scraped from the core

1 cup milk
1 beaten egg
1 cup bread or cracker crumbs
2 tablespoons butter or margarine
⅔ cup grated cheese
salt and freshly ground black pepper to taste
    Combine all of the ingredients in a well-greased 1½ quart casserole and
stir gently to mix. Bake until set (about 30 minutes). Makes 4 to 6 servings.

Cattail pollen

When baked, cattail pollen is delicious and has a flavor all of its own. It is one
of those things in life that you would never miss if you never tasted it, but
once you do, you're hooked.

    The first step is to collect the pollen, and some methods work better than
others. Attempting to shake the pollen into a container usually results in
most of it floating away. The following method is suggested:

    Holding a gallon pail in one hand, raise it up toward the level of the spike.
With the other hand gently bend the spike downward into the pail and slap it
sharply against the inside. The pollen will slide down the inside surface of the
pail into the bottom. Release that spike and go on to the next—if you bend
the spikes gently they will spring back unbroken. (It is important to move
slowly and quietly in a cattail marsh in order not to disturb nesting birds—
red-winged blackbirds will no doubt scold you anyway.)

    Each spike should yield about 1 teaspoon of pollen unless it's been taken
by wind or rain. Collect more pollen than you think you will need, because
some of what you collect will be fuzz. This, along with a few insects, can be
sifted out easily once you are home. After the pollen is sifted, it is ready to
use. To store it for later use, freeze it in tightly sealed containers.

Cattail pollen pancakes

2 eggs, separated
1½ cups milk (more or less depending on the size of the eggs)
2 tablespoons honey or granulated sugar
1 teaspoon vanilla
¼ cup cattail pollen
1½ cups all-purpose flour
2 teaspoons baking powder
½ to 1 teaspoon salt
    Beat the egg whites until stiff but not dry, then set them aside. Put the egg

yolks, milk, honey or sugar, and vanilla into a large bowl and mix with a fork or whisk until blended. Sift the dry ingredients together, then add them to the milk mixture, stirring only until well blended.

Gently fold the beaten egg whites into the batter. Pour the batter onto a hot, lightly greased griddle, using about ⅓ cup for each pancake (a ⅓-cup measuring cup makes a handy ladle for dipping out the batter). Allow the pancakes to cook until bubbles appear and remain around the edges (usually less than a minute). Turn each pancake and cook for about 30 seconds or so. This recipe should serve 4, but be prepared to make another batch.

A few ripe mulberries stirred into the batter just before cooking make a good addition. For an especially elegant meal, place a dollop of sour cream or vanilla yogurt on a stack of buttered cattail-pollen pancakes and top with chunky mulberry syrup (recipe on page 127).

Pancakes may be made ahead of time, frozen in a tightly closed container with waxed paper in between, and reheated in a toaster just before serving. It is important to freeze them in as flat a position as possible so that they will slide easily into the toaster—also, toast them while they are still frozen. This method works well when serving large groups.

Sunshine muffins

400 degree oven
1 cup milk
1 egg
¼ cup cooking oil
⅓ cup honey
1 ½ cups all-purpose flour
½ cup cattail pollen
2 teaspoons baking powder
½ to 1 teaspoon salt

Combine the milk, egg, oil, and honey in a bowl and beat with a fork or whisk until blended. Sift the dry ingredients together and add them to the liquid. Stir only enough to mix. Pour the batter into greased muffin pans and bake until the muffins are raised and lightly browned—about 20 minutes. Makes 24 muffins. Fresh mulberries make a good addition.

Gold-nugget cream puffs

425 degree oven
¾ cup + 2 tablespoons all-purpose flour
¼ cup cattail pollen

½ cup (1 stick) margarine or butter
½ teaspoon salt (optional)
1 cup water
4 eggs
  Grease two cookie sheets with margarine and set them aside. Measure the flour and pollen, stir them together until blended, and then set them aside, also.
  Cut the margarine or butter into several pieces so it will melt easily, then put these pieces, the salt, and the water into a medium pot over high heat. Heat and stir only until the water boils and the margarine or butter is melted. Turn off the heat and immediately add the flour-pollen mixture. Stir vigorously until the mixture is smooth and forms a soft mass that tends to hold together. Add the eggs, one at a time, beating vigorously with a large spoon after each is added.
  Drop the batter by heaping tablespoonsful onto the cookie sheets. Bake at 425 degrees for 15 minutes; then turn the temperature to 325 degrees and bake for 20 minutes more. Remove puffs from the cookie sheets; allow to cool on wire racks. Slit puffs along one side. Filled with vanilla pudding or ice cream they make a delicious dessert. Filled with creamed chicken or vegetables, they make a delicious luncheon entree. Makes about 24 puffs.

Cattail pollen pound cake

325 degree oven
1 ¼ cup margarine or butter (room temperature)
2 ¼ cups granulated sugar
½ teaspoon salt
7 eggs
2 cups all-purpose flour
½ cup cattail pollen
¼ cup cold water
2 teaspoons vanilla extract
  Thoroughly grease a 10-inch bundt pan or two 9 x 5 x 3–inch loaf pans with margarine or butter—do not use cooking oil or the cake will stick and be difficult to remove. Take time to make certain you have not missed any spots, then dust the pan or pans with flour and set aside.
  In a large bowl, cream the margarine or butter, the sugar, and the salt with an electric mixer. Add the eggs one at a time and beat well after each addition. Add 1 cup of the flour and all of the pollen, then beat well. Add the remaining flour and beat again. Add the water and vanilla and beat until

smooth and thoroughly blended. Spoon the batter into the prepared pan (or pans) and smooth it out toward the sides with the back of a spoon.

Bake the cake until the surface has browned and springs back when touched lightly—about 55 to 60 minutes for a bundt pan, about 40 to 45 minutes for loaves. Remove the cake from the oven and allow it to cool in the pan on a wire rack until is comfortably warm to the touch but not yet cool. (To prevent sticking, the cake must be removed while it is still warm). Typically, the cooling time for a bundt pan will be about 1 to 1½ hours and for loaf pans, about 30 to 45 minutes.

To remove the cake from a bundt pan, use a table knife to loosen the edges around the outside and the hole, then turn the pan over onto a plate and, holding the pan and plate together, make several sharp jerking motions so that the cake falls out onto the plate. With loaves, after loosening the edges, simply turn each pan over and shake gently. Allow the cake to finish cooling, then lightly sift powdered sugar over the top and cover the cake until it is to be cut and served.

If frozen in a tightly covered container, this cake, whole or sliced, will keep for several months.

Cattail pollen bread
350 degree oven
1 cup milk
1¼ cups cold water
⅓ cup honey or granulated sugar
2 to 4 teaspoons salt
3 packages (2 teaspoons each) dry yeast
2 eggs
½ cup cattail pollen
5½ cups all-purpose flour
6 tablespoons cooking oil

Scald the milk, then remove it from the heat. Add the cold water, sugar, and salt and stir until blended. Pour this into a large mixing bowl. Check the temperature—when lukewarm, add the eggs and beat well with an electric mixer. Add the yeast and stir until it is dissolved. Add the cattail pollen and half of the flour, then beat with the mixer. Add 5 tablespoons of the oil and beat until well blended. Remove the mixer from the batter.

Stir in the remaining flour with a large spoon, then with the spoon or with your hands, work the dough until it is well blended and holds together. Pour the remaining tablespoon of cooking oil over the dough, turning the dough so that the entire surface becomes lightly coated with oil. Put the dough into a large container and cover it with a lid or towel.

If the bread is not desired until the following day, place the dough in a refrigerator to rise overnight. If it is to be made directly, place it in a warm place to rise. Either way, allow the dough to rise until doubled in bulk, then turn it out onto a lightly floured surface and knead it until smooth.

To make three loaves of braided bread, divide the dough into 3 parts, then divide each of these into 3 more parts. Roll each part into a rope about 18 inches long. For each loaf, loosely braid 3 ropes together on a greased cookie sheet. (It is important that the braid be loose so that the dough will have room to expand.) Once the loaf is braided, look it over and adjust its shape as needed. Shortening the braid slightly by pulling the loops of the braid out a little on either side results in a better-looking loaf.

Using a spray bottle, spray the loaves with fresh water, then set them aside in a warm place to rise until doubled. Spray them with water several times during this period so that the surface does not become dry. Bake for about 25 minutes or until lightly browned.

Remove the loaves from the cookie sheets and allow them to cool for 10 minutes on wire racks. *After that, it is important to cover the loaves so they do not dry out.* A good method is to cover them with a kitchen towel, then a sheet of plastic, then with another kitchen towel. When cooled, store the loaves in plastic bags or other air-tight containers, freezing them if they are to be used later.

This bread is delicious plain—but toasted, buttered, and served with jelly, it is even better.

Field mint, wild mint
Mentha arvensis L.

Peppermint
Mentha piperita L.

Spearmint
Mentha spicata L.

Mint family: Lamiaceae

Description: These mints are perennial herbs that spread by rhizomes and sometimes by seed. Field mint is native, and although both peppermint and spearmint were introduced, they have naturalized widely. As is typical of the mints, all three of these species have square stems and opposite leaves. The stems may stand erect or trail over the ground but rarely reach more than 18 inches in length. The leaves are medium to dark green with serrate margins. The flowers, which are small, tubular, and two-lipped and vary in color from lavender to white, occur in the axils of leaves and at the tips of branches. The fruits are very small dry nutlets that are commonly called seeds.

Distribution: Scattered throughout the United States and into Canada except arid places; in scattered sites throughout the Great Plains, but rare in the southwest portion.

Habitat: Rich, moist soil along streams and ditches, often in marshes and wet meadows.

Edible parts: Leaves and stems, cooked or uncooked.

Seasons to collect: Anytime plants can be found.

Cautions: Be sure you have mint—test plants for minty odor. Do not collect from areas that might be polluted. For safety, grow your own plants.

Additional information and recipes: Throughout history, mints have been treasured by all societies that have had access to them. Before settlers came to the Great Plains, Plains Indian people used wild mint not only for tea and for flavoring food, but also to help prevent spoilage in meats and fats. Dried meat was stored with alternating layers of mint, and the leaves were worked into certain fats, particularly those used medicinally. Sometimes a person who was breaking a horse would rub mint on his own body to obscure the human odor and thus reduce the horse's fear.

When settlers came, they brought cuttings of favorite mints with them, but they gathered wild mint as well, laying up large quantities for use in winter. Mint tea, mainly enjoyed as a pleasant drink, was also believed to aid digestion and to calm the nerves. More recently, Asian newcomers have brought cuttings of mint plants with them for use in cooking, particularly with meat. One reason mints are transported is that they are so easily rooted.

To root your own mint, simply stand several branches in a small jar of water. In a few days, white roots will begin to grow from the nodes near the lower end of the branches. When these roots reach ½ inch or so in length, carefully plant the branches in moist soil, then water frequently, especially while they are getting started. Mints do better outdoors than in, but if pots are placed where the plants receive plenty of sunlight, they can usually be wintered-over indoors.

Mints may be collected anytime during the growing season, but leaves are at their best in early summer before the plants blossom. Also, they are more flavorful if picked in the cool of the morning. Although similar in appearance, each of the species mentioned above has its own flavor and fragrance. Because wild mint is usually found near water, watch for it when collecting cattails. If you notice a minty odor, look around—you may discover mint plants close by, perhaps even at your feet.

Mint makes an attractive garnish for nearly any food, but is often overlooked as a flavoring for meats and vegetables. Mint jelly with lamb is well known, but mint leaves fried with lamb or with other meats are good, also. Surprisingly, when combined with a little lemon juice, freshly chopped mint leaves make a fairly good substitute for salt on stir-fried vegetables such as carrots, broccoli, or cabbage. Perhaps best known is mint tea brewed with dried leaves, but the fresh leaves can be used to make a refreshing drink.

To dry mint

The common way to hang mint leaves to dry is to make a sack cover that will allow circulation of air but protect the leaves from dust. To do this, poke a small hole in the bottom of a paper sack, then turn it upside down and pull a branch of mint, topside down, through the hole from inside the sack—pull through only enough branch to allow hanging. When thoroughly dry, strip the leaves from the branches and store them in tightly covered containers. (The branches need not be discarded—tied in small bundles, they impart a fresh scent to closets and cupboards.)

A more time-consuming method, but one that results in even better flavor, is to wash the plants, shake them well, pat them thoroughly dry with a towel, then pluck the leaves from the branches and lay the leaves in a single layer between white tissues or thin paper towels in a book. After about 10 days, the leaves will be brittle dry. At that point, remove the leaves from the book and place them, whole, in a container with a tightly fitting cover and store them in a cool place. This is too much bother for a large harvest, but it's nice to have at least one jarful to use for special occasions.

Hot mint tea

To brew dried mint for tea, crumble the leaves just before using, allowing 1 teaspoon of coarsely crumbled leaves for each cup. To use fresh mint, allow 1 8-inch branch for each cup.

Heat twice as much water as will be needed for the tea. When the water boils, pour half into the teapot to heat it, then pour it out. Immediately place the mint, either loose or in a tea ball, inside the teapot and again fill it with boiling water. Set the lid in place and cover the teapot with a cloth so that the tea will stay hot. Allow the tea to steep for 5 to 10 minutes. Serve hot; if desired, add honey or sugar.

Fresh mint cooler

1 large handful of fresh mint leaves and branches
4 cups cold water
honey or granulated sugar to taste

Place the mint and water in an electric blender and blend on high speed only until the water becomes green. Pour the liquid through a strainer to remove the fibrous plant material. Return the liquid to the blender, add honey or sugar, and blend again. Pour over cracked ice in chilled glasses. Makes 4 servings. May be varied by adding lemon or ginger ale.

Mint jelly

1 cup loosely packed mint leaves
1 package powdered pectin
3 cups water
4 cups granulated sugar
few drops of green food coloring (optional)

Read about jelly making, Appendix A.

Put the mint leaves into a large, heavy kettle and crush them with a potato masher. Add the water and heat just to the point of boiling, but do not allow it to boil. Remove the kettle from the heat, cover it with a lid, and allow the mint to steep in the water for about 5 minutes. Strain the liquid through a damp jelly cloth and measure. If necessary, add water to make 3 cups. Measure the sugar and set it aside.

Pour the liquid into the kettle; add the pectin and stir well. If desired, add the green food coloring. Place the kettle over high heat and stir the liquid constantly until it reaches a full boil. Immediately add the sugar all at one time and stir until the jelly again reaches a full boil. Watch a clock and, continuing to stir, allow the jelly to boil for 1 minute. Remove from the heat, quickly skim off the foam, and pour the jelly into hot, sterile jars, leaving ¼ inch headspace. Cap the jars with two-piece screwband lids and process for 5 minutes in a boiling water bath. Makes a little more than 4 cups of jelly.

Mint and apple jelly
Read about jelly making, Appendix A.

This recipe may be made with nearly any amount of apples. Use approximately 1 cup of coarsely chopped fresh mint leaves for 8 cups of quartered apple. For best results, use crab apples or underripe cooking apples and don't peel them.

Cut the apples into quarters and remove the seeds, then put them into a large kettle. Add water to about ¾ the depth of the apples. Cover the kettle with a lid and simmer until the apples are tender—about 30 minutes. Crush the chopped mint and stir it into the hot apples and juice. Remove the kettle from the heat, again cover with the lid, and allow the contents to cool for about 10 minutes.

Remove as much mint as possible, then pour the apples into a damp jelly cloth and extract the juice. (Discard the apple pulp and skins.) Measure the juice and allow ¾ cup granulated sugar for each cup of juice.

Place the juice and sugar in the kettle and stir well. If desired, add a few drops of green food coloring. Place over medium-high heat and allow to boil until the jelling point is reached. Test for doneness with a thermometer or use the spoon or cold saucer method. When done, remove the jelly from the heat, quickly skim off the foam, and pour into hot, sterile jars, leaving ¼ inch headspace. Cap the jars with two-piece screwband lids and process for 5 minutes in a boiling water bath. One batch (8 cups of apples) makes about 2 cups of jelly.

Day-lily
Hemerocallis fulva L.

Lily family: Liliaceae

Description: The day-lily is an introduced perennial herb. It grows in clumps from a fibrous root system having numerous small, fleshy tubers. The leaves rise from the base of the plant, are long and narrow, and appear to be folded lengthwise. The flower buds are green and oblong and of various sizes, depending on their stage of development. These buds and the subsequent flowers are borne at the top of leafless stalks, which may stand as much as 3 feet tall. The flowers, which are large and orange, are *not* spotted like some of the true lilies. Each flower lasts but a single day—hence the name day-lily. The fruits are light green and fleshy at first, but become dry and light tan as they ripen.

Distribution: Eastern United States with scattered populations elsewhere; in yards and gardens throughout the Great Plains, occasionally escaped and naturalized, particularly in the southeastern portion.

Habitat: Roadsides, ditches, stream banks, meadows; often found around abandoned farmsteads.

Edible parts: Tubers, cooked or uncooked; young leaves, up to about 5 inches long, cooked or uncooked; flower buds and flowers, cooked.

Seasons to collect: Leaves, in spring; flower buds and flowers, throughout summer; tubers, anytime they can be found.

Cautions: Use day-lilies only; never experiment by eating other flowers that resemble them. (Note that although day-lilies belong to the lily family, they are not considered to be true lilies; true lilies, such as the Easter lily and tiger lily, are not edible.)

Be aware that at the green and fleshy stage, the fruits (seed capsules), which *are not* edible, resemble the flower buds, which *are* edible. Both may be present at the same time, but they can be distinguished from each other by cutting them crosswise; the fruit has 3 chambers, the bud has layered petals.

When trying day-lily leaves for the first time, eat only a very small amount—they tend to have a laxative effect and cause indigestion for some persons.

Additional information and recipes: Day-lily leaves are best used in early spring when they are young and tender. A few are good added to tossed salads or cooked in soups and stews.

Day-lily tubers may be dug anytime the weather permits. Select firm tubers and simply wash and scrub them well. They do not require peeling. Sliced or whole tubers may be added fresh to salads or cooked and mixed in with other vegetables.

Although individual flowers wilt after only a day, flowers are produced throughout much of the summer, with each plant having many blossoms. Day-lily tubers transplant easily, and a good harvest of buds and flowers may be obtained from even a small patch. Flower buds are best if picked when 1 inch or more in length. Flowers may be used fresh or when slightly wilted. Stuffed with cheeses and prepared like a relleno, the fresh flowers make an outstanding hors d'oeuvre (recipe appears below).

Day-lily buds
Remove and discard any part of the stem that may be attached. Stir-fry the buds in a small amount of vegetable oil until tender or boil or steam them about 8 minutes and drain off the cooking water. Top the buds with sour cream or yogurt, or sprinkle them with seasoned salt or grated cheese. The flavor of day-lily buds is usually mild, but occasionally you may find a spicy one.

Stuffed day-lily hors d'oeuvres
16 fresh day-lily flowers
1 eight-ounce package cream cheese
1 piece cheddar cheese approximately ¾ x 1 x 3 inches
¼ cup all-purpose flour (approximate)
2 eggs
2 teaspoons water
salt to taste
vegetable oil for frying

Remove and discard the center parts of the flowers, then set the flowers aside. Cut the cream cheese and cheddar cheese into 16 thin slabs each and don't fret if they are not perfectly shaped—they are all going to melt out of shape, anyway.

Using your hands, mold a piece of cream cheese over each piece of cheddar to make 16 egg-shaped lumps with the cheddar in the center. Slip one of these into each flower and secure the ends by gently twisting the petals and tucking them under. Sprinkle the stuffed flowers with flour until they are well coated all around. Shake the flowers gently to remove excess flour and place them on a cookie sheet; refrigerate for at least an hour.

Meanwhile, combine the eggs and water in a small bowl and blend them together with a fork. Remove the stuffed flowers from the refrigerator. Pour the oil into a skillet to a depth of about ¼ inch and set the heat at medium-high.

Using a slotted spoon, dip each flower into the egg mixture, then place it into the hot oil. Fry the flowers, turning them with a spatula, until they are a light golden brown on all sides, then carefully remove them to paper towels to drain. Serve hot. For an elegant garnish, tuck a few fresh day-lily flowers around the stuffed flowers just before serving. Makes 16 hors d'oeuvres.

Day-lily hors d'oeuvres may be varied by using flavored cream cheese or by placing bits of cooked crab, slices of olives, or toasted nuts alongside the cheddar cheese in the stuffing.

Common elderberry, black elderberry, elderberry

Sambucus canadensis L.

Honeysuckle family: Caprifoliaceae

Description: The common elderberry is a native shrub growing to a height of about 7 feet and usually occurring in groups. Young plants are only slightly woody and are tinged with green. Older plants are woody, but the stems and branches contain large pithy centers and can be broken easily. The bark is light brown with small corky dots. The leaves are alternate and pinnately compound with from 5 to 7 leaflets arranged in opposite pairs with a terminal leaflet. The leaflets are green and smooth above; the underside is pale green and slightly hairy, especially along the midvein, and the margins are serrate. The flowers have 5 petals and are small and creamy white with a sweet fragrance. They occur in dense, slightly rounded or flat branched clusters with the flower buds in the center of the cluster opening first. The fruits occur in clusters and are small and round, each containing 3 to 5 very small nutlets (usually simply called seeds). When ripe, the fruits are juicy and deep purplish black. By midsummer, it is common to find clusters of buds and flowers and ripe fruits on the same shrub.

Distribution: Eastern United States and into Canada; southern and eastern portions of the Great Plains with scattered populations north and west. (Note that other species of elderberry occur elsewhere in the United States and Canada; some but not all of them are edible.)

Habitat: Along roadsides, fence rows, stream banks, and edges of woods; usually in rich moist soils and in full sun.

Edible parts: Flowers and flower petals, called elderblow, cooked (as in pancakes) and dried for tea; ripe fruits, cooked (see page 224).

Seasons to collect: Flowers (and elderblow), late spring through late summer; fruit, midsummer through autumn.

Cautions: It is important to remember that at first glance, elderberry leaves and flowers resemble those of water hemlock (*Cicuta maculata*), an extremely poisonous plant sometimes found in moist areas. However, the *fruits* of the two plants are *not* similar, the fruit of water hemlock being dry and not at all berrylike. Also, the stems of water hemlock are green, often with purple mottling, especially on the lower portions, and not woody. Flower clusters of both plants are small and white, but the petals of elderberry flowers are joined together and, when given a gentle tug, will come off in a single ring—the petals of water hemlock flowers are separate. To make certain you have the right plant, check with a plant authority such as your county extension agent.

Some cautions apply to elderberry fruit; see page 224.

Additional information and recipes: With their graceful beauty and edible flowers and fruit, elderberries would seem a good choice for yard planting, but probably because of their tendency to spread, they are not commonly planted in yards. However, if you have plenty of space or if you don't mind keeping them in check by hoeing, elderberries make attractive screening hedges or specimen plantings. In spring, shoots from around the base of older elderberry shrubs are easily transplanted.

Elderberry flowers have long been used to make tea and wine and to flavor baked goods such as muffins and pancakes. The flavor is pleasant and flowerlike, but in baked goods, the flowers go a long way. Often more flowers are collected than can be used—for most recipes two flower clusters are more than enough.

Also remember that without flowers, there can be no fruit. With elderberry, it is especially important to be moderate in picking the flowers, so that later in the year, wild birds that rely on elderberry fruit will not suffer for lack of food. Fortunately, with the elderberry there is a way to solve this problem and satisfy both birds and humans. It has to do with the fact that as the ovaries of elderberry flowers develop into fruit, the small rings of petals loosen and fall. Where elderberries are abundant, the fallen petals blow and drift in the wind, leading to their being called elderblow. By shaking a head of flowers over a bucket you can collect an abundance of elderblow while leaving the ovaries in place to develop into fruit. If the petals don't fall easily, the flowers have likely just opened recently—simply wait a few days and try again. For tea, elderblow may be used fresh or dried, but for baked goods, it is better used fresh.

If you do take entire heads of flowers, you will find that although the flowers are sweet, the tiny branchlets to which they are attached are slightly bitter. A few won't matter, especially up close to the flowers, but as much as possible, snip these branchlets away with scissors.

To dry elderblow

Elderberry petals are difficult to wash, so collect in an area away from dust or other pollution. Shake the heads of the flowers over a pail or other container, catching the elderblow as it falls. Once home, shake the elderblow out onto cookie sheets lined with kitchen towels, spreading it in a shallow layer for quick drying. Place the cookie sheets in a light, airy place away from direct sunlight and allow the elderblow to dry thoroughly—usually several days. When the elderblow is dry, shake it into glass jars having lids or double bag it in paper sacks, closing the sacks tightly.

Elderblow tea
For each cup of tea:
1 to 2 tablespoons dried elderblow
1 cup boiling water
   To make 1 cup, put the elderblow into a tea ball in a cup, add boiling water, and steep for several minutes. Remove the tea ball.
   To make a potful, heat the pot by filling it with boiling water, then pouring it out. Put the elderblow into a tea ball or directly into the pot. Add the boiling water and steep for several minutes. Remove the tea ball; if the petals are loose in the pot, use a strainer when pouring the tea. Add lemon, honey, or sugar as desired.

Elderblow pancakes
2 cups all-purpose flour
2 teaspoons baking powder
2 tablespoons honey or granulated sugar
½ to 1 teaspoon salt
1⅔ cups milk
4 eggs, separated
1 cup elderblow (or 1½ cups elderberry flowers, snipped from their branchlets)
margarine or butter
honey or powdered sugar
   Sift the flour, baking powder, sugar, and salt together into a large bowl. Add the milk and egg yolks, stirring only until the batter is well blended. Add the elderblow or flowers and stir again. Beat the egg whites until stiff, then gently fold them into the batter.
   Pour the batter onto a hot, lightly greased griddle, using ⅓ cup for each pancake. Allow the pancakes to cook until bubbles appear and remain around the edges (only 30 to 60 seconds), then turn them over and allow them to cook on the other side for the same amount of time. Spread the pancakes with butter or margarine, then drizzle with honey or sprinkle with

powdered sugar. (Flavored syrups overpower the delicate flavor of the petals). Serve immediately. Makes about 16 pancakes.

This recipe may be halved or doubled, but the batter does not store well, so if you have extra, make it into pancakes and freeze them to reheat in a toaster later. (Make sure the pancakes are lying flat when they freeze—if bent, they won't fit into the toaster slots.)

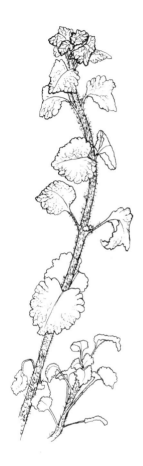

Common horehound, horehound, hoarhound

Marrubium vulgare L.

Mint family: Lamiaceae

Description: Often grown in herb gardens, common horehound is an introduced perennial herb that has escaped and naturalized in some areas. Under good growing conditions plants may reach a height of 30 or more inches but often stand less than 20 inches at maturity. The leaves, stems, and branches are covered with fine white hairs, giving the plant a gray, wooly appearance. The leaves are opposite and oval, with scalloped or toothed margins. The flowers are small, tubular, two-lipped, and white and are borne in clusters around the stems and branches at the axils of leaves. The fruits ("seeds") are small and numerous.

Distribution: In scattered areas throughout the United States and into Canada; in the Great Plains, mostly in the southeastern portion.

Habitat: Yards, gardens, and open areas where soil has been disturbed; along roadsides and sometimes along creek banks, but more often in drier soil, usually in full sun.

Edible parts: Fresh or dried leaves and stems used to flavor candylike lozenges.

Seasons to collect: Early summer to frost.

Cautions: If collecting horehound when the flowers are in bloom, take care to avoid being stung by bees.

Additional information and recipes: With horehound there seems no middle ground—people either like it or dislike it strongly. Even those who like horehound rarely consume it on a regular basis, but instead take it from time to time medicinally or to satisfy a craving for its unique bittersweet flavor.

Many persons were introduced to horehound as children, the candy lozenges once being the standard treatment for a sore or scratchy throat. Today, although no longer easily available over the counter, homemade horehound lozenges are still used.

Unlike most strongly flavored plants, horehound has little or no odor. For this reason, cooks often use too much, with the result that the candy is so bitter the interesting horehound flavor can't be detected. Furthermore, should the cook taste the water in which the horehound has boiled, he or she may be discouraged from proceeding on because at that point the flavor is very unappealing. Only when cooked and in combination with the other ingredients is the intriguing horehound flavor obtained.

Also, it is important to know that the flavor of dried horehound is a lot stronger than that of fresh horehound. For example, the recipe that follows calls for 4 branches of *fresh* horehound, each about 6 inches long, or 2 *dried* branches of that same length (including, of course, the leaves). When picking, select the uppermost branches of the plant and, if possible, those that have not yet bloomed.

Horehound picked and dried in summer can be used in winter to make interesting holiday gifts. I usually gather 50 or so branches, each about 6 inches long, and allow them to hang upside down until brittle dry. (Microwaving is not recommended: it alters the flavor, and the wooly hairs tend to catch fire.) Then, inasmuch as 2 dried branches of horehound are needed for each batch of lozenges, I use 25 baby food jars and crumble two branches (about ¼ cup) into each, storing the jars in a cool, dark place. In December, I make one batch of horehound lozenges and divide the pieces into 25 portions, placing each portion in a plastic sandwich bag. From this, 25 gifts can be put together, each containing a jar of dried horehound, a little bag of lozenges, and a copy of the recipe for making them. Gathered up inside a square of brightly colored calico and tied with yarn, this makes a unique gift. Do be aware, however, that not everyone appreciates the flavor of horehound.

Old-fashioned horehound lozenges
TO MAKE THE HOREHOUND-FLAVORED WATER
4 six-inch branches fresh horehound or 2 dried branches (about ¼ cup crumbled dried leaves and stems, loosely packed)
1 cup water
Put the horehound and water into a saucepan and heat to boiling, then reduce the heat to medium, cover the pan with a lid, and allow the water to simmer for 10 minutes. Remove the pan from the heat and strain the liquid through a sieve. Discard the plant material and measure the liquid. If necessary, add enough water to make ½ cup.
TO MAKE THE LOZENGES
½ cup horehound-flavored water
1 cup light corn syrup (or part corn syrup, part honey)
2 cups granulated sugar
butter or margarine the size of a pea
¾ cup granulated sugar for coating the lozenges

Grease a cookie sheet with margarine or butter and set it aside.

Combine the horehound water, corn syrup, first amount of sugar, and the butter or margarine in a large, heavy kettle and stir well. Place the kettle over medium-high heat and allow the mixture to boil for about 7 to 9 minutes or until it reaches 300 degrees on a candy thermometer. If you do not have a thermometer, test by dropping a little hot syrup into very cold water; when it hardens immediately and is brittle, the candy is done. This candy burns easily, so you must watch it closely throughout the cooking period.

When the candy is done, remove it from the heat and allow it to cool for 5 minutes before pouring it into the greased pan, then allow it to cool 3 to 4 minutes more. Using a pizza cutter or a table knife, press a crease into the candy and watch to see if it flows back together again. If it does, wait another minute and check again. Check often because once this candy begins to harden, it does so rapidly.

As soon as the crease holds, use the cutter or knife to score the candy into pieces about ¾ inch square. When the candy is cool, work a knife or spatula under it and then, using your fingers, break it into pieces along the creased lines.

Place the ¾ cup of sugar into a paper bag and add about 1 cup of the pieces. Shake the sack lightly until the candy is well coated with sugar—this prevents the pieces from sticking together. Repeat until all of the pieces are coated. Makes about 225 lozenges.

Store candy lozenges in a tightly covered container in a cool place. During hot weather, lozenges are best stored in a refrigerator or freezer.

Milkweed buds and flowers

Please read the general comments about milkweeds, beginning on page 54.

Milkweed buds

Not long after milkweed shoots grow too tall and coarse to be edible, small green clusters of flower buds appear and soon open into flowers. Both buds and flowers are edible and are often present on a plant at the same time in early or midsummer.

Milkweed flower buds may be collected at any size but, like the shoots, are best if collected just before cooking.

To cook milkweed buds

Wash the buds and put them into a pot. Pour in enough boiling water to cover and allow them to boil gently for 7 to 10 minutes. Drain and discard the water. Serve buds plain with simple seasoning or add them to soups or casseroles—they are especially good in combination with cheese. Do remember that they must be properly prepared by boiling (and the cooking water discarded) before they can be incorporated into any other recipe.

Milkweed flowers

Growing your own patch of milkweed is handy and having even a single clump near your house will let you know when various parts are ready for harvest in the wild. The best time to transplant milkweed is in late autumn or early spring, but the best time to select plants is while they are in bloom. (Ask permission if you want to dig milkweed along a road or in a field—most rural landowners will gladly grant your request.) Choose plants having deep rose flowers and mark them so you can return to dig later on. If waiting is not possible, cut the plants back to about 10 inches before digging. Either way, replace the soil and firmly tamp it back into place.

Fritters made with milkweed flower clusters are exceptionally delicious. The slender, more delicate pedicels of common milkweed make it the better choice, but showy milkweed will certainly do. With either kind, choose the flowers with deeper color because they are more flavorful. At first glance the following recipe for fritters may appear to be complicated, but once you've made it, the next time will seem easy.

Two things are especially important for tender, crisp fritters: first, make the batter several hours ahead of time (or even several days before) and refrigerate it until you are ready to dip and fry the flower clusters, and second, use peanut oil for frying. The resting time in the refrigerator not only chills the batter but alters its chemical make-up; using peanut oil allows the fritters to fry at a high temperature. These details make a remarkable difference in the finished product.

Do be cautious—hot oil is dangerous. Whether using an electric fryer or a heavy flat-bottomed pot on the stove, fill it no more than half full of oil and be aware that even a drop of moisture in hot oil will cause it to pop and sputter. To avoid this, heat the oil slowly so any moisture present will have evaporated by the time the oil has reached the right temperature for frying. Never leave hot oil unattended and never heat oil to the point of smoking. In case of an oil fire, use a fire extinguisher or smother the flames with flour or a large pot lid.

Milkweed flower fritters

BATTER

1 egg white
cold water
¼ cup unsifted all-purpose flour
¼ cup cornstarch
½ teaspoon baking powder
1 teaspoon granulated sugar
¼ teaspoon salt

Put the egg white into a measuring cup and add enough cold water to make ½ cup. Pour the egg white and water mixture into a small bowl and beat it with a whisk or egg beater until slightly frothy, then set aside. Stir the dry ingredients together in a medium bowl. Add the egg white and water mixture and stir only enough to combine. Cover the bowl and refrigerate for several hours or up to 4 days.

FLOWER CLUSTERS

10 to 12 clusters of milkweed flowers

Wash the flower clusters under running water to remove ants. Shake off as much water as possible and drain the clusters on kitchen towels. Using a sharp knife, cut off the stem that once attached the cluster to the plant, then divide each cluster by carefully cutting it apart at the back where it is held together (thus making 2 smaller clusters). Refrigerate the clusters until ready to fry them.

FRYING THE FRITTERS

peanut oil for deep-fat frying

Pour the oil into the deep-fat fryer or heavy pot to a depth of 4 to 5 inches and heat it to 350 to 375 degrees, or test by putting a drop of batter into the hot oil—if it sinks to the bottom and slowly rises, the oil is not hot enough;

if it stays at the surface without sinking, the oil is too hot. At the proper temperature, a drop of batter will sink but rise quickly, expanding rapidly at the surface.

Remove the batter from the refrigerator and stir. Using a fork, dip each cluster into the batter, then place it carefully into the hot oil. Fry each cluster, turning once, until crisp and lightly browned. Remove the fritters with a slotted spoon and drain them on paper towels. Sprinkle them with a mixture of ½ cup granulated sugar and 1 teaspoon ground cinnamon. Serve them hot. Makes 20 to 24 fritters.

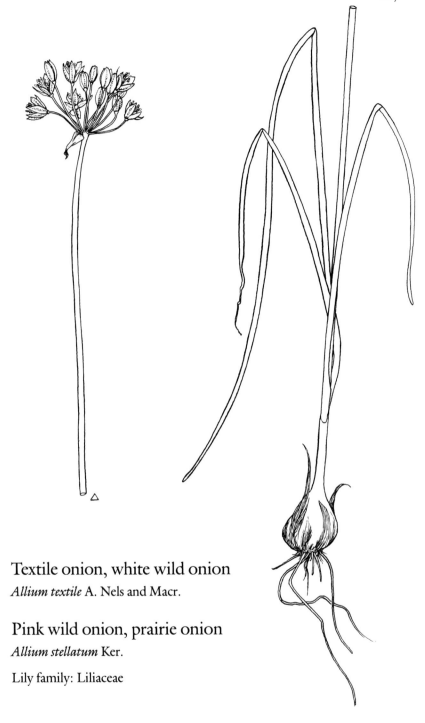

Textile onion, white wild onion
Allium textile A. Nels and Macr.

Pink wild onion, prairie onion
Allium stellatum Ker.

Lily family: Liliaceae

Description: These native onions are strongly scented perennial herbs growing from bulbs and reproducing by seeds. Textile onion stands about 8 to 10 inches high at the time it blooms in late spring or early summer. The bulb is oval to conical in shape, with a fibrous covering resembling woven textile. (This covering is loose and somewhat soft and may remain belowground when the bulb is pulled from the soil.) The leaves are smooth, narrow, and channeled (grooved), and typically occur two per stem. The flowers are usually white, occasionally pink, and are borne in clusters at the top of a single stem. The seeds are black.

Pink wild onion is different in several ways. It usually stands about 1 foot tall by the time it blooms in late summer or fall. The bulb is oval to conical in shape and covered with smooth, thin skin not unlike that of garden onions. The several narrow leaves rise from the base of the plant and may be deeply channeled to nearly flat. The clusters of flowers are pink. The seeds are black.

Distribution: Widely distributed throughout the United States and into Canada, with textile onion more commonly found in the west and pink wild onion in the east. In the Great Plains, textile onion is found in the north and west and as far south as western Kansas (with scattered populations elsewhere); pink wild onion is found in the north and east and south to Texas.

Habitat: Moist meadows or along streams, but both textile onion and pink wild onion are found in drier areas as well, with textile onion common on prairies, often on rocky slopes, and pink wild onion on prairies, rocky slopes, and along roadsides, often in richer soil.

Edible parts: Bulbs cooked or uncooked; tender young leaves, cooked or uncooked.

Seasons to collect: Anytime of year they can be found.

Cautions: Be aware that plants in the genus *Zigadenus* (sometimes spelled *Zygadenus*), commonly called death camas (also spelled camass), look much like wild onions and are poisonous, some species particularly so. Be aware also that these plants may grow in the same places that wild onions grow. Although most species of death camas have bulbs that look like onions, none have the characteristic onion or garlic odor. Consequently, when collecting wild onions, it is necessary to smell each and every bulb *and it is important to* *do this in such a way that odor lingering on your hands from handling true wild onions doesn't fool you into thinking that subsequent bulbs are passing the test.*

In the past, all wild onions and garlics were generally considered edible, but recent information from the American Medical Association warns against eating certain wild *Allium* species, two of which are reported in the Great Plains. The species not recommended are wild garlic, *Allium canadensis* L., and field garlic, *Allium vineale* L., both of which typically develop bulblets among the flowers at the top of the plant. Some varieties of *Allium canadensis* produce seeds, but the warning appears to be directed only toward those that produce bulblets. Apparently, these species contain toxins that may cause severe stomach upset, particularly in young children. Also of concern, according to the warning, is that over a period of time, eating the bulblets can interfere with the absorption of iodine by the thyroid, causing susceptibility to goiter.

Additional information and recipes: Smaller, wild onions look and smell like garden onions and may be used in much the same way. Because the flavor of wild onions is usually stronger, however, use them more sparingly.

Regardless of whether you use wild or garden onions, it is important to cut them properly. When onions are simply cut crosswise, they remain in small, round chunks even after cooking. A better way is to cut them *diagonally* into thin slices so that the layers are more apt to separate and the flavor will blend in with other ingredients.

Persons who recall attending country schools long ago say that they often ate wild onions on the way to school and that friends would tease each other by exhaling oniony breath into each other's faces. Today wild onions are not widely used, even for children's fun, and when they are used, they are usually cooked.

Slices of wild onion are good stir-fried with other vegetables, wild or domestic, or may be added to greens, dressings, stews, or soups. They are particularly good with cheese in scrambled eggs.

Scrambled eggs with wild onions and cheese
2 tablespoons margarine or butter
2 to 4 tablespoons wild onion slices, including tops
8 eggs
2 tablespoons milk
salt and freshly ground black pepper to taste
¾ cup grated cheese

Melt the margarine or butter in a skillet over medium heat, add the onion slices, and stir until tender but not browned. Add the eggs and milk and stir with a fork until combined. Continue stirring until the eggs are nearly firm. Turn the heat to low, sprinkle the cheese over the egg mixture, cover the skillet with a lid, and allow the mixture to cook for a few minutes, checking to see that the eggs do not overcook. Makes 4 servings.

This recipe is good cooked over a campfire and may be varied by adding bits of crisp bacon, chopped and cooked cactus pad, or wild greens such as watercress, dandelion, stinging nettle, or violet. Slices of young cattail shoot (cut diagonally) also make a good addition, but cook them in the skillet (the same goes for greens or bacon) before adding the eggs.

Red mulberry, black mulberry
Morus rubra L.

White mulberry, black mulberry
Morus alba L.

Mulberry family: Moraceae

Description: The red mulberry is a native tree that often grows to a height of 60 feet or more. Typically, it has a straight trunk and a rounded crown, but some specimens are more shrublike. The leaves of the red mulberry may be irregularly lobed but frequently are unlobed and very pointed at the tip; the upper surface is smooth to rough, and the underside is entirely covered by very minute hairs.

The white mulberry (sometimes called black mulberry) is an introduced tree and is now the most common mulberry in the Great Plains. Typically, it is shorter and shrublike, but some trees resemble the red mulberry and grow to a height of 40 feet or more. The leaves of the white mulberry are usually lobed on one or both margins and taper to a blunt, not sharp, tip; the upper surface is smooth to shiny, and hairs on the underside occur only on the veins.

Mulberries bear female and male flowers separately, and often a tree will bear only one sex—this is particularly true of the white mulberry. The female flowers are borne in small, inconspicuous hanging clusters less than 1 inch in length; the male flowers occur in catkins up to 2 inches long. Fruits of the red mulberry are deep purple to black; those of the white mulberry may be white, lavender, purple, or black.

Distribution: Red mulberry: scattered throughout much of the south-central and eastern United States and into eastern Canada; in the Great Plains, eastern and central Nebraska and Kansas, into Oklahoma and Texas (more common in Missouri). White mulberry: throughout much of the eastern United States and into eastern Canada, scattered (wherever introduced) in the western United States; in the Great Plains, southeastern South Dakota, eastern and central Nebraska, throughout Kansas and scattered south (also in Iowa and Missouri).

Habitat: Red mulberry: rich, moist soil in woods, on flood plains, and along creek banks, less frequently in yards. White mulberry: moist or drier soils in woods, on flood plains, along creek banks, roadsides, and fence rows, often planted in yards and shelter belts.

Edible parts: Ripe fruits, cooked or uncooked; slightly unripe fruits, cooked only.

Seasons to collect: Late spring through midsummer, but location and species make a difference.

Cautions: Some persons are sensitive to the milky sap of mulberry leaves and branches and some cannot tolerate the underripe fruits, but in the Great Plains it is a common practice to add a few slightly underripe mulberries to the ripe ones when making jelly or jam. I have never heard of anyone experiencing problems as a result of that practice.

Additional information and recipes: To botanists, "red" and "white" (and sometimes "black") refer to different species of mulberry and not to the color of the fruit. However, in describing the use of the fruit, I will use "black" and "white" to refer to the color of the fruit.

Older persons whom I interviewed often remembered mulberry picking from their youth. Apparently some families looked forward to each year's mulberry season with enthusiasm, whereas others considered mulberries merely survival fare to be used when other fruits were unavailable. However, as children, nearly everyone prized mulberries, and some persons spoke at great length about particularly memorable picking excursions when they were young.

I, too, came to love mulberries at an early age, no doubt as the result of summer visits to the farm of my Uncle Waldo and Aunt Dora near Lyons, Nebraska. When I was a child, I thought there was no place in the world as good as that farm. It seemed that everything a child would ever dream of was there—a farm dog, eggs to gather, a huge yawning barn to explore, and beside it, a feedlot with a wonderful mulberry tree growing just inside the fence. Two things were memorable about that tree: its enormous sweet, black, juicy fruit and the fact that it grew close enough to the fence that we children could use the rails like rungs of a ladder. Being a child, I did not make an association between the feedlot and the exceptional quality of the fruit, but I have wondered about it since, for nowhere else have I found mulberries so lush and flavorful.

Over the years, in an attempt to locate a comparable tree, I have sampled fruit from many mulberry trees and in doing so, have learned that the flavor, size, and juiciness of mulberries vary significantly from tree to tree. This is particularly true of the white fruits, which are not necessarily inferior to black fruits as is commonly believed. Although some white-fruited mulberry trees bear fruit of flat, uninteresting taste, others produce fruit that is very flavorful and nearly as sweet as candy.

As an adult, I went back to Lyons and to the farm, but with some sadness knowing that after lives that had stretched into their nineties, my uncle and aunt would not be there. The house was still lived in, but the barn and the mulberry tree were gone. So I will never know for sure. Maybe it was the nutrients from the feedlot, maybe it was just an unusually fine mulberry tree, or maybe it is simply nostalgia, but in my mind each of those fruits was remarkable, and when I remember back to picking them—even dishpansful—it seems that we were having the greatest of fun.

As an adult I learned to harvest mulberries by spreading a sheet under the tree and shaking the branches vigorously. Then a friend pointed out that once you are home, the fruit has to be sorted through by hand anyway. I thought about this, then tried it both ways: harvesting by hand and harvesting by shaking the branches. The result was that, all told, each method takes about the same amount of time. Today I handpick the mulberries from the lower branches and use the sheet-and-shake method to harvest those beyond my reach.

In whatever manner you take mulberries from the tree, transport them home in shallow containers so that the bottom layers of fruit will not be crushed. To avoid spoilage and to remove the tiny insects that are sometimes present between the segments of the fruit, sort the mulberries as soon as possible after they have been picked, then soak them for about 3 minutes in salt water—¼ cup salt to 1 gallon of water. Drain the salty water and very gently rinse the mulberries with clear water. It is important to handle the fruits gently. Because mulberries soon become moldy even when refrigerated, it is best to keep them no more than 24 hours after they have been picked. Some cookbooks direct readers to remove the stems from mulberry fruits, but I have never felt that was necessary and have had no complaints.

Mulberries are versatile. They are particularly good with dairy products and blend well with other fruits. White or lavender mulberry fruits are best used fresh, but the purple or black fruits are good either fresh or cooked. Although often eaten plain as a snack or with milk and sugar, they can be cooked in numerous ways and are easily frozen for later use.

Mulberry juice or syrup made with the dark fruits may be used to flavor and color desserts, salads, and drinks. Even a small amount added to lemonade creates a beautiful, refreshing drink, and a tablespoon or two stirred into a milk shake makes an extraordinary "purple cow." For the recipes that follow, I suggest using dark mulberries—purple or black—but you may want to experiment by using the lighter ones.

Mulberries have a low acid content and are nearly always improved by the addition of a little lemon or rhubarb juice. (See instructions for making rhubarb juice in Appendix B.) Where directions call for crushing mulberries, a potato masher is recommended, but if handled carefully, even a pop bottle will do.

To freeze mulberries

Read about freezing, Appendix A.

Although mulberries may be frozen with or without sugar, when frozen without, they will lose some flavor. If using sugar, allow 1 to 2 tablespoons for each cup of mulberries and stir only until the fruit is coated with sugar. Freeze in tightly covered containers.

To extract mulberry juice

Use all or mostly fully ripe mulberries—a few slightly underripe mulberries may be added for tartness. Add ¼ cup water for each cup of mulberries. (A workable amount seems to be 8 cups of mulberries and 2 cups of water.) Put the mulberries into a large, heavy kettle and crush them thoroughly. Add the water, stir well, and cover the kettle with a lid. Place over medium heat and allow the mulberries to simmer until tender—about 20 minutes. Stir several times during cooking so that the fruit does not burn. Remove the pot from the heat and allow the contents to cool enough to handle, then strain through a damp jelly cloth.

As already noted, the juiciness of mulberries varies considerably from tree to tree, but typically, when prepared according to the instructions above, each cup of mulberries will yield about ½ cup of juice. The juice may be used as a drink (plain or sweetened with sugar or honey), made into jelly or syrup, or used in other recipes.

Mulberry jelly

4 cups mulberry juice
⅓ cup lemon or rhubarb juice
1 package powdered pectin
5½ cups granulated sugar

Read about jelly making, Appendix A.

Measure the sugar and set it aside. Place the juices and pectin in a large, heavy kettle and stir well, then place over high heat and bring to a boil. Add the sugar all at one time. Stir well and continue stirring until the mixture again reaches a full boil. Begin timing and allow to boil for 1 minute, stirring constantly. Remove from the heat, quickly skim off the foam, and pour the jelly into hot, sterile jars, leaving ¼ inch headspace. Cap the jars with two-piece screwband lids and process for 5 minutes in a boiling water bath. Makes about 7½ cups of jelly.

Mulberry-rhubarb jelly
1½ cups mulberry juice
1½ cups rhubarb juice
1 package powdered pectin
4 cups granulated sugar
    Proceed as for mulberry jelly above. Makes about 5½ cups of jelly.

Mulberry jam
3 cups ripe mulberries
1 cup slightly underripe mulberries
2½ cups granulated sugar
½ cup lemon or rhubarb juice
¼ teaspoon each of cinnamon and nutmeg (optional)
    Read about jam making, Appendix A.
    Crush the mulberries in a large, heavy kettle. Stir in the sugar and juice—also the spices if you choose to use them. Place over low heat and stir until the sugar is thoroughly dissolved. Increase the heat to medium-high, and stirring constantly to prevent burning, cook until thick enough to hold a slightly rounded shape in a spoon—from 7 to 10 minutes. Or use the cold saucer test. When done, remove from the heat and skim off the foam, then stir well and ladle the jam into hot, scalded jars. Put the lids in place but do not screw them on tightly. Cool to room temperature, then tighten the lids. Store in a refrigerator or freezer. Makes about 3 cups of jam.

Mulberry-rhubarb syrup
4 cups ripe mulberries
1 cup diced rhubarb stalk
1 cup water
few grains of salt
granulated sugar in an amount equal to the juice
    Read about syrup making, Appendix A.
    Crush the mulberries in a large, heavy kettle. Add the rhubarb and water and stir well. Cover with a lid, place over low heat, and simmer until the mulberries and rhubarb are tender—about 20 minutes. (To prevent burning, stir several times during cooking.) Remove from the heat and allow to cool until comfortable to handle, then strain the mixture through a damp jelly

cloth. (Note: the pulp remaining in the jelly cloth need not be discarded. Sweetened with sugar or honey, it makes a good sauce—or use it in the filled-cookie recipe found later in this section.)

Measure the juice and return it to the kettle, then measure an equal amount of sugar and add it and the salt to the juice. Heat to boiling and boil for about 7 minutes. Remove from the heat, quickly skim off the foam, and pour the syrup into hot, scalded jars, leaving ½ inch headspace. Cap the jars with two-piece screwband lids and process for 10 minutes in a boiling water bath. Makes about 2½ cups of syrup.

Chunky mulberry syrup

4 cups ripe mulberries
2¼ cups granulated sugar
½ cup lemon or rhubarb juice
few grains of salt

Read about syrup making, Appendix A.

Crush the mulberries in a large, heavy kettle. Add the sugar, the lemon or rhubarb juice, and the salt. Place over medium heat and cook for 7 to 10 minutes, stirring frequently to prevent burning. Remove from the heat and skim off the foam, then pour the syrup into hot, scalded jars. Put the lids in place but do not screw them on tightly. Cool to room temperature, then tighten the lids. Store in a refrigerator or freezer. Makes 4 cups of syrup.

This syrup is especially good on yogurt or ice cream. For some reason—perhaps simply the particular combination of flavors—it is remarkably good drizzled over a scoop of sour cream or vanilla yogurt on top of cattail pollen pancakes (recipe on page 90).

Mulberry gelatin

1 envelope unflavored gelatin or 1 teaspoon powdered (not flaked) agar
⅓ cup granulated sugar
1 cup water
1 cup mulberry juice
2 tablespoons lemon juice

If using gelatin, combine it and the sugar in a bowl and stir until well mixed. Heat the water to boiling, add it to the mixture in the bowl, then stir until the sugar and gelatin are dissolved. Set aside to cool. If using agar, combine it with the sugar and water in a saucepan. Heat and stir over medium heat until the agar has dissolved. Cool only slightly.

Add the mulberry and lemon juices to the gelatin or agar mixture and stir to combine. Pour into a 2-cup dish or mold (an 8 x 8 x 2–inch square dish works well). Refrigerate until firm. Makes 4 to 6 servings.

Chilled mulberry-lemon dessert
½ cup cold water
2 envelopes unflavored gelatin or 2 teaspoons powdered (not flaked) agar
1 cup mulberry juice
2 eight-ounce packages cream cheese
6 tablespoons granulated sugar
1 cup milk
1 12-ounce can frozen lemonade concentrate, slightly thawed
4 cups fresh mulberries, chilled

Put the cold water into a medium-sized bowl and sprinkle the gelatin or agar over it, stirring well to moisten. In a small saucepan, bring the mulberry juice to the point of boiling, but do not allow it to boil. If using gelatin, pour the hot juice into the softened gelatin and stir until the gelatin has dissolved. Set aside to cool. If using agar, stir the moistened agar into the hot juice, then stir and cook over medium-low heat until the agar has dissolved. Cool only slightly.

In a large mixing bowl, beat the cream cheese and sugar with an electric mixer. Continue beating and gradually add the milk, gelatin or agar mixture, and lemonade concentrate in that order. Beat only until well blended. Pour into a 6-cup ring mold or bowl. Refrigerate until set (overnight for gelatin, 2 hours for agar).

Just before serving, prepare the plate on which the dessert will be served by holding it under cold running water, then set it aside, allowing it to remain wet. Next, fill a sink or dishpan with comfortably hot water. Loosen the edges of the dessert by running the blade of a table knife around the rim of the mold and, if using a ring mold, don't forget to do the inner rim as well as the outer. Lower the mold into the hot water for a few seconds only, being careful not to let water flow over the rim. Remove the mold from the hot water and place the serving plate over the mold. Quickly turn both mold and plate over together, jerking sharply. This action should cause the dessert to fall from the mold onto the plate—if it doesn't, repeat the process, beginning with lowering the mold into the hot water. Or wrap the pan for a short time in a towel wrung out in hot water.

Once the dessert has released, the wet surface of the plate will allow it to be moved slightly with a spatula in case it is off-center. Fill or surround the dessert with chilled mulberries. Makes 8 to 10 servings. (Recipe may be halved or doubled.)

Perhaps because our mother was so fond of mulberries, my brothers and I always assumed that whenever we found mulberries and brought home a large panful, she would make a mulberry pie. I don't recall ever being disappointed. Sometimes she made combination pies mixing mulberries with wild gooseberries or with rhubarb from her garden. All were delicious.

Of course, in those days we had never heard of zucchini squash, but later, when Mother learned about the versatility of this abundant vegetable, she began experimenting and came up with the mulberry-zucchini pie that appears below. Hers, too, are the filled mulberry cookies, a treat that down through the years has remained a family favorite.

Mulberry pie
425 degree oven to start
pastry for a 2-crust 8-inch pie
3 cups ripe mulberries
¼ cup lemon or rhubarb juice
3 tablespoons all-purpose flour
¾ cup granulated sugar
1 tablespoon margarine or butter
1 tablespoon granulated sugar
dash of cinnamon and nutmeg

Roll out the pastry, arrange the bottom crust in the pie pan, and set it aside.

Combine the mulberries and the lemon or rhubarb juice in a bowl and stir gently. Stir the flour and first amount of sugar together and add this to the mulberries, again stirring gently. Pour the mixture into the bottom crust. Cut the margarine or butter into pieces and scatter these over the surface. Cover with the top crust; seal and trim the edges. Make a 2-inch slash in the top crust to allow steam to escape during baking.

Combine the second amount of sugar and spices; sprinkle this over the top crust. Bake at 425 degrees for 10 minutes, then reduce the heat to 375 degrees and bake for an additional 25 minutes. Remove the pie from the oven and allow it to cool on a wire rack. Makes 6 servings.

Mulberry-rhubarb pie
425 degree oven to start
pastry for a 2-crust 9-inch pie
2 cups ripe mulberries
2 cups diced rhubarb stalks

4 tablespoons all-purpose flour
1 cup granulated sugar
1 tablespoon margarine or butter
1 tablespoon granulated sugar
dash of cinnamon and nutmeg

Roll out the pastry, arrange the bottom crust in the pie pan, and set it aside.

Combine the mulberries and rhubarb chunks in a bowl. Mix the flour and first amount of sugar together and add this to the mulberries and rhubarb, stirring gently to combine. Proceed as directed for mulberry pie, above. Makes 6 to 8 servings.

For variety, substitute gooseberries for the rhubarb. Note that with gooseberries, both the stems and blossom ends must be removed.

Mom's mulberry-zucchini pie

425 degree oven to start
pastry for a 2-crust 9-inch pie
2 cups ripe mulberries
3 cups grated zucchini squash
½ cup lemon or rhubarb juice
3 tablespoons cornstarch
1 cup granulated sugar
1 tablespoon margarine or butter
1 tablespoon granulated sugar
dash of cinnamon and nutmeg

Roll out the pastry, arrange the bottom crust in the pie pan, and set it aside.

Combine the mulberries, zucchini, and juice in a bowl. Mix the cornstarch and first amount of sugar together and sprinkle this over the mulberries and zucchini, stirring gently to combine. Proceed as directed for mulberry pie, above. Makes 6 to 8 servings.

Mulberry filled cookies

350 degree oven
DOUGH
½ cup granulated sugar
½ cup (1 stick) margarine or butter
2 eggs
1 teaspoon vanilla extract

2 cups all-purpose flour

1 teaspoon baking powder

Using an electric mixer, beat the sugar with the margarine or butter until light. Add the eggs one at a time, then the vanilla, beating well after each addition. Sift the flour and baking powder together, then add this to the other ingredients and beat again. Place the dough in a covered container and chill well. (Dough may be frozen for later use.)

FILLING

1 teaspoon margarine or butter

2 teaspoons cornstarch

1 cup ripe mulberries

1 cup diced rhubarb stalk

½ cup granulated sugar

1 teaspoon vanilla extract

With the back of a spoon, work the cornstarch into the margarine or butter to make a smooth paste, then set aside.

Place the mulberries in a heavy pot and crush them with a potato masher. Add the diced rhubarb and sugar. Stir to combine and place over medium heat, stirring constantly until the sugar has dissolved and the mixture begins to boil. Reduce the heat to low, cover the pot with a lid, and cook for 3 to 4 minutes or until the rhubarb is soft. Stir a small amount of the hot fruit mixture into the cornstarch and margarine (or butter) paste, then stir this back into the fruit mixture in the pot. Stirring constantly, cook for about 2 minutes or until the mixture is quite thick. Remove from the heat and stir in the vanilla. Allow the mixture to cool. Makes about 1 cup of filling.

ASSEMBLING THE COOKIES

Lightly grease 2 cookie sheets with margarine or butter and set them aside.

Dust a pastry cloth or hard surface heavily with powdered sugar. Remove the dough from the refrigerator and cut it in half. Place one of the halves on the powdered surface and return the other to the refrigerator so that it will remain chilled. With a rolling pin, roll the dough out to a thickness of ⅛ inch or less. Cut out circles approximately 2½ inches in diameter. (An empty 12-ounce frozen juice can is just the right size and easier to handle than most cookie cutters.)

Count and divide the circles—half will be bottoms, half will be tops. Using a spatula, carefully place the bottoms on a greased cookie sheet and heap 1 rounded teaspoon of filling in the center of each. Again using the spatula, lift the tops and place one over each mound of filling. The edges will seal themselves during baking, but prick the top of each cookie with a fork so that steam can escape. Repeat with the other half of the dough. Bake until lightly browned—about 15 minutes.

Remove the cookies from the cookie sheets and allow them to cool on wire racks. When cool, place the cookies in a tightly covered container. If not used the same day they are baked, refrigerate them and use within a few days. Makes 20 to 24 cookies.

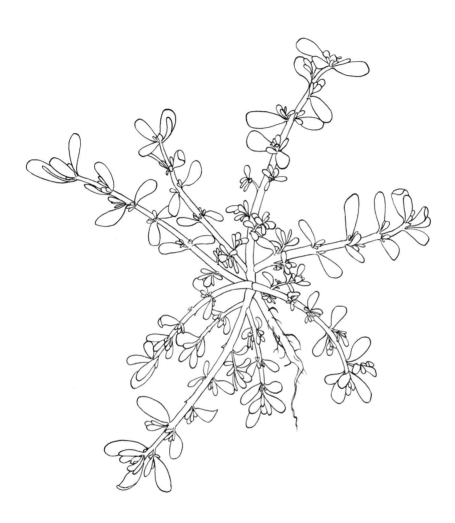

Purslane, pusley

Portulaca oleracea L.

Purslane family: Portulacaceae

Description: Purslane is an introduced low-growing annual herb with numerous branches originating from a central root. Both branches and leaves are smooth, fleshy, and often tinged with red or purple. The plant may lie flat on the ground like a mat or stand mostly upright, but the branches are rarely more than 8 inches long. The leaves are flat and bluntly oval and occur in a nearly opposite, somewhat random arrangement on the branches. The flowers are small and yellow and occur in the axils of the leaves, but because they mostly open in mornings and only when there is sunshine, they may be overlooked. The seeds are minute and borne in a small capsule, the upper half of which opens like a lid.

Distribution: Throughout much of the United States and into Canada; common throughout the Great Plains.

Habitat: Yards, gardens, cultivated fields, and along roadsides; prefers full sun and can tolerate fairly high temperatures.

Edible parts: Leaves and branches, cooked or uncooked. (Flowers and seeds are edible but too small to collect in quantity.)

Seasons to collect: Early summer and throughout the growing season.

Cautions: Commonly considered a weed, purslane in lawns or public places is sometimes sprayed with herbicide. Collect only from plants that look fresh and healthy—better yet, grow your own.

Additional information and recipes: In early summer as garden lettuce is becoming too bitter to eat, purslane leaves are just becoming large enough to pick. Although they are small, fresh purslane leaves are good in sandwiches and do not wilt in association with mayonnaise as lettuce often does. The flavor is slightly sour, and, interestingly, the texture is both crunchy and slightly slick. In many parts of the world, purslane is grown in gardens and sold in markets as a vegetable.

Purslane may offer other benefits as well. Recently, a study at the National Institute on Alcohol Abuse and Alcoholism in Bethesda, Maryland, identified purslane as the richest known source of omega-3 in leafy greens. Egg yolks from chickens fed purslane were reported to contain 10 times the amount of omega-3 fatty acids (believed to reduce cholesterol) as yolks from typical supermarket eggs. No doubt more research on this subject is forthcoming.

Purslane leaves are good on hamburgers and exceptionally good on tacos. Both the leaves and the tender chopped stems may be added to soups, stews, scrambled eggs, and omelets. To serve purslane alone as a vegetable, it may be steamed, boiled, or stir-fried in a little cooking oil, then seasoned to taste. The flavor blends well with onions, and stir-fried purslane and onions make a good side dish with potatoes, rice, or meat.

As you begin to look at purslane with an eye to eating it, you will notice that some plants have larger leaves than others. Purslane starts easily from cuttings, so to provide yourself with larger-leaved plants, simply snip a few branches from a hearty specimen and plant them about 2 inches deep in moist soil. Purslane does not do well as a long-term houseplant, but by planting a few branches in a clay pot in late autumn and keeping the pot in a sunny window, you can pick leaves well into winter before the plants become too scraggly. Whether plants are in a flower pot or outside, always select young leaves and stems from the upper portions of the plant and remember that because this plant grows close to the soil, leaves and branches must be thoroughly washed to remove dirt or sand.

Purslane freezes well and makes a good addition to various recipes in winter.

To freeze purslane

Read about freezing, Appendix A.

Have ready a bowl of ice water and a 1-cup freezer container. Put 2 cups of purslane and 1 cup of water into a pot over high heat, cover with a lid, and boil for 3 minutes. Remove the pot from the heat and pour the mixture into a strainer to drain. Put the strainer into the ice water so that the purslane will cool quickly. When cold, drain and put the purslane into the container, cover, and freeze. Makes about 1 cup.

Purslane and oxtail soup

2 pounds of oxtails, disjointed
8 cups water
1 cup coarsely cut onion
1 medium carrot, cut diagonally into ¼ inch slices
½ cup barley
2 cups purslane leaves and chopped stems
salt and freshly ground black pepper to taste

Put the oxtails and water into a large pot. Cover with a lid and cook over low heat for 3 to 3½ hours or until the meat is tender. Remove from the heat. Drain the broth and chill it so that the fat may be removed and discarded. When the oxtails are cool enough to handle, separate the meat from the bones and fat, keeping only the meat. Pour the broth back into the pot and add the onion, carrot, barley, salt, and pepper. Cover the pot with the lid and cook the soup over medium heat for 20 minutes. Stir in the purslane and meat; cook for 10 minutes more. Makes 4 to 6 servings.

This recipe may be varied (and the servings increased) by adding 1 cup of tomato juice with the vegetables and barley or by adding other vegetables.

Buffalo currant, black currant

Ribes odoratum Wendl.

Currant family: Grossulariaceae

Description: Buffalo currant is a slender, branched native shrub growing to about 5 feet in height under good conditions. The leaves are alternate, usually as broad as long, and deeply lobed; the margins are usually toothed. The flowers occur in hanging clusters in early spring and are bright yellow, with 5 petals and a pleasant, spicy odor. The fruits hang in small clusters, with some fruits much larger than others. They are yellowish at first but turn black and juicy when fully ripe; they contain numerous seeds.

Distribution: Northwestern United States and into Canada; scattered east and south; throughout much of the Great Plains; cultivated as a garden plant.

Habitat: Hillsides, ravines, rocky ledges, borders of woods, and along fence rows.

Edible parts: Ripe fruits, cooked or uncooked.

Season to collect: Early summer.

Cautions: No particular cautions apply.

Additional information and recipes: The wild black currant, *Ribes americanum* Mill., occurs in the central and northern Great Plains but is less flavorful than the buffalo currant. The flowers of wild black currant are white to pale yellow green and lack the spicy fragrance of buffalo currant flowers. The ripe fruits are juicy and black, but they do not ripen until late summer. In some parts of the Great Plains, wild black currant is more common than buffalo currant.

The word "currant" usually brings to mind the small dried fruits, similar to raisins, which are sold in grocery stores. Those, however, are actually small grapes, not true currants. Among the true currants, both wild and domestic, much variation occurs. Some of the wild currants are too dry to be used for anything other than survival food, and some are juicy but not particularly flavorful. The buffalo currant is both juicy and flavorful and, like its garden cousins, makes excellent jelly, syrup, and jam. In addition, it can be used to make an exceptionally rich, black pie.

Buffalo currant bushes transplant well and make attractive yard plants. Choose a well-drained, sunny location and give them an occasional watering, especially in spring.

To extract currant juice

4 cups buffalo currants

½ cup water

Combine the currants and water in a heavy kettle and place over medium heat. Cover the kettle with a lid and allow the fruit to boil gently until tender—about 10 minutes. Remove from the heat and allow the fruit to cool until comfortable to handle, then strain through a damp jelly cloth. Yields about 2 cups of juice.

Buffalo currant jelly

2 cups buffalo currant juice

2 cups granulated sugar

Read about jelly making, Appendix A.

Stir the juice and sugar together in a large, heavy kettle. Place this over medium-high heat, bring to a gentle boil, and allow it to cook until it reaches the jelling point. Test for doneness with a jelly thermometer or use the spoon or cold saucer method. When done, remove from the heat, quickly skim off the foam, and pour the jelly into hot, sterile jars, leaving ¼ inch headspace. Cap the jars with two-piece screwband lids and process for 5 minutes in a boiling water bath. Makes a little more than 2 cups of jelly.

Buffalo currant syrup

2 cups buffalo currant juice

1 ½ cups granulated sugar

½ cup light corn syrup

Read about syrup making, Appendix A.

Combine the currant juice and sugar in a large, heavy kettle; place over medium-high heat and boil for 5 minutes. Slowly add the syrup and reheat to boiling. Boil for 2 minutes, then remove from the heat and skim off the foam. Pour the syrup into hot, scalded jars, leaving ½ inch headspace. Cap jars with two-piece screwband lids and process for 10 minutes in a boiling water bath. Makes 2 ½ cups of syrup.

Chunky currant topping

2 cups granulated sugar

1 cup water

4 cups buffalo currants

honey, to be added later

Read about syrup making, Appendix A.

Combine the sugar and water in a large, heavy kettle over high heat and bring the mixture to boiling. Boil for 2 minutes, then add the currants, 1 cup at a time, stirring after each addition. Reduce the heat to medium, bring to a gentle boil, and allow to boil for 7 minutes. Remove from the heat and quickly skim off the foam. Pour the topping into hot, sterile jars, leaving ¼ inch headspace. Cap the jars with two-piece screwband lids and process for 5 minutes in a boiling water bath. Makes about 4 cups of topping.

To serve, add ¼ cup honey to each cup of topping; stir well. This is especially good on yogurt or hot oatmeal.

Buffalo currant jam

buffalo currants
water
granulated sugar

Read about jam making, Appendix A.

Measure the amount of currants, then mash them in a large, heavy kettle and stir in 2 tablespoons of water for each cup of currants. Place over medium-high heat and stir constantly until the juice flows and begins to bubble. Reduce the heat to medium, cover the kettle with a lid, and cook, stirring often, until the currants are soft—about 10 minutes. Remove the kettle from the heat and allow to cool until comfortable to handle. Press the currants through a sieve to remove the seeds. Measure the pulp.

Combine the pulp and an equal amount of sugar in a heavy kettle and place over medium heat. Cook, stirring constantly, until the mixture is thick enough to hold a slightly rounded shape in a spoon—about 5 minutes. Or test for doneness using the cold saucer method. When done, remove from the heat and skim off the foam, then stir the jam well and ladle it into hot, sterile jars, leaving ¼ inch headspace. Cap the jars with two-piece screwband lids and process for 5 minutes in a boiling water bath. Makes about ⅔ as much jam as the original amount of currants.

Buffalo currant pie

400 degree oven
pastry for a two-crust 9-inch pie
4 cups buffalo currants
1 tablespoon lemon juice
1 cup granulated sugar
2 tablespoons cornstarch or 3 tablespoons all-purpose flour
dash of salt

dash of powdered ginger or nutmeg (optional)
1 tablespoon margarine or butter

Roll out the pastry and arrange the bottom crust in the pie pan; set aside. Place the currants in a medium bowl and sprinkle them with the lemon juice. Mix the sugar, cornstarch or flour, salt, and spices together and stir this into the currants. Pour the mixture into the pie crust. Cut the margarine or butter into pieces and scatter this over the filling. Place the top crust over all and seal around the edges, then make a 2-inch slit to allow escape of steam during baking. Bake at 400 degrees for about 40 to 45 minutes. Makes 6 to 8 servings. Serve warm with vanilla ice cream.

Sandcherry

Prunus pumila L. var. *besseyi* (Bailey) Gl.

Rose family: Rosaceae

Description: The sandcherry is a short native shrub, usually much branched and typically growing to a height of less than 2½ feet. Branches are sometimes upright, but often bend to the ground with upturned ends. The leaves are alternate with fine irregular teeth along the margins, the upper surface dark green and smooth, the lower surface paler and with a slightly waxy covering that wipes off easily. The leaves tend to cluster toward the tips of the branches. The flowers, which bloom in spring, are small and white with 5 petals. The fruits are about the size and shape of bing cherries but the color may be purple black, reddish, or yellow red, often with some mottling. Fruits may hang singly or in groups, and each contains a single seed called a stone or pit.

Distribution: Northern half of the Great Plains south into central Kansas; also eastern Wyoming and northeastern Colorado.

Habitat: Hillsides, creek banks, sandbars, open prairies, and along roadsides and fence rows, particularly in sandy areas and often among grasses; usually in full sun.

Edible parts: Ripe fruits, cooked. Ripe sandcherries may be eaten uncooked, but are too astringent for most tastes.

Season to collect: Early summer.

Cautions: Sandcherries growing along roadsides are sometimes sprayed with herbicides. Do not use fruits from plants that bear signs of spray, such as yellow, wilted, or dead leaves or discolored fruit.

When working with sandcherries, do not crush the seeds. Sandcherry seeds contain a cyanide-forming compound that can cause illness or even death if consumed in large amounts. Note that the seeds of several other kinds of fruits, including orchard cherries, contain this compound. Freezing or ordinary cooking and processing of the fruits is not harmful.

Additional information and recipes: Sandcherries are one of the most interesting and delicious wild fruits of the Great Plains. Often hidden by grasses or other plants, these hardy little bushes can produce tremendous amounts of fruit. Although the yield varies from year to year, a heavy crop is produced about every third year. Sandcherries transplant well when young and make attractive yard plants. Although they need protection from fruit borers, they seem relatively free of disease and other insect infestation. If you try transplanting, dig them early in spring or late in autumn. Although sandcherry bushes, advertised as native, are sold through commercial nurseries in the Great Plains, it is likely that much of this stock has been grown from plants brought from outside the United States. The fruits are similar to our native sandcherry and of equal quality, but the plants are taller and more upright.

Larger and earlier to ripen than chokecherries, sandcherries often appear to be ripe before they are, and sometimes look unripe when in fact they are ready to pick. Tasting may be the only way to determine their readiness—if they seem especially tart, a week or so longer on the bush may result in their being considerably sweeter. When uncooked, sandcherries have a flavor that ranges from astringent to moderately sweet, but when cooked, the flavor is delicious.

Once an important food for Indian people living in the Great Plains, sandcherries were cooked in season or were pounded into a mush, seeds and all, then dried in patties and stored for winter. That the seeds contained a toxic substance was well known to these people, but they had learned that by proper drying, the compound could be broken down, rendering the patties safe to eat. Some persons still make these patties in the traditional way. When I was conducting interviews about plants in the 1970s, a Lakota (Sioux) elder described how, when he was a child, families or groups of friends would go together on picking excursions. He remembered that such outings were greatly enjoyed, but that serious attention was given to the way plants were harvested. He said that if not picked properly, sandcherries will be bitter. He explained this by comparing the sandcherry to the houseplant called "sensitive plant." "When you touch that, the leaves fold together," he said, "that's a *physical* reaction; when you touch the sandcherry, the flavor changes—that's a *chemical* reaction." Sandcherries, he said, must be picked as quickly and gently as possible with little or no talking, and it is best to approach the bushes against the wind.

Thoroughly intrigued with sandcherries, I interviewed descendants of settlers as well. They, too, recalled going out as families and with groups of friends to gather sandcherries, and also remembered such outings as being great fun. They said that when time did not permit group outings, one or perhaps a few family members picked the fruit.

Often, what happened in farming areas was that when men working in their fields saw that fruit was ripe, they reported it to the women in the family, who would then do the gathering, usually with their children. In ranching areas where men traveled much greater distances during a day, the wild fruit they spotted would often be miles from the house. Those who were so inclined stopped and picked what they could carry in saddlebags or came prepared with containers the following day, bringing the fruit back so the women could cook or can it. A man in eastern Wyoming said he rarely felt he had time to pick wild fruit, but when he saw sandcherries he got off his horse. There was nothing in the world that compared to sandcherry pie or jelly, he said.

Not only are sandcherries delicious, but their large size allows the use of an ordinary hand-operated cherry pitter. This makes it possible to substitute sandcherries for sour cherries in most recipes. To prepare the fruit for pitting, simply wash it and remove any stems that are still attached. Although I've heard that they do occur, I have yet to find a wormy sandcherry.

To freeze sandcherries
Read about freezing, Appendix A.

Pit the sandcherries. Measure, and add ¼ cup granulated sugar for each cup of sand cherries and juice. Stir well so that the sugar is evenly distributed. Spoon the sandcherries into containers having tightly fitting lids. With the back of the spoon push the fruit down so that it is covered by the juice. Freeze.

To freeze sandcherries for making jelly later, do not pit and do not add sugar. Simply wash the fruit, allow it to drain well, measure it into 8-cup amounts, and freeze it in heavy freezer-grade plastic bags until ready to use. When making jelly, proceed the same as for fresh sandcherries.

To extract sandcherry juice
8 cups sandcherries
2 cups water

Combine the sandcherries and water in a large, heavy kettle over medium heat. Cover with a lid and allow to boil gently until the fruit is soft—about 20 minutes. Remove from the heat and allow to cool until comfortable to handle. Pour the fruit into a damp jelly cloth and squeeze to extract the juice. Makes a little more than 3 cups of juice.

Sandcherry jelly
3 cups sandcherry juice
1 package powdered pectin
4½ cups granulated sugar

Read about jelly making, Appendix A.

Measure the sugar and set it aside. In a large, heavy kettle combine the sandcherry juice and pectin. Stir well. Place the kettle over high heat and, stirring constantly, bring the juice to a full boil. Begin timing and, still stirring, allow the jelly to boil hard for 1 minute. Remove from the heat and quickly skim off the foam; pour the jelly into hot, sterile jars, leaving ¼ inch headspace. Cap the jars with two-piece screwband lids and process for 5 minutes in a boiling water bath. Makes 5 cups of jelly.

Sandcherry–wild plum jelly

2 cups sandcherry juice
2 cups wild plum juice
3 cups granulated sugar

See instructions for making wild plum juice on page 197. Read about jelly making, Appendix A.

Combine the juices in a large, heavy kettle; place over medium-high heat and allow to boil gently for 5 minutes (do not cover). Add the sugar and stir until it is dissolved. Allow to boil, stirring occasionally, until the jelling point is reached. Test for doneness with a jelly thermometer or use the spoon or cold saucer method. The amount of time required will vary with the amount of pectin in the wild plum juice, but 15 minutes is typical. Remove from the heat and quickly skim off the foam; pour the jelly into hot, sterile jars, leaving ¼ inch headspace. Cap the jars with two-piece screwband lids and process for 5 minutes in a boiling water bath. Makes about 3½ cups jelly.

Sandcherry jam

4 cups pitted and finely chopped sandcherries and juice
1 package powdered pectin
5 cups granulated sugar

Read about jam making, Appendix A.

Measure the sugar and set it aside. Stir the pectin into the sandcherries in a large, heavy kettle. Place over high heat and, stirring constantly, bring to a full boil. Add the sugar all at once and continue stirring. When the mixture again reaches a full boil, begin timing and, still stirring, allow it to boil hard for 1 minute. Remove from the heat, skim off the foam, then stir well and ladle the jam into hot, sterile jars, leaving ¼ inch headspace. Cap the jars with two-piece screwcap lids and process for 5 minutes in a boiling water bath. Makes 6 cups of jam.

Sandcherry topping

1 cup pitted sandcherries and juice

½ cup water
½ cup granulated sugar
1 tablespoon cornstarch
1 tablespoon margarine or butter
2 drops almond extract

Place the sandcherries, juice, and water in a heavy medium pot. Mix the sugar and cornstarch together until well blended. Add this to the sandcherry mixture and stir well. Place over medium heat and cook, stirring constantly, until the mixture thickens. Cook, still stirring, until the mixture clears—about 2 minutes. Remove from the heat, add the margarine or butter and the almond flavoring. Stir until combined. Sandcherry topping may be served hot or cold. To store, cover and allow to cool to room temperature, then refrigerate. Makes about 1½ cups of topping.

Traditional sandcherry pie
425 degree oven to start
pastry for a two-crust 9-inch pie
4 cups pitted sandcherries and juice
2 drops almond extract
3 tablespoons cornstarch or quick-cooking tapioca
1 cup granulated sugar
2 tablespoons margarine or butter

Roll out the pastry, arrange the bottom crust in the pan, and set it aside.

Put the sandcherries, juice, and almond extract into a large bowl. Mix the cornstarch or tapioca with the sugar, stir this into the sandcherries, and allow the mixture to stand for 15 minutes. Stir, then pour the mixture into the pie crust. Cut the margarine or butter into pieces and scatter them across the filling. Cover the filling with the top crust and seal the edges. Make a 2-inch slash in the top crust so steam can escape during baking. If desired, sprinkle the top crust with 1 tablespoon granulated sugar mixed with a dash of cinnamon.

Place the pie in the oven and bake at 425 degrees for 10 minutes. Reduce the heat to 350 degrees and allow it to bake for another 40 minutes or until lightly browned. Makes 6 to 8 servings.

Ainsworth sandcherry pie
350 degree oven
pastry for a two-crust 9-inch pie
3 cups pitted sandcherries and juice
½ package black raspberry-flavored gelatin (not artificially sweetened)

1 cup boiling water
1 cup granulated sugar
3 ½ tablespoons quick-cooking tapioca

Roll out the pastry, arrange the bottom crust in the pie pan, and set it aside.

Put the sandcherries and juice in a heavy medium-sized pot. In a small bowl combine the gelatin and boiling water, stir until dissolved, then add to the sandcherries. Mix the sugar and tapioca together and stir this into the sandcherries also. Allow the mixture to stand for 3 minutes to soften the tapioca, then cook for 2 or 3 minutes over medium heat, stirring constantly.

Remove the pot from the heat and allow to cool slightly, then pour the mixture into the pie crust. Add the top crust and seal around the edges. Make a 2-inch slash in the top crust to allow steam to escape. Bake for 1 hour or until the crust is lightly browned. Makes 6 to 8 servings.

When the following recipe came to me, it was titled simply "cherries jubilee" and it called for canned bing cherries. It was delicious, but I think the substitution of sandcherries makes it even better.

Sandcherries jubilee

3 cups pitted sandcherries: fresh, frozen, or canned
¾ cup granulated sugar (omit if using sweetened frozen or canned sandcherries
1 cup currant jelly (see buffalo currant jelly, page 139)
½ cup brandy
1 quart vanilla ice cream

If you are using fresh sandcherries, put them into a pot with the sugar; stir well. Place over medium heat, cover with a lid, and cook until tender—about 10 minutes. From this point on, the process is the same for fresh, frozen, or canned sandcherries.

Drain the juice from the sandcherries and set them aside. (The cook may drink the juice.) Melt the jelly in a chafing dish or saucepan, then add the drained sandcherries. Heat slowly until the jelly is completely melted and bubbly. While the sandcherries are heating, spoon the ice cream into individual serving dishes on a serving tray.

When the sandcherry mixture is ready, turn off the heat under the chafing dish or saucepan. (High heat could cause the brandy to explode.) Then, without stirring, slowly pour the brandy into the center of the sandcherries—the brandy should float on top. Light a kitchen match (nothing shorter) and touch it to the brandy. As soon as it ignites, spoon the flaming fruit over the ice cream. Serve immediately. Makes 6 generous servings.

(Note: do not serve anything containing alcohol without first informing your guests. The belief that alcohol cooks out and cannot become a problem for alcohol-sensitive persons is not true.)

Low juneberry, juneberry, sarvisberry, low serviceberry, saskatoonberry

Amelanchier humilis Wieg. (Pursh) DC.

Juneberry, sarvisberry, saskatoon serviceberry, saskatoon-berry

Amelanchier alnifolia Nutt.

Juneberry, tree juneberry, sarvisberry, serviceberry

Amelanchier arborea (Michx. f.) Fern.

Rose family: Rosaceae

Description: The first two species listed above are shrubs and very similar to each other. Both reproduce by underground stems. Although under good conditions these shrubs may reach a height of 10 feet or so, often they are considerably shorter. In prairie, juneberry shrubs no more than 2 feet tall may bear fruit. *A. arborea,* the tree form of juneberry, has a single trunk (occasionally several), reproduces by seed, and may reach heights of 30 feet or more. Leaves of all species are alternate and have serrate or partly serrate margins. When the leaves first emerge, they are folded lengthwise and are densely covered with soft hairs. As the leaves grow, the upper surface becomes smooth, the underside smooth or slightly hairy. The leaves of *A. alnifolia* are rounded, usually with a blunt tip, whereas those of *A. humilis* and *A. arborea* are oval with a more rounded or pointed tip. The flowers are white with 5 petals and are borne in clusters at the ends of the branches, appearing before or with the emerging leaves. The fruits also occur in clusters and when ripe are round, juicy, and deep blue black, much like blueberries. Each fruit contains several seeds.

Distribution: *A. humilis*: scattered in the eastern United States and into Canada; throughout much of North Dakota, scattered in South Dakota and into Nebraska. *A. alnifolia*: scattered in the northern and western United States and Canada; throughout much of North Dakota, scattered in South Dakota and into Nebraska. *A. arborea*: scattered in the eastern United States; along the Missouri River in southeastern Nebraska, into eastern Kansas and Oklahoma (and western Missouri).

Habitat: *A. humilis* and *A. alnifolia* on hillsides, in prairies, ravines, open woods, and along streams; *A. arborea* in open, often rocky woods, frequently on slopes or at the top of ravines or buffs.

Edible parts: Fresh or dried, cooked or uncooked ripe fruits.

Seasons to collect: Early summer to midsummer, depending on latitude; *A. arborea* in early summer, usually June; *A. humilis* and *A. alnifolia* in early to midsummer, usually July, sometimes into August.

Cautions: Juneberries are so good tasting that it is easy to overeat and suffer intestinal upset, especially the first time.

Additional information and recipes: In North Dakota these fruits are usually known as juneberries. In the Black Hills of South Dakota they are sarvisberries (usually spelled serviceberries or service berries), and in Canada they are saskatoonberries or simply saskatoons. By whatever name, these fruits are delicious eaten fresh or made into pie, jam, syrup, or sauce—the sauce being particularly good with meat. The seeds are chewable and have a subtle but delicious flavor reminiscent of almond.

Although still gathered by the bucketsful in parts of North and South Dakota, juneberries are no longer common in many areas where they were once abundant. Historically, juneberries were one of the fruits used in pemmican, a mixture of dried meat, dried fruit, and fat, originated by Native people and later adopted by trappers and others who found the mixture to be both convenient and tasty. Explorers and early botanists praised the fruit of the juneberry in their journals, and settlers made extensive use of it for pie and sauce. Pemmican is still made today, and dried juneberries are now used much like raisins or other dried fruit.

Gathered wild in many areas, juneberries are also grown in yards and are available through many nurseries. With their showy white blossoms and attractive foliage, they make excellent yard plants. My experience with the juneberry tree is limited, but I can verify that both shrubby species produce a surprisingly large amount of delicious fruit, and even though they may spread, they do so slowly and can be kept in check by hoeing. In some areas wild juneberries are infected by rust or subject to insect infestation, but the urban plantings of juneberries I have observed have been free of both insects and disease.

Of all wild fruits, juneberries are perhaps the easiest to pick and prepare. Usually a simple washing is all that is required. Like other low-acid fruits, cooked juneberries are improved by the addition of lemon or rhubarb. Directions for making rhubarb juice appear in Appendix B.

Juneberry-rhubarb sauce

5 cups juneberries
10 cups diced rhubarb stalk
7 cups water
4 cups granulated sugar

Put berries, rhubarb, and water into a large, heavy kettle over high heat and bring to a boil. Do not cover. Reduce the heat and boil gently for about 10 minutes or until the juneberries and rhubarb are tender—stir several times while the mixture is cooking. Add the sugar. Continue to stir and cook until the sugar has dissolved and the sauce is thick and bubbly. Remove from the heat. Pour the sauce hot or cooled into containers having tightly fitting lids. Refrigerate or freeze to store—see general instructions for freezing, Appendix A. Best when served slightly thawed. Makes 8 pints of sauce.

Juneberry topping

6 tablespoons granulated sugar
2 tablespoons cornstarch
2 cups juneberries
¼ cup water
2 tablespoons margarine or butter
2 tablespoons lemon juice

In a small bowl, mix the sugar and cornstarch together until well blended; set aside.

In a medium pot, combine the berries and water. Place over medium heat, cover with a lid, and cook only until the juice begins to flow—about 3 minutes. Add the mixture of dry ingredients, stirring gently until mixed. Cook, stirring constantly, until the mixture bubbles and the juice thickens and clears. Remove from the heat and stir in the margarine or butter and the lemon juice. Cover and allow to cool to room temperature, then refrigerate to store. Makes about 2 cups of topping.

Juneberry topping is particularly good over cheesecake or chilled vanilla pudding.

Juneberry pie

450 degree oven to start
pastry for a two-crust 9-inch pie
4 cups juneberries
2 tablespoons lemon or rhubarb juice
¼ cup all-purpose flour
¾ cup granulated sugar
¼ teaspoon salt
2 tablespoons margarine or butter
1 tablespoon granulated sugar mixed with a dash of cinnamon

Roll out the pastry, arrange the bottom crust in the pie pan, and set it aside.

In a medium bowl stir the berries with the juice. Sift the flour, the first amount of sugar, and the salt together, then sift this over the juneberries. Stir gently until mixed, then pour the mixture into the bottom crust. Cut the margarine or butter into pieces and scatter them over the berry mixture. Cover the filling with the top crust and seal the edges. Make a 2-inch slash in the top crust to allow steam to escape during baking. Combine the second amount of sugar and the cinnamon and sprinkle this over the crust. Bake at 450 degrees for 10 minutes, then reduce the heat to 375 degrees and allow the pie to bake for 30 minutes more. Remove the pie from the oven and allow it to cool on a wire rack. Makes 6 to 8 servings.

Juneberry-gooseberry and juneberry-rhubarb pies are also delicious. In the recipe above, simply substitute gooseberries or diced rhubarb stalk for half of the juneberries, increase the sugar to 1 ½ cups, and omit the lemon or rhubarb juice.

Juneberry jam
4 cups juneberries
½ cup rhubarb juice
3 cups granulated sugar
  Read about jam making, Appendix A.
  Crush the berries in a large, heavy kettle; add the rhubarb juice and stir. Place the kettle over medium heat and stir constantly until the juice flows and comes to a boil. Reduce the heat and allow the mixture to boil gently, stirring occasionally, for about 10 minutes. Add the sugar, stir well, and cook until thick—about 15 minutes. Stir often during this last period of cooking so that the jam does not burn. Remove from the heat and skim off the foam. Pour the jam into hot, sterile jars leaving ¼ inch headspace. Cap the jars with two-piece screwband lids and process for 5 minutes in a boiling water bath. Makes about 4 cups of jam.

To dry juneberries
Wash the juneberries and look them over, discarding any undesirable fruit. Then shake them out in a single layer onto cookie sheets or trays and place in a light, dry place away from dust and insects. Juneberries may be dried in the sun or in the shade, but if they are dried outdoors, the trays must be brought inside during the night to protect the fruit from moisture and animals. When dry, shake the fruit into containers having tightly fitting lids and store in a cool place.

The following recipe can be varied in a number of ways. All white or all whole wheat flour may be used in place of the half-and-half flour mixture.

For persons who do not use sugar, the puffs may be served without frosting; honey lovers need only drizzle the unfrosted puffs with honey. The addition of toasted pecans makes this one of the fastest recipes ever for pecan rolls.

Frosted juneberry puffs
425 degree oven to start

PUFFS

½ cup (1 stick) margarine or butter

1 cup water

4 eggs

½ cup all-purpose flour

½ cup whole wheat flour

½ cup fresh or dried juneberries

2 tablespoons grated orange rind (optional)

Lightly grease a large cookie sheet with margarine or butter and set it aside. (To avoid sticking, do not use cooking oil for greasing.) Stir the flours together and set aside also.

Cut the margarine or butter into at least 4 pieces and put these and the water into a pot over medium-high heat. Stir so that the margarine or butter melts completely. As soon as the water reaches the boiling point, turn the heat to low and add the flour all at once. Stir quickly until the flour and water are well blended, then keep stirring until the mixture holds together—this will take less than a minute. Remove from the heat and allow to cool for about a minute. Add the eggs one at a time, beating well with a spoon after each addition. Add the juneberries (and the orange rind, if desired). Stir only until well mixed.

Drop the batter from a spoon onto the greased cookie sheet, making 12 to 15 puffs. Bake for 15 minutes at 425 degrees, then reduce the temperature to 325 degrees and bake for another 25 minutes or until the puffs are a light brown. Remove from the oven and the pans; allow to cool on a rack until comfortable to handle. Spread the puffs with powdered sugar frosting while still warm.

FROSTING

½ stick margarine or butter

1 ½ cups powdered sugar

2 tablespoons boiling water

1 teaspoon vanilla

2 tablespoons grated orange rind (optional)

Place the powdered sugar, margarine or butter, and water in a large bowl and beat until smooth with an electric mixer or by hand. Add the vanilla and beat again. If using orange rind, stir it in with a spoon. Frost rolls while they are still slightly warm.

To make pecan rolls, toast ⅔ cup pecan meats in a 350 degree oven for 10 minutes or until they taste done. Remove and cool, then shake into a shallow dish. After frosting the rolls, press each roll, upside down, into the pecans.

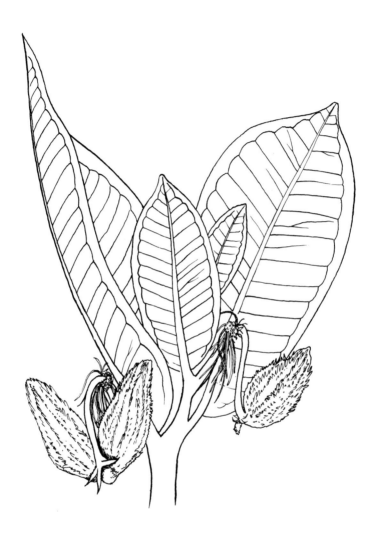

Milkweed pods

Please read general comments about milkweeds, beginning on page 54.

As the flowers of milkweed pass their prime, the familiar seed cases, or pods, begin to form. Often, people are surprised to learn that these pods are edible.

If possible, milkweed pods should be picked just before cooking—the longer the lapse between picking and cooking, the greater the tendency for the undesirable milky juice to remain in the pods. Also, it is important to select only young, firm, green pods. Those that have become spongy to the touch will not be tender when cooked.

To cook milkweed pods

Wash the pods well under running water. Put them into a pot and add enough boiling water to cover, then place over medium-high heat and allow them to boil gently for about 8 to 10 minutes. Drain and discard the cooking water. After cooking, small pods may be pickled or added whole to soup or stew; larger ones may be split lengthwise and the lump of soft, immature seeds removed—but don't discard that lump. Those immature seeds are one of the milkweed's tastiest parts, and when chopped and mixed with other ingredients, they make a good filling. Depending on the ingredients in the stuffing, milkweed pods may be served as a main course or as hors d'oeuvres.

Stuffed milkweed pod casserole

16 to 20 medium-size milkweed pods
2 tablespoons margarine or butter
½ cup diced mushrooms
2 green onions, sliced into thin, diagonal slices
1 cup diced cooked chicken
salt and pepper to taste
2 cups chicken broth or one can cream of chicken soup

Cook the milkweed pods according to the directions above. Drain well and when cool enough to handle, slit each pod lengthwise and remove the lump of seeds inside. Chop or make several cuts through each lump of seeds, then set them aside to be mixed with the remaining ingredients.

Heat the margarine or butter in a skillet; add the mushrooms and onions. Stir and cook until tender. Add the chicken, chopped milkweed seeds, and seasonings; stir until well combined. Stuff the milkweed pods with filling and place them in a shallow baking dish. Spoon the remaining stuffing around the pods. Pour the chicken broth or soup over all and bake for 20 to 30 minutes. Makes 4 servings.

Milkweed hors d'oeuvres

1 quart fresh young milkweed pods (about 1 pound)
3 cups water
2 tablespoons lemon juice
½ teaspoons salt
    Cooked, chopped seafood, cream cheese, or rice for stuffing (see below).

Cook the milkweed pods according to the directions above. Drain them well, then add the water, lemon juice, and salt and bring to a boil again. Boil gently for 15 minutes; drain and allow to cool. Slit each pod lengthwise and remove the lump of immature seeds. Chop or make several cuts through each lump, then mix this with a combination of cooked, chopped seafood such as shrimp or crab, sour cream or cream cheese, or cooked, seasoned rice. Carefully stuff each pod with the filling. Serve hot or cold. Makes about 40 small hors d'oeuvres.

Milkweed pod pickles

3 quarts fresh young milkweed pods (about 3 pounds)
6 small hot chilies (optional)
6 cloves garlic, peeled
¼ cup celery seed
¼ cup mustard seed
6 teaspoons dill seed
2 cups apple cider vinegar
2 cups water
2 to 3 teaspoons salt, depending on preference
2 tablespoons granulated sugar
    Read information about canning, Appendix A.

Put the milkweed pods into a large kettle or use two smaller kettles. In another pot, heat to boiling enough water to cover the pods. Pour the boiling water over the pods and allow them to boil gently for 5 minutes, then drain and discard the water. Repeat, again boiling for 5 minutes and draining. Allow the pods to cool until comfortable to handle.

Meanwhile, sterilize 6 pint jars and set them aside. Peel the garlic, and if using chilies, slit each one lengthwise, then hold it under cold running water and remove the seeds and membranes. (Chile juice tends to remain on the fingers, so wear plastic gloves or wash your hands well with soap after this step.) Into each jar put 1 clove garlic, 1 chile, 2 teaspoons celery seeds, 2 teaspoons mustard seeds, and 1 teaspoon dill seeds. Pack the milkweed pods rather tightly into the jars.

Stir the vinegar, water, salt, and sugar together in a large pot and heat to boiling. Continue stirring and cook for 2 or 3 minutes or until the sugar and salt are dissolved. Pour the liquid over the pods immediately and fill the jar, leaving ½ inch headspace. Cap the jars with two-piece screwband lids and process for 10 minutes in boiling water bath. Store in a cool, dark place. Allow pickles to mellow at least 1 week before using. Makes 6 pints.

Black raspberry
Rubus occidentalis L.

Red raspberry
Rubus idaeus L. subsp. *sachalinensis* (Levl.) Focke var. *sachalinensis*

Rose family: Rosaceae

Description: The black and red raspberries are native shrubs usually growing in patches or thickets. Although the rootstocks are perennial, the above-ground stems, called canes, are mostly biennial. Raspberry canes may be erect or arching, with those of the black raspberry measuring up to 6 feet or more and armed with stout, sharp, hooked prickles; those of the red raspberry are typically shorter and have numerous slender, weak prickles or sometimes few or no prickles. First-year canes are called primocanes and produce leaves but not flowers or fruit. In their second year, the canes, then called floricanes, produce branches that bear flowers and fruit. After the fruit has ripened, the canes usually die (but the plant itself continues to live, each year sending up new canes). The leaves of both the black and the red raspberry are alternate and divided into 3 to 5 irregularly toothed leaflets, the upper surface dark green with few hairs, the lower surface so densely covered by soft hairs that it appears to be white. The flowers are borne in clusters and are white with 5 petals. Ripe fruits of black raspberry are purple black; those of red raspberry are deep rose. The juicy, rounded, somewhat bumpy cap considered to be a single raspberry fruit is actually several to many small, single-seeded fruits attached together. When ripe, this cap easily separates from the small, rounded base, called a receptacle, which remains attached to the plant. Noticing this will help you distinguish raspberries from blackberries—with blackberries, the receptacle detaches along with the ripe fruit.

Distribution: Black raspberry: in the eastern and central United States, some scattered populations west and into Canada; in the eastern Great Plains; common in Missouri with scattered populations west and into Oklahoma. Red raspberry: in the northern Great Plains and into Canada, south into western Iowa, also scattered east, south, and west.

Habitat: Open woods, ravines, along streams, fence rows, and roadsides; often in rocky areas and in partial shade.

Edible parts: Ripe fruits, cooked or uncooked; leaflets, dried and brewed for tea.

Seasons to collect: Black raspberry fruit from early to midsummer; red raspberry fruit from mid to late summer; leaflets of either black or red raspberry, in summer.

Cautions: To avoid being stuck by the prickles, wear tightly woven fabrics (such as blue jeans) and move slowly. For the sake of the plant, do not harvest leaflets in spring when the plant is making its greatest growth, and when you do harvest, take only a few leaflets from each plant.

Additional information and recipes: Wild raspberry fruits are sometimes described as being small and seedy, but likely this is because the fruits were collected from plants growing in dry soil. Plants growing along streams or in other areas where they can draw enough moisture produce plump, juicy fruit and are one of nature's most outstanding treats.

Ripe raspberries are exceptionally tender and bruise easily. For this reason, small berry boxes such as those used in grocery stores are recommended for picking. Also, fruits will transport better if only loosely covered.

Once home, a quick rinse in cold water is all that is needed to prepare raspberries for eating. They are so delicious fresh that many persons prefer to eat them just as they are, or to merely add milk and sugar. (See recipe for berry milk in Appendix B.)

Raspberries freeze well and make wonderful jam, jelly, syrup, and topping. Raspberries also form the basis for some very elegant desserts. In fact, several desserts can be made from a basic raspberry puree, which can be prepared ahead of time and frozen for later use.

Basic raspberry puree
4 cups black or red raspberries
1 cup water
⅔ cup granulated sugar
1 tablespoon lemon juice
few grains of salt

Stir the raspberries, water, and sugar together in a heavy pot. Heat to boiling, then adjust the heat so that the mixture will boil very gently. Begin timing and boil, stirring frequently, for 4 minutes. Turn off the heat and allow the mixture to cool for 10 minutes.

Remove the seeds by pressing the mixture through a sieve—use the back of a serving spoon, pressing and scraping until most of the pulp has been pushed through the sieve. Be sure to scrape off and save any pulp clinging to the outside of the sieve. Add the lemon juice and salt and stir well. Makes a little more than 2 cups of puree.

This puree may be used as a topping for yogurt or ice cream and makes a particularly good dressing for fresh fruits such as peaches and oranges.

To store the puree for use within a few days, refrigerate it in a covered container. For longer storage, freeze the puree in a tightly covered container.

Raspberry ice
2 cups basic raspberry puree
1 cup water
2 tablespoons light corn syrup

Combine the ingredients and stir until blended, then pour into a shallow dish and freeze for at least 3 hours before serving. To serve, cut the ice into squares and place it in the individual dishes—after a few minutes at room temperature, it will soften enough to eat with a spoon. Makes 4 to 6 servings. If the raspberry ice is not to be used the same day it is made, freeze it in a tightly covered container.

Raspberry sherbet
2 cups basic raspberry puree
1 cup light cream
2 tablespoons light corn syrup

Proceed as for raspberry ice.

For a truly elegant dessert, scoop each serving into a ball and top it with a single fresh raspberry and a mint leaf or drizzle it with extra raspberry puree. Makes 4 to 6 servings.

To freeze raspberries
4 cups black or red raspberries
½ cup granulated sugar

Read about freezing, Appendix A.

Rinse the raspberries in ice water, but do not allow them to soak. Drain the raspberries by placing them in a colander, then shake gently to remove as much water as possible. Place the raspberries in a large bowl, sprinkle with sugar, and toss them lightly until coated. Shake the raspberries into containers having tightly fitting covers. Freeze immediately.

To extract raspberry juice
5 cups black or red raspberries
½ cup water

Place the raspberries in a large, heavy pot and crush them with a potato masher. Add the water, then place over medium heat and stir until the mixture begins to simmer. Turn the heat to low, cover the pot with a lid, and allow the fruit to simmer for about 8 minutes. Remove from the heat. When cool enough to handle, pour the raspberries into a damp jelly cloth and squeeze.

The amount of juice obtained will depend not only on the juiciness of the fruit, but on whether red or black raspberries are used. A typical yield for black raspberries is about 1½ cups of juice; for red raspberries, about 2 cups.

Raspberry syrup
raspberry juice
granulated sugar

Read about syrup making, Appendix A.

Measure the raspberry juice and an equal amount of sugar and stir both together in a heavy kettle. Place over high heat and stir until the juice begins to boil. Reduce the heat but do not cover the kettle. Allow the syrup to boil gently for about 7 minutes. Remove from the heat, quickly skim off the foam, and pour the syrup into hot scalded jars, leaving ½ inch headspace. Cap the jars with two-piece screwband lids and process for 10 minutes in a boiling water bath. Makes about half as much syrup as the amount of juice.

Red raspberry jelly
4 cups red raspberry juice
1 box powdered pectin
5½ cups granulated sugar

Read about jelly making, Appendix A.

Measure the sugar and set it aside. Stir the juice and pectin together in a large, heavy kettle, then place over medium-high heat and, stirring constantly, bring to a full boil. Add the sugar all at once and continue stirring. Again bring to a boil, then begin timing. Stirring constantly, boil for 1 minute. Remove from the heat, quickly skim off the foam, and pour the jelly into hot, sterile jars. Cap the jars with two-piece screwband lids and process for 5 minutes in a boiling water bath. Makes about 6 cups of jelly.

Black raspberry jelly
4½ cups black raspberry juice
1 box powdered pectin
6½ cups granulated sugar

Follow directions for making red raspberry jelly. Makes about 6½ cups of jelly.

Raspberry jam
5 cups red or black raspberries
1 box powdered pectin
7 cups granulated sugar
    Read about jam making, Appendix A.
    Measure the sugar and set it aside. Crush the raspberries with a potato
masher. (If fewer seeds or no seeds are desired, press a portion or all of the
crushed fruit through a sieve and discard the seeds.) Put the crushed fruit
into a large, heavy kettle. Add the pectin, and stir until well combined. Place
over medium-high heat and stir constantly until the mixture boils. Add the
sugar all at one time and continue to stir. Again bring to a boil, then begin
timing and, still stirring, allow the mixture to boil hard for 1 minute. Remove from the heat and skim off the foam, then stir the jam well and ladle
into hot, sterile jars, leaving ¼ inch headspace. Cap the jars with two-piece
screwband lids and process for 5 minutes in a boiling water bath. Makes a little more than 8 cups of jam.

Raspberry-honey topping
2 cups raspberries
¼ cup honey
¼ cup water
    Crush the raspberries with a potato masher, then press them through a
sieve to remove the seeds. Combine the raspberry pulp, honey, and water in
a heavy kettle and stir well. Place over medium heat and cook for 4 to 5 minutes, stirring several times during the cooking period. Remove from the heat
and allow the contents to cool. Pour the topping into a container having a
tightly fitting lid, then refrigerate. Makes about 1 cup of topping. Recipe
may be doubled, tripled, or more.
    This topping is particularly good drizzled over yogurt or vanilla ice cream
and makes an excellent, not-too-sweet syrup for pancakes or cooked cereals.

Dried raspberry leaflets can be brewed alone to make a mild-flavored tea or
mixed with stronger-flavored components. The leaflets are lightweight and
tend to float even when crumbled or cut, and the soft fuzz on their undersur-
face causes the pieces to cling together, so when brewing raspberry tea, either plain or in a mixture, it is helpful to use a tea ball. If the leaf material is
placed directly into the teapot, stir well several times while the tea is brewing.
Crushed raspberry leaf is used as a filler with other ingredients in various
commercial herb tea mixes.

To dry raspberry leaflets

Wash the leaflets well under running water, pat dry with a nonfuzzy towel, then lay them in a single layer on a kitchen towel in a large flat pan with sides. Cover the pan with a thin cloth and put it in a light, airy place away from direct sunlight until the leaflets are brittle dry. Crumble or cut the leaflets, then store them in tightly covered jars in a cool place.

Raspberry leaf tea

To brew the tea, use 1 cup water and 1 tablespoon crumbled (or cut) leaflets for each cup of tea desired. Use a tea ball or place the tea directly into a cup or heated pot. Add boiling water and cover the pot with a cloth to retain the heat. Allow to steep for 5 minutes. Remove the tea ball or pour the hot tea through a strainer. Serve with sweetening if desired.

Highbush blackberry, blackberry
Rubus ostryifolius Rydb.

Highbush blackberry, blackberry
Rubus pensilvanicus Poir.

Common blackberry, highbush blackberry, blackberry
Rubus allegheniensis Porter

Rose family: Rosaceae

Description: All of these blackberry species are native shrubs having erect or arching stems called canes that are armed with sharp prickles. The rootstocks of blackberries are perennial, but the canes are mostly biennial. First-year canes, called primocanes, grow rapidly and produce leaves but not flowers or fruit. In their second year, the canes, then called floricanes, produce branches that bear flowers and fruit. After the fruit has matured, the canes usually die (but the plant itself continues to live, each year sending up new canes). The leaves are alternate and mostly divided into 3 to 5 leaflets—leaves on the floricanes typically have 3, but sometimes are simple. Smooth and dark green above, they are softly hairy and lighter colored below, but not white like raspberry leaves. The margins of the leaflets are sharply to broadly toothed. The flowers are white with 5 petals and occur in small clusters. The immature fruits are first green, then red, and finally ripen to a juicy, glossy black about midsummer. Blackberry fruits look like small, bumpy caps, but are usually considerably larger than raspberries, and when they are ripe, the receptacle on which the fruit rests detaches and comes off with the fruit.

Habitat: Prairies, ravines, open woods, and along roads and fence rows.

Distribution: Widely scattered areas of the United States and southern Canada; in the Great Plains, southeastern portion only (into Iowa and Missouri).

Edible parts: Ripe and slightly underripe fruits, cooked or uncooked.

Season to collect: Midsummer.

Cautions: To avoid being stuck by the prickles, wear tightly woven fabrics (such as blue jeans) and move slowly.
   Blackberry plants spread rapidly and are difficult to control—not a good choice for most yards.

Additional information and recipes: Wild blackberries are some of the most prickly of the wild brambles. It is nearly impossible to pick even a few without getting scratched, but that fact does not stop blackberry lovers. Some blackberry shrubs have long, arching canes with easy-to-reach fruits. Others are more bushlike with the largest, juiciest fruits occurring low, often on inner branches, and for these a good tactic is to use a stick to push aside the outer branches while you reach in and pick the fruit with your other hand. As a long-time blackberry picker once advised me, "You can't hardly pick blackberries without your getting yourself a little stick."

Once home, blackberries are easy to prepare. You will notice small hair-like projections on the surface of the fruits—these are neither harmful nor even noticeable when consumed. Simply wash the fruits and remove any of the leafy, starlike bases that may still be attached at the stem ends. The blackberries are then ready to eat or to freeze for later use.

Note that some blackberry recipes call for rhubarb or lemon juice. Instructions for making rhubarb juice are in Appendix B.

To freeze blackberries

Read about freezing, Appendix A.

Blackberries freeze very successfully with or without granulated sugar. If you use sugar, add 2 tablespoons for each cup and stir gently to coat each fruit. By spreading the fruits loosely on a cookie sheet so that they freeze separately, any amount may be stored. Later, whatever measure is desired may be shaken out just as though the fruits were fresh.

To extract blackberry juice

6 cups blackberries
⅔ cup water

If the juice is to be used in a recipe for jelly that does not call for added pectin, select some slightly underripe blackberries to be added to the ripe ones. Sometimes fully ripe blackberries do not have enough pectin to cause jelly to set. A good ratio is 4 cups ripe blackberries to 2 cups slightly underripe blackberries.

Place the blackberries in a large, heavy kettle and thoroughly crush them with a potato masher. Stir in the water, then place over high heat, cover with a lid, and allow to boil gently for 5 minutes. Remove the kettle from the heat, allow the fruit to cool until comfortable to handle, then pour it into a damp jelly cloth and squeeze to extract the juice. The amount of juice will vary with the juiciness of the fruit, but 3 cups is a typical yield.

Blackberry jelly without added pectin

3 cups blackberry juice
1 ½ cups granulated sugar

Read about jelly making, Appendix A.

Pour the juice into a large, heavy kettle. Heat to boiling and allow to boil gently for 5 minutes. Add the sugar and stir until dissolved. Adjust the heat so that the juice boils gently without boiling over, then allow it to cook, stirring occasionally, until it reaches the jelling point—about 10 minutes. Test for doneness with a jelly thermometer or use the spoon or cold saucer method. When done, remove from the heat and quickly skim off the foam, then pour the jelly into hot, sterile jars, leaving ¼ inch headspace. Cap the jars with two-piece screwband lids and process for 5 minutes in a boiling water bath. Makes only 2 cups of jelly, but it's superb!

Blackberry jelly with pectin

3 cups blackberry juice
½ cup rhubarb or lemon juice
1 package powdered pectin
5 cups granulated sugar
    Read about jelly making, Appendix A.
    Measure the sugar and set it aside. Put the juices and pectin into a large, heavy kettle and stir well. Place over high heat and stir constantly until the liquid reaches a full boil. Add the sugar all at once and continue to stir. Again bring to a full boil, then begin timing. Still stirring, allow to boil for 1 minute. Remove from the heat, quickly skim off the foam, and pour the jelly into hot, sterile jars, leaving ¼ inch headspace. Cap with two-piece screwband lids and process for 5 minutes in a boiling water bath. Makes 6 cups of jelly.

Blackberry jam without added pectin

6 cups blackberries (4 cups ripe, 2 cups slightly underripe)
3 cups granulated sugar
    Read about jam making, Appendix A.
    Thoroughly crush the blackberries in a large, heavy kettle. Place over medium heat and stir constantly until the juice flows and begins to boil. Add the sugar and stir well until it is dissolved. Adjust the heat so that the mixture will boil gently without boiling over. Stir frequently and cook until the jam is thick enough to hold a slightly rounded shape in a spoon—usually 12 to 15 minutes—or test doneness with the cold saucer method. When done, remove from the heat and skim off the foam, then stir the jam well and ladle it into hot, sterile jars, leaving ¼ inch headspace. Cap the jars with two-piece screwband lids and process for 5 minutes in a boiling water bath. Makes about 4 cups of jam.

Blackberry jam with pectin
6 cups blackberries
½ cup rhubarb or lemon juice
1 package powdered pectin
7 cups granulated sugar
  Read about jam making, Appendix A.
  Measure the sugar and set it aside. Thoroughly crush the blackberries in a
large, heavy kettle. Heat the fruit to boiling and allow it to boil gently for
about 3 minutes. Remove from the heat and allow it to cool. Add the lemon
or rhubarb juice and the pectin to the cooled blackberries and stir well. Place
over high heat and, stirring constantly, bring the mixture to a full boil. Add
the sugar all at once, and stirring constantly, again bring to a full boil. Begin
timing and allow to boil for 1 minute. Remove from the heat and skim off the
foam, then stir the jam well and ladle it into hot, sterile jars, leaving ¼ inch
headspace. Cap the jars with two-piece screwband lids and process for 5
minutes in a boiling water bath. Makes about 6 cups of jam.

Chunky blackberry syrup
6 cups blackberries
1 ½ cups granulated sugar
  Read about syrup making, Appendix A.
  Thoroughly crush the blackberries in a large, heavy kettle. Place over high
heat and stir constantly until the juice flows and begins to boil. Reduce the
heat and allow the juice to simmer gently for about 5 minutes. Add the sugar
and again bring to boiling. Allow to cook for about 5 minutes more or until
the mixture is syrupy. Remove from the heat and skim off the foam, then stir
the syrup well and pour it into hot, sterile jars, leaving ½ inch headspace. Cap
the jars with two-piece screwband lids and process for 10 minutes in a boiling water bath. Makes a little more than 5 cups.

Blackberry pie
425 degree oven to start
pastry for a two-crust 9-inch pie
6 cups blackberries
2 tablespoons rhubarb or lemon juice
1 ½ cups granulated sugar
½ cup all-purpose flour

2 tablespoons margarine or butter

1 tablespoon sugar

dash of cinnamon and nutmeg

Roll out the pastry, arrange the bottom crust in the pie pan, and set it aside.

Place the blackberries in a large bowl and sprinkle the rhubarb or lemon juice over them; stir to mix. Sift the first amount of sugar and flour together over the blackberries, then stir only until the fruit is well coated. Pour the blackberries into the pastry-lined pie pan. Cut the margarine or butter into several pieces and scatter it over the blackberries.

Make a 2-inch slash in the top crust so that steam can escape during baking, then put it in place over the filling and seal the edges. Brush the top crust lightly with water. Combine the second amount of sugar with the spices and sprinkle this over the top. Bake at 425 degrees for 10 minutes. Reduce the heat to 375 degrees and continue baking for another 40 to 45 minutes. Remove the pie from the oven and allow it to cool on a metal rack. Makes 6 to 8 servings.

Blackberry cake

350 degree oven

2 cups all-purpose flour

1 teaspoon soda

1 teaspoon cinnamon

1 ½ cups granulated sugar

½ cup margarine or butter

1 egg

1 cup buttermilk

1 cup blackberries

Grease a 9 x 12–inch baking pan and set it aside. Sift the flour, soda, and cinnamon together and set them aside also.

Using an electric mixer, cream the sugar and margarine or butter; add the egg and beat until the mixture is light and fluffy. Add half of the buttermilk and stir well. Stir in half of the flour mixture, then add the remainder of the buttermilk and beat well with the mixer. Gently mix the blackberries with the remaining half of the flour until all of the blackberries are coated with flour (this helps prevent them from sinking to the bottom). Gently fold the blackberries and flour into the batter, stirring only until well mixed. Pour the batter into the prepared pan and bake until the center springs back when lightly touched—about 40 minutes. Remove the cake from the oven and allow it to cool for at least 15 minutes. Served warm, with butter, this makes an excellent coffeecake; cooled and topped with ice cream or whipped cream, it is delicious as a dessert. Makes 9 to 12 servings.

Blackberry dumplings

DUMPLING DOUGH

1 cup all-purpose flour
4 teaspoons granulated sugar
1 ½ teaspoons baking powder
½ teaspoon salt
½ cup milk
3 tablespoons melted butter or cooking oil

Sift the flour, sugar, baking powder, and salt together into a medium bowl. Add the milk and butter or oil, and stir until well combined. Set aside.

BLACKBERRY SAUCE

⅔ cup granulated sugar
2 tablespoons cornstarch
⅔ cup water
1 tablespoon margarine or butter
2 cups blackberries
dash of nutmeg

Combine the sugar and cornstarch in a small bowl and mix well. Use a large, heavy kettle and, if possible, a domed lid. (Water that condenses during cooking will follow the curvature of the lid and run down the sides instead of dripping on top of the dumplings.) Put the water into the kettle, add the sugar–cornstarch mixture and stir until blended. Place over medium heat and, stirring constantly, bring the mixture to a boil. Continue cooking until the mixture becomes thick and clear. Stir in the margarine or butter, blackberries, and nutmeg; again bring to a boil.

Gently place the dumpling dough by teaspoonsful into the hot blackberry mixture. Set the heat on low, cover the kettle with the lid and allow to simmer for about 12 minutes. Do not lift the lid during the cooking time, because it is important that the steam not escape.

Remove the kettle from the heat. The dumplings may be served warm or cold, but I think they are best if served quite warm with very cold cream. Makes 4 to 6 servings.

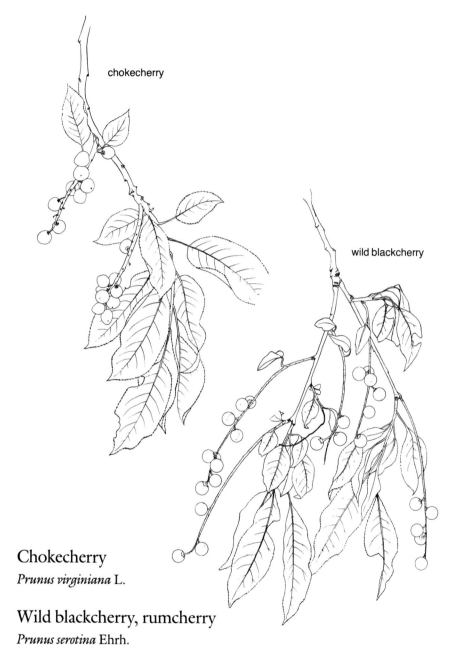

chokecherry

wild blackcherry

Chokecherry
Prunus virginiana L.

Wild blackcherry, rumcherry
Prunus serotina Ehrh.

Rose family: Rosaceae

Description: The chokecherry is a small native tree often occurring in thickets. Under good conditions, it may attain a height of 20 feet or more, but it usually stands no more than 12 feet. The leaves are alternate with finely serrate margins, the upper surface dark green and smooth, and lower surface pale green and smooth or with some hairs on the veins. The flowers are white with 5 petals and are borne in long clusters, as are the fruits. The fruits are round and smooth, becoming juicy and turning a deep red purple to black when ripe. Each contains a single seed called a stone or pit.

The wild blackcherry is a native tree sometimes growing 50 feet tall. It reproduces by seed and does not form thickets. The leaves are alternate with finely serrate margins, but narrower than those of the chokecherry. The upper surface of the leaves is dark green and smooth; the lower surface, lighter green and smooth. The flowers are similar to those of chokecherry, as are the fruits.

Distribution: Chokecherry: scattered throughout many areas of the United States, except the extreme south and southeast, and into Canada; common throughout the Great Plains. Wild blackcherry: scattered throughout much of the eastern United States and into Canada; in the southeastern Great Plains from southeastern Nebraska south into Kansas, Oklahoma, and Texas.

Habitat: Hillsides, open woods, along streams, roadsides, and fence rows, in rich or sandy soil; in full sun or partial shade, but plants growing in shade usually do not produce fruit.

Edible parts: Ripe fruits, cooked. (Uncooked fruits are not harmful, but are simply too astringent to be palatable, although they are much liked by birds.)

Season to collect: Mid to late summer—in hot, dry years, fruits may ripen earlier.

Cautions: Chokecherries and wild blackcherries growing along roadsides may be sprayed with herbicides. Do not use fruits from plants that bear signs of spray, such as yellow, wilted, or dead leaves or discolored fruit.

When working with chokecherries or wild blackcherries, do not crush the seeds. The seeds contain a cyanide-forming compound that can cause illness, or even death, if consumed in large amounts. Note that the seeds of several other kinds of fruits, including orchard cherries, contain this compound; frozen or cooked and processed fruits are not harmful.

Additional information and recipes: Wild blackcherries were once better known as rumcherries because years ago they were often added to rum and brandy. The result was a smooth, slightly sweet liqueur having a mellow cherry flavor and a deep wine-red color. Although wild blackcherries make exceptional syrup and jelly, there is little record of such use. Perhaps because the fruit is so popular with birds, finding enough for anything other than flavoring may have been difficult. However, where wild blackcherry trees are numerous, I have noticed that birds sometimes ignore certain trees. To my taste, the fruit on these trees is sweeter and more flavorful than the fruit they so eagerly consume. Readers may want to investigate this phenomenon for themselves.

Like sandcherries, chokecherries were once a staple food for Plains Indian people. Both chokecherries and sandcherries were crushed and dried as patties for use in winter. The drying process altered the harmful compounds in the seeds so that the patties were safe to eat. When cooked, dried chokecherries impart a delicious flavor to various foods, especially meat. Persons in some parts of Nebraska and South Dakota (perhaps elsewhere as well) still make these patties and use them in the traditional way.

Among settlers, chokecherries soon became an important part of the diet. I once interviewed an older woman about her memories of growing up in eastern South Dakota in the late 1800s. "There is nothing in the world quite like chokecherries," she told me, "I wish I had a handful right now; I'd eat them without even cooking!" She proceeded to describe the many jars of syrup her mother put up, as well as the quantities of syrup and jelly that she herself had canned as an adult with a young family. Other women said much the same thing: nothing quite compares to that unique bitter-sweet-tart chokecherry flavor, and no matter how many years go by, it seems a person never forgets how good that flavor is.

A Nebraska man said that his mother used to make a chokecherry pie he remembered as wonderful. I was surprised at that. The seed in a chokecherry is usually larger than the flesh around it, so pitting enough chokecherries to make a pie seemed nearly impossible. When he said it was called half-hour pie, I said I thought it would take longer to make than that—it would have to be called three- or maybe four-hour pie, and even then, I couldn't see how anyone could pit enough chokecherries to make a pie. He said that was just the point, it took so long that his mother didn't pit them—she made the pie with whole chokecherries. When the pie was served, removing the pits became the responsibility of the eaters. "Half-hour" referred to how long it took to eat a slice of the pie. I made the pie and thought it quite good, but perhaps a dessert to be eaten only in the company of close friends and family. (The recipe is included below.)

Since learning about half-hour pie, I have heard several accounts of chokecherry pie for which each fruit was pitted by hand. All have been described as labors of love. One woman told me that each summer she handpitted chokecherries and made a pie for her husband because it was his favorite. She said it took a long time and that he got only one such pie a year. Apparently the recipe is the same as for an ordinary cherry pie.

Another unusual chokecherry recipe is the one for gumdrops. Other wild fruit juices can be substituted in this recipe, but there is something about the flavor of chokecherry, especially when the gumdrops are dipped in chocolate, that make it outstanding.

Of course, the well-known uses of chokecherries are for juice, jelly, jam, and syrup, but it often happens that at the time that chokecherries are ripe, people are too busy with other summer activities to do much cooking. Fortunately, chokecherries may be frozen just as they are, or the juice may be extracted and canned. However you prepare chokecherries, wash them first, remove any part of the stem that may have remained attached, and drain well.

To freeze chokecherries

Read about freezing, Appendix A.

A convenient amount for freezing is 8 cups of fruit (enough for a batch of jelly or jam). Put into heavy freezer-grade plastic bags or large containers having tightly fitting lids and freeze them as soon as possible. To use frozen chokecherries, proceed the same as for fresh chokecherries.

To extract chokecherry juice

8 cups chokecherries

3 cups water

Put the chokecherries and water into a large, heavy kettle over medium-high heat. Bring the water to boiling, then reduce the heat to low, cover the kettle with a lid, and allow the fruit to boil gently for 30 minutes. Remove the kettle from the heat and allow it to cool until comfortable to handle.

Meanwhile, arrange a damp jelly cloth in a cone-shaped colander so that the center of the cloth is at the bottom of the cone and the edges of the cloth are hanging over the rim of the colander. Pour the fruit into the jelly cloth and allow the juice to drip through, then gently squeeze to extract more juice. This yields about 3 cups of juice, more or less, depending on the juiciness of the fruit. If less, and you plan to make jelly, add a little water to make 3 cups.

After the juice has been removed, the fruit that is left in the colander may be pureed and used to make jam (see recipes for puree and jam below.)

To can chokecherry juice

See general instructions for canning in Appendix A.

In a heavy kettle bring the chokecherry juice to the boiling point, then allow it to simmer for about 3 minutes. Pour the juice into hot, scalded jars, leaving ½ inch headspace. Cap the jars with two-piece screwband lids and process in a boiling water bath for 10 minutes. Remove the jars from the canner and allow to cool away from drafts.

Chokecherry jelly

3 cups chokecherry juice
1 package powdered pectin
4½ cups granulated sugar

Read about jelly making, Appendix A.

Measure the sugar and set it aside. Stir the juice and pectin together in a large, heavy kettle. Place over medium-high heat and, stirring constantly, allow the mixture to come to a full boil. Add the sugar all at once and continue stirring. Again bring to a boil, then begin timing. Still stirring, boil for 1 minute. Remove from the heat, quickly skim off the foam, and pour the jelly into hot, sterile jars, leaving ¼ inch headspace. Cap the jars with two-piece screwband lids and process for 5 minutes in a boiling water bath. Makes about 6 cups of jelly.

Chokecherry–wild plum jelly

1 cup chokecherry juice
1 cup wild plum juice
1½ cups granulated sugar

See instructions for extracting plum juice on page 197.

Combine all of the ingredients in a large, heavy pot. Place over medium-high heat until the liquid comes to a full boil, then adjust the heat and allow it to boil gently for about 10 minutes. Test for doneness with a thermometer or use the spoon or cold saucer method. Remove the kettle from the heat, skim off the foam, and pour the jelly into hot, sterile jars, leaving ¼ inch headspace. Cap the jars with two-piece screwband lids and process for 5 minutes in a boiling water bath. Makes about 2 cups of jelly.

Chokecherry syrup
chokecherry juice
granulated sugar
   Read about syrup making, Appendix A.
   Combine equal amounts of chokecherry juice and sugar in a heavy kettle, stir well, then boil gently for 10 to 15 minutes. Remove from the heat, quickly skim off the foam, and pour the syrup into hot, scalded jars, leaving ½ inch headspace. Cap the jars with two-piece screwband lids and process for 10 minutes in a boiling water bath. Makes ½ to ⅔ cup syrup for each cup of chokecherry juice.
   Chokecherry syrup has many uses. It is good on pancakes, ice cream, and yogurt and can be used to flavor and color desserts and drinks. Only ½ cup of this syrup added to a pitcher of lemonade makes an especially delicious, refreshing drink, and ¼ cup mixed in with the ingredients for apple pie or apple crisp will give a rosy color and that unique chokecherry flavor.

Chokecherry fizz
For each serving:
3 to 4 tablespoons of chokecherry syrup (or ¼ cup chokecherry juice plus 2 teaspoons granulated sugar)
¾ cup tonic water or ginger ale
squeeze of orange or lime
ice
   Put the chokecherry syrup (or the sweetened juice) into a tall glass, add cracked ice about halfway up, fill with tonic water or ginger ale, add the orange or lime, and stir well.

Chokecherry puree
8 cups chokecherries
3 cups water
   Put the chokecherries and water into a large, heavy kettle over medium-high heat. Bring the water to boiling, then reduce the heat to low, cover the kettle with a lid, and allow the fruit to simmer for about 30 minutes. Remove from the heat and allow to cool until comfortable to handle. Pour the fruit into a cone-shaped colander and press the pulp through with the pestle. Makes 3 to 4 cups of puree.

Note that puree can also be made from the fruit that is left after extracting chokecherry juice. Simply return what is left in the jelly cloth to the kettle and add about 2 cups of water. Heat and stir the mixture for several minutes, then allow it to cool until comfortable to handle. Pour the mixture into the cone-shaped colander and extract the pulp by pushing it through with the pestle. Yields will vary, but the amount will be less than for puree made without first extracting the juice.

Chokecherry jam without pectin
chokecherry puree
granulated sugar
    Read about jam making, Appendix A.
    Put equal amounts of chokecherry puree and sugar into a large, heavy kettle over medium heat. Cook, stirring constantly, for 7 to 10 minutes or until the jam holds a slightly rounded shape in a spoon. Or use the cold saucer method. Be aware that chokecherry jam burns easily, so constant stirring is important. When done, remove from the heat and skim off the foam, then stir the jam well and ladle it into hot, sterile jars, leaving ¼ inch headspace. Cap the jars with two-piece screwband lids and process for 5 minutes in a boiling water bath. Makes about 1 ⅓ cups for every cup of puree used.
    Chokecherry is so richly flavored that this jam is too strong for most tastes. The two recipes that follow make jams that are milder, yet still have that unmistakable chokecherry flavor.

Chokecherry jam with pectin
4 cups chokecherry puree
1 package powdered pectin
5 cups granulated sugar
¼ cup lemon juice
    Read about jam making, Appendix A.
    Measure the sugar and set it aside. Stir the puree and pectin together in a large, heavy kettle. Place over high heat and, stirring constantly, allow the mixture to come to a full boil. Add the sugar all at once and continue stirring. Again bring to a boil, then begin timing and, still stirring, boil for 1 minute. Remove from the heat and stir well, then skim off the foam and ladle the jam into hot, sterile jars, leaving ¼ inch headspace. Cap the jars with two-piece screwband lids and process for 5 minutes in a boiling water bath. Makes 7 to 8 cups of jam.

Chokecherry–wild plum jam

3 cups chokecherry puree
4½ cups wild plum juice
3 cups granulated sugar

Read about jam making, Appendix A. See instructions for making plum juice on page 197.

Stir all three ingredients together in a large, heavy kettle. Place over high heat and bring to a full boil. Reduce the heat and allow the jam to boil gently for 10 minutes. Stir frequently during the first 5 minutes; stir constantly for the last 5 minutes—this jam burns easily. Remove from the heat and skim off the foam, then stir the jam well and ladle it into hot, sterile jars, leaving ¼ inch headspace. Cap the jars with two-piece screwband lids and process for 5 minutes in a boiling water bath. Makes about 6 cups of jam.

This jam is particularly good with cream cheese on whole wheat crackers or in peanut butter sandwiches.

Chokecherry-yogurt dessert

2 envelopes unflavored gelatin or 1 teaspoon powdered (not flaked) agar
½ cup cold water
1 cup chokecherry juice
4 tablespoons granulated sugar or honey (more or less, as desired)
2 cups (16 ounces) plain yogurt

Put the water into a large bowl. Add the gelatin or agar and stir until completely moistened. Stir in the sugar or honey. In a saucepan heat the chokecherry juice to just boiling. If using gelatin, pour the hot juice into the softened gelatin and stir until the gelatin has dissolved. If using agar, add the softened agar to the juice in the saucepan and cook and stir until the agar has dissolved (do not overcook). Return the mixture to the bowl. Allow the mixture to cool to room temperature, then add the yogurt and stir well. Pour the mixture into a dish or mold and refrigerate until it is firm. Makes 4 servings.

Half-hour pie

375 degree oven
pastry for a two-crust 8-inch pie
1 cup sugar
1 tablespoon cornstarch
dash of salt
2 cups chokecherries

2 cups peeled and diced apples

Roll out the pastry, arrange the bottom crust in the pan, and set it aside. Stir the sugar, cornstarch, and salt together until well blended. Put the chokecherries and diced apple into a bowl, then add the sugar-cornstarch mixture and stir until mixed. Put this into the bottom crust and cover with the top crust. Make a slash in the top crust to allow steam to escape. Bake until lightly browned—about 45 minutes. Remove the pie from the oven and allow it to cool. Makes 6 to 8 servings. Serve with a small side dish for the pits.

Chokecherry gumdrops

1 package powdered pectin
¾ cup chokecherry juice
½ teaspoon baking soda
1 cup granulated sugar
1 cup light corn syrup
few grains of salt

For this recipe you will need a clock with a minute hand, a heat-resistant pan approximately 8 x 8 x 2 inches, two long-handled spoons, and two heavy pots: one medium and one large. (A separate spoon must be used for each pot so that sugar does not come into contact with the pectin until just the right moment.)

In the large pot combine the sugar, corn syrup, and salt. Stir these together with a long-handled spoon and leave it in the pot. In the medium pot combine the pectin, juice, and soda (the soda will cause the mixture to foam). Place both pots over high heat and cook, alternately stirring each with its own spoon, until the sugar-syrup solution has reached a full boil and most of the foam has disappeared from the juice—this will take 3 to 4 minutes.

Now you are ready to combine the contents of the two pots. To avoid splattering, pour the chokecherry solution in a thin stream into the sugar-syrup solution, stirring as you pour. Use medium-high heat and stir constantly until the contents are well blended and have again reached a full boil. Now, begin timing and, still stirring, allow to boil hard for 1 minute. (Constant stirring and correct timing are necessary to prevent burning.)

Remove the pot from the heat and immediately pour the contents into the heat-resistant pan; allow to stand uncovered at room temperature until thoroughly cool and firm—usually at least 3 hours.

Place about ¾ cup granulated sugar in a shallow bowl. Use a knife dipped into warm water to cut the gumdrops; make 9 or 10 cuts across the pan horizontally and vertically. Carefully remove the gumdrops from the pan and gently roll them in the sugar, then refrigerate or freeze them in tightly covered containers. Makes about 100 gumdrops.

Once frozen, gumdrops may be stored for up to a year, but when getting them ready for the freezer, space them far enough apart that they do not touch. Waxed paper laid between layers will prevent them from sticking together.

I often make gumdrops in summer, using chokecherry and other juices, then freeze and store them until November or December. Different juices make gumdrops of different colors and flavors. A plate of these jewellike candies passed around after Thanksgiving dinner in the interim when no one is yet ready for pie makes an elegant treat. Saved for December and mixed in with holiday cookies, they provide a special touch with their clear, deep colors and unusual flavors.

The combination of chokecherry and chocolate is particularly delicious, and if left unsugared, these gumdrops can be used as the center for dipped chocolate candies. Reminiscent of chocolate-covered cherries, these candies are truly outstanding.

Chocolate-covered chokecherry jells

1 recipe chokecherry gumdrops cut into ¾-inch squares, but *not* rolled in sugar
1 16-ounce package semisweet chocolate chips (real chocolate, not imitation)

Place the gumdrops in a freezer until thoroughly frozen. Meanwhile, cover two cookie sheets with waxed paper and set them aside.

Melt the chocolate chips in a microwave or put them into the top of a double boiler over boiling water and stir until melted. (If using a microwave, take care to not overcook the chips—overcooking not only alters the flavor of the chocolate, but also harms the texture, causing it to be lumpy.) Once the chocolate is melted, stir it only until it is smooth and well blended. Using a spoon, dip each frozen gumdrop into the warm chocolate, then place it on the waxed paper. Allow the candies to remain undisturbed until the chocolate has again become firm—this can take several hours or, if the kitchen is warm, even longer. Firming can be hastened by putting the candies (still on the cookie sheets) into a refrigerator. When firm, carefully transfer the candies to a container that has a tightly fitting lid, separating the layers with waxed paper. Refrigerate or freeze to store. Makes about 100 pieces of candy.

The recipe for gumdrops can also be used to make a glaze for fresh apples. The result is something like candied apples, but not as sticky.

Chokecherry-glazed apples
1 recipe chokecherry gumdrops
12 medium apples, chilled
12 blunt wooden sticks such as those used for candied apples

It is important that the apples be thoroughly chilled before you begin. Have ready a heat-resistant bowl to pour the glaze into after it has cooked. The apples will be dipped into the glaze, so choose a bowl deep enough to accommodate one whole apple. Prepare two cookie sheets by spreading them with double layers of waxed paper; set them aside.

Follow the directions for chokecherry gumdrops, except after cooking, pour the hot glaze into the bowl described above (instead of a shallow pan). Let the glaze cool until it thickens slightly—otherwise it will run off the fruit. While the glaze is cooling to the right consistency for dipping, prepare the fruit.

Remove the fruit from the refrigerator. Dry the apples and insert a wooden stick into the stem end of each. Test the glaze—when still slightly warm and the consistency of thick syrup, proceed with the dipping.

Handle the apples by their sticks, turning each in the glaze so that it becomes covered. When well coated, remove the apple but hold it above the bowl for a few moments to allow excess glaze to drip back in, then place the apple on the waxed paper. Space the apples far enough apart that they do not stick together. Allow them to remain until the glaze is set—usually about an hour. Any leftover glaze may be allowed to stand until firm, then treated like gumdrops.

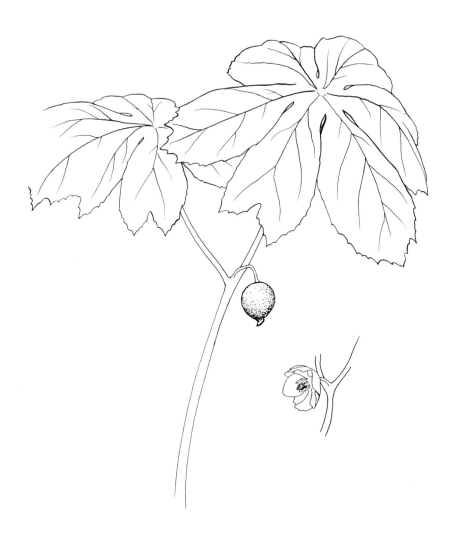

May-apple

Podophyllum peltatum L.

Barberry family: Berberidaceae

Description: The may-apple is a native perennial herb reproducing mostly by creeping rhizomes. May-apples often form large, dense patches with some plants standing up to 20 inches tall. First-year plants do not flower but produce a single petiole with 1 umbrella-like leaf, which has 3 to 9 lobes and toothed margins. Typically, second-year plants produce a stem with 2 leaves and a single white 6- or 9-petaled nodding flower in the fork between the petioles. The fruit is a plump, oval, many-seeded berry, which ripens to a lemon yellow.

Distribution: Eastern United States and into Canada; in the Great Plains, the southeastern portion only.

Habitat: Rich soil in wooded areas and along damp roadsides or stream banks.

Edible parts: Ripe berries, cooked; uncooked berries in moderation.

Season to collect: Mid to late summer.

Cautions: Use ripe berries only—all other parts of the may-apple are poisonous if eaten. The cooked berries seem to be generally agreeable, but overeating of uncooked fruits can cause indigestion and severe abdominal pain.

Additional information and recipes: Although a may-apple plant produces but a single fruit each year (and some will produce none), if you live where may-apples grow, finding enough fruit may not be difficult because the plants usually form very large patches.

May-apples transplant well and require little care other than watering, but plant them where they will be shaded much of the day. Although they form large patches, they increase slowly and can be controlled by hoeing. May-apples make an especially attractive planting under tall trees.

May-apple fruit has a wonderful flavor all its own and makes good juice, jelly, and jam. To prepare the fruits, simply wash them well.

To extract may-apple juice

Cut the berries into halves and measure the amount. Use 1 cup water for each 6 cups of fruit. Put the fruit and water into a large, heavy kettle, place over medium-high heat, and bring to a boil, then reduce the heat, cover with a lid, and allow the fruit to simmer until tender—about 15 minutes.

Remove the mixture from the heat and allow it to cool until comfortable to handle, then pour it into a sieve or damp jelly cloth and allow the juice to drip through. For drinking, sweeten to taste or combine with other juices or with ginger ale—serve chilled or pour over cracked ice. For making jelly, add sugar only after adding the pectin.

May-apple jelly

3 cups may-apple juice
1 package powdered pectin
5 cups granulated sugar

Read about jelly making, Appendix A.

Measure the sugar and set it aside. Combine the juice and pectin in a large, heavy kettle. Place over high heat and, stirring constantly, bring to a boil. Add the sugar all at one time. Stir and again bring to a full rolling boil. Begin timing, and allow to boil hard for 1 minute. Remove from the heat and quickly skim off the foam, then pour the jelly into hot, sterile jars, leaving ¼ inch headspace. Cap the jars with two-piece screwband lids and process for 5 minutes in a boiling water bath. Makes about 5 ½ cups of jelly.

May-apple jam

PREPARING THE PULP

8 cups may-apple berries cut into halves
1 cup water

Put the fruit and water into a large, heavy kettle. Place over medium-high heat and bring to a boil. Reduce the heat to low, cover with a lid, and allow to simmer gently for about 15 minutes or until tender. Stir several times during the cooking–may-apple berries burn easily. Remove the kettle from the heat and allow the fruit to cool until comfortable to handle. Pour the fruit into a cone-shaped colander and press the pulp through with the pestle. Discard the seeds and any skins that remain.

MAKING THE JAM

4 cups may-apple pulp
2 tablespoons lemon juice
1 box powdered pectin
5 ½ cups granulated sugar

Read about jam making, Appendix A.

Measure the sugar and set it aside. Combine the pulp and pectin in a large, heavy kettle and stir well. Place over medium-high heat and, stirring constantly, bring the pulp to a full boil. Add the sugar all at once, stir, and again bring to a full boil. Begin timing and allow to boil hard for 1 minute, stirring constantly. Remove from the heat and skim off the foam, then stir the jam well and ladle it into hot, sterile jars, leaving ¼ inch headspace. Cap the jars with two-piece screwband lids and process for 5 minutes in a boiling water bath. Makes a little more than 6 cups.

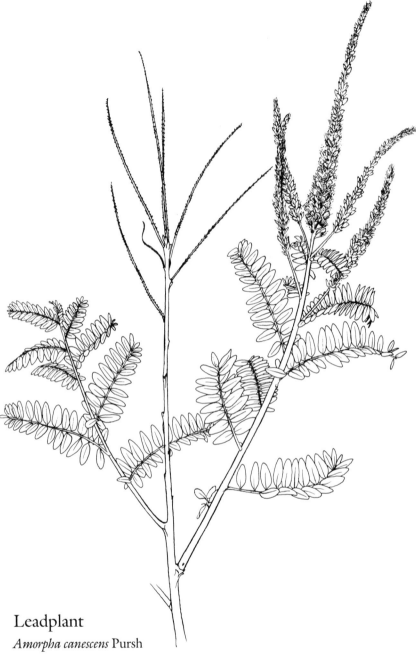

Leadplant

Amorpha canescens Pursh

Bean family: Fabaceae

Description: Leadplant is a short native shrub with 1 to several branched stems. The leaves are alternate and pinnately compound, typically with 17 to 20 pairs of small opposite leaflets, plus a smaller terminal leaflet. Both upper and lower surfaces of the leaflets are covered with fine hairs, giving the plant a silvery or leadlike appearance. The flowers are small, with 1 heart-shaped purple to lavender petal, and are borne in spikelike clusters at the tips of the branches. The fruits are small wooly pods, each containing a single seed.

Distribution: Throughout much of the Great Plains, into Canada and western Missouri, with scattered populations in surrounding states.

Habitat: Well-drained prairies, pastures, hillsides; often along roadsides and fence rows; in full sun.

Edible parts: Dried leaflets brewed for tea.

Seasons to collect: Late summer to early autumn.

Cautions: Remember that except in winter, all plants need leaves to live and grow, so it is best to delay harvesting until late summer when growing has nearly ceased. Even then, harvest only a small amount from each of many plants rather than many leaflets from any one plant.

Additional information and recipes: Leadplant tea is an old-time favorite, enjoyed by various prairie peoples who, along the way, have given this plant some interesting names. Translated, the old Omaha-Ponca name means "buffalo bellow plant," referring to the fact that its blooming period coincides with the rutting season of the bison (buffalo), a time when the behavior of the bulls includes much bellowing. Among settlers it was known as "shoestring plant" because as plows cut through the virgin sod, the roots of leadplant broke with a snapping sound like that of shoestrings breaking. Settlers called the tea "prairie tea."

Although greatly diminished in numbers over the years by cultivation and overgrazing, leadplant can still be found in scattered native prairies and along some roadsides. Even so, it is better to grow your own. For good reason, collecting from native prairies is usually prohibited and although seeds for planting can safely be harvested from roadsides, it is better to collect leaves for making tea from areas less apt to be polluted. The tiny hairs that cover the leaves of leadplant tend to catch and hold roadside dust and residues—materials you'd not want in your tea.

Fortunately, leadplant makes an attractive, easy-care yard plant. In the future it may be possible to buy these shrubs at nurseries, but now it is likely that you will need to start your own from seed. Collect the seeds in autumn and refrigerate them in a tightly closed container until planting time in spring. Leadplant seeds are very small but sprout rather easily if they have been given that cold treatment and then are soaked overnight in water just before planting. For a permanent location, choose a place that is sunny and has well-drained soil. It is advisable to encircle each plant with wire mesh to protect it from rabbits and deer.

Leaflets are harvested by simply stripping them from the midvein of the leaf (again, remember not to take too many leaflets from any one plant). Use a cloth or paper bag for collecting and transporting the harvest—plastic is not recommended because it traps heat and moisture inside the bag and, in even a short time, that combination can cause the leaflets to deteriorate.

To dry leadplant leaflets

Once home, shake the leaflets out in a single layer onto a kitchen towel laid in a large pan with sides. Cover the pan with a light towel or with cheesecloth to protect the leaflets from dust (the sides of the pan will hold the cover up off the leaflets). Place the pan in a light, airy place away from direct sunlight until the leaflets are brittle dry—usually about 10 days. Even if the leaflets seem to be dry in less time, the flavor is much improved if they are allowed to cure for at least 10 days after being picked. When thoroughly dry, shake the leaflets into glass jars with tightly fitting lids. Store in a cool, dry place away from sunlight.

Besides having a pleasant, mellow flavor, leadplant has a remarkable property in that the leaflets may be brewed more than once with little loss of flavor; in fact, they are usually good for at least 3 brewings. After the first brewing, simply refrigerate the wet leaflets in a covered container, then reuse within 2 days.

Leadplant tea

For each serving:
1 tablespoon dried leaflets
1 cup water

Place the leaflets and water in a pot over high heat and stir until the water reaches the boiling point. Reduce the heat to its lowest setting and cover the pot with a lid. Allow the tea to steep for about 5 minutes, then pour through a strainer, but save the leaflets to use again (as suggested above). Tea may be served hot or iced and, if desired, sweetened with honey or sugar.

Wild plum

Prunus americana Marsh.

Rose family: Rosaceae

Description: Wild plum is a small native tree sometimes reproducing by seeds but more often by suckers (shoots from the roots) to form dense thickets. The branches are smooth and have many sharp-tipped twigs. The leaves are alternate, dark green, and smooth on the upper surface, lighter green and sparsely hairy on the under surface. Margins are finely and sharply serrate. Flowers are round and white with 5 petals. The fruits are round to oval and contain a single seed called a stone or pit. When ripe, the fruits are fleshy and juicy and may be various shades of yellow, rose, or purple.

Distribution: Scattered populations throughout the United States, except the arid southwest, and into Canada; widely distributed throughout the Great Plains.

Habitat: Along roadsides, fence rows, stream banks, and the edges of prairies or woods; in rich, rocky, or sandy soils, usually in full sun.

Season to collect: Late summer.

Edible parts: Ripe fruits, cooked or uncooked.

Cautions: Serious poisoning has occurred from eating unripe plums. When picking, be mindful of the sharp twigs and caution children about them.

Additional information and recipes: Wild plums grow well in yards and are easily transplanted in spring. They do spread but can be controlled by spading and hoeing. At least one variety of wild plum does not spread and is available from some nurseries.

It is not possible to write other than passionately about wild plums, because no matter what time of year you find a patch of them, something special will be there. The fruits are ripe in late summer or early autumn, and in a good year, hang so thickly you can fill a bucket standing under one tree. In winter, the tracks of animals—mice, rabbits, sometimes coyote or deer—crisscross the snow under the thickets. When there is no snow, hundreds of plum pits, bearing tiny, uniform grooves made by the gnawing of mice; can be found scattered on the ground among the dried leaves.

Spring is perhaps the best of all. Although the fragrance of plum blossoms may reach you on the wind, to really know the magic of a plum thicket in spring you have to be there among the trees. In order not to disturb the bees above your head it is best to go in bending low or on your hands and knees. If the branches are not high enough for that, sit alongside and listen to the humming and inhale the blended fragrance of warm, sweet flowers and cool, moist earth.

Information handed down in the oral histories of Plains Indian societies indicates that earlier people relied heavily on wild plums for food, fresh in season, but also dried in winter. Wild plums also played an important role in the diet of settlers, who, like Native people, ate plums fresh in season, but who preserved plums by canning. Plum sauce was served with meat or for dessert, and plum jelly and jam were prized for bread and toast. Plum juice, without sugar, was canned by the quart—and usually as many quarts as the woman of the house could manage to put up, for a good plum crop is not to be found every year.

There was a reason for so much plum juice. Like apples, plums are high in pectin, the substance that causes jam and jelly to set. Even under the best of conditions, several years of growth are required before apple trees will produce enough fruit to satisfy the needs of a family—and after waiting several years for a fruit crop, settlers in drier parts of the Great Plains found that orchard fruit trees were not well suited to the harsh weather conditions of their area. Many families came to rely considerably on wild fruits, and when wild plums were plentiful, they gathered and preserved all that they could. Plum juice, they had learned, not only jelled, but when mixed with other fruits caused *them* to jell, too. (see the recipes for chokecherry–wild plum jelly and jam on pages 179 and 182.) But plum jelly and jam were not solely for spreading on bread. Some families used these condiments for basting roast meat, particularly wild game, and when they could buy spices and wanted to be fancy, they made a spiced jam specifically for that purpose.

Although it is tempting to take plums from the tree before they are fully ripe, this will only lead to disappointment because plums don't ripen much after they are picked. Be aware also that in seeking ripe fruit, you can't go by looks alone. Size is not necessarily a determining factor, and the color of ripe fruit varies from tree to tree. For example, yellow fruits on one tree may be hard and sour; yellow fruits on another tree may be sweet and juicy. Juiciness and flavor are probably the most reliable characteristics to look for and a single bite will tell you what you need to know. When ripe, wild plums are not only good tasting, but have relatively thin skin; underripe plums are astringent and have thicker, slightly bitter skin. Of course, plums can become too ripe, and at that stage they are mushy and will not make good cooked products.

Look your harvest over and discard fruits having wormholes, then give the fruit a thorough washing and pick out any debris. Some recipes, such as plum upside-down cake, require cutting the fresh fruit to remove the pits, but for jelly and jam the pits may be left in until after the first cooking.

A few more words about plum jelly and jam—it has long been a practice to make both jelly and jam from the same batch of fruit. After the plums are cooked, the juice and pulp are separated; the juice is made into jelly and the pulp is made into jam. The recipe that follows came from South Dakota and is nearly a hundred years old. It has been updated only in regard to the modern type of lids used and the boiling water bath processing.

To extract wild plum juice and pulp
Although the yield will vary with the juiciness of the plums, 1 gallon of plums usually makes about 5 cups of jelly and about the same amount of jam and is a good amount to work with. For each gallon of plums use 4 cups of water. (Again, you do not need to remove the pits.)

Divide the plums and water into two batches or whatever amounts are reasonable for the size of your kettle. Work with one batch at a time, repeating the following steps for each batch. Put the plums and water into a large, heavy kettle. Bring to a boil, reduce the heat to low, cover with a lid, and allow the plums to simmer until they are soft—about 25 minutes. Remove the kettle from the heat and allow the plums to cool until comfortable to handle.

In extracting the juice from so large an amount of fruit, it helps to use a cone-shaped colander to support the jelly cloth. Simply arrange the damp cloth in the colander so that the center of the cloth is at the bottom of the cone and the edges of the cloth hang over the rim of the colander.

Pour a quart or so of the cooled plums into the jelly cloth and allow the juice to drip through into a large container, then squeeze gently to extract more juice. Turn what is left (the pulp, skins, and pits) out into still another large container. Repeat with another quart or so of plums and continue, each time collecting the juice for jelly and saving the rest for jam. After all of the juice has been extracted, set it aside while you separate the pulp from the skins and pits.

Return the mass of pulp, skins, and pits to the large kettle but do not reheat. You may or may not need to add a little water, depending on how much juice was removed. The mixture should be something like soft pudding. If too dry, add water—about ¼ cup at a time—and stir until the right consistency is reached. Remove the jelly cloth from the colander. Place the pulp-skins-pits mixture in the colander and press the pulp through with the pestle, then set it aside for jam; discard the skins and pits. Repeat this procedure for each kettle of plums.

Wild plum jelly

4 cups plum juice
3 cups granulated sugar
Read about jelly making, Appendix A.

Put the juice and sugar into a large, heavy kettle and stir well. Place over high heat and bring to a boil, then reduce the heat and allow the liquid to boil gently until it reaches the jelling point. Typically, the boiling time will be 20 to 25 minutes. Test for doneness with a jelly thermometer or use either the spoon or cold saucer method. When done, remove the kettle from the heat and quickly skim off the foam, then pour the jelly into hot, sterile jars, leaving ¼ inch headspace. Cap the jars with two-piece screwband lids and process for 5 minutes in a boiling water bath. Makes about 5 cups of jelly.

Wild plum jam

4 cups plum pulp
3 cups granulated sugar
Read about jam making, Appendix A.

Put the pulp and sugar into a large, heavy kettle over medium heat and stir until the sugar has dissolved, then proceed as directed above for plum jelly, except the jam will be done when it thickens and forms a rounded heap in a spoon. Expect the jam to be done in much less time than the jelly, perhaps in less than 10 minutes. Also, note that jam burns easily, so stir frequently, especially toward the end of the cooking. When done, remove the kettle from the heat and quickly skim off the foam, then pour the jam into hot, sterile jars, leaving ¼ inch headspace. Cap the jars with two-piece screwband lids and process for 5 minutes in a boiling water bath. Makes about 5 cups of jam.

To can wild plum juice

After extracting the juice as directed above, return it to the kettle and heat it to boiling, then begin timing and allow to boil for 5 minutes. Pour it into hot, sterile jars, leaving ½ inch headroom. Cap the jars with two piece screwband lids and process in a boiling water bath for 10 minutes.

Wild plum combination jelly

It doesn't always work, but when mixed half and half with other juices, wild plum juice will often cause the combined mixture to jell. Work with 6 cups or less of combined juice at a time. Measure the juice, then put it into a large, heavy kettle and add ¾ cup granulated sugar for each cup of juice. Place over high heat until the juice boils, then reduce the heat so that it boils gently.

Cook until it reaches the jelling point—usually about 25 minutes. Test for doneness with a jelly thermometer or use the spoon or cold saucer method. Remove the kettle from the heat and skim off the foam. Pour the jelly into hot, sterile jars, leaving ¼ inch headspace. Cap jars with two-piece screwband lids and process for 5 minutes in a boiling water bath. (Keep in mind that should the mixture fail to jell, it will make excellent syrup.)

The following recipe calls for fresh ginger root, which is available in the produce department of many grocery stores. Peel a small portion of root and use a garlic press to extract the juice. If you don't have a garlic press, cut several thin slices of ginger root and allow them to marinate for at least a week in the sauce—remove them before serving.

Spiced wild plum sauce

1 cup wild plum jam
1 tablespoon apple cider vinegar
½ teaspoon minced dried onion
¼ teaspoon dry mustard
dash each of nutmeg and cloves
few grains of salt
freshly ground black pepper to taste
¼ to ½ teaspoon fresh ginger root juice (if it is unavailable, use ⅛ teaspoon ground ginger)

Combine all of the ingredients except the ginger juice in a small saucepan and stir until well blended. Place over medium heat and stir until the mixture begins to boil. Reduce the heat, then stirring constantly, allow it to cook for 1 minute. Remove from the heat and stir in the ginger juice. Cool. Makes about 1 cup of sauce.

Plum sauce may be served as an accompaniment for meat at the table or may be used to baste meat while it is roasting. To baste, brush the sauce lightly over the surface of the meat several times during the last half hour or so of baking. To store, plum sauce must be refrigerated or kept frozen.

Wild plum upside-down cake

350 degree oven
SAUCE
3 cups pitted plums, cut into pieces
½ cup water
2 cups granulated sugar

1 tablespoon margarine or butter

1 teaspoon vanilla

dash of nutmeg

Put the plums and water into a heavy pot. Cover and cook over medium-low heat until soft—about 5 minutes—but check and stir often to guard against burning. Remove the lid, add the remaining ingredients, and stir. Do not replace the lid. Adjust the heat so that the mixture boils gently, then cook until well blended—usually 2 to 3 minutes. Remove from the heat and allow the plums to cool while you make the cake batter.

CAKE

½ cup milk

1 tablespoon margarine or butter

2 eggs

1 cup granulated sugar

¼ teaspoon salt

1 cup all-purpose flour

1 teaspoon baking powder

1 teaspoon vanilla extract

Grease a 7 x 11 x 2–inch cake pan with margarine or butter and set it aside.

Put the milk and the margarine or butter into a small saucepan and heat to scalding (bubbles will appear around the edge). Do not allow the milk to boil. Turn off the heat and leave the milk mixture in the pan while you put together the other ingredients.

With an electric mixer, beat the eggs until foamy, then add the sugar *gradually* and continue beating until the mixture is light colored and very thick— at least 4 minutes at high speed. Sift the flour, baking powder, and salt together, then add this to the egg mixture. With the mixer set at its lowest setting, beat only until the egg and flour mixtures are blended. Add the hot milk mixture and the vanilla. Using a large spoon, gently stir until mixed.

Pour the cooked plum mixture into the pan, then pour the cake batter over it. Bake for about 35 minutes or until the cake springs back when lightly touched in the center.

Remove the cake from the oven and allow it to cool at least 15 minutes on a wire rack. The cake may be cut and served directly from the pan or it may be turned out and then cut. To turn the cake out, run a knife along the edges while it is still warm, then turn it over onto the serving dish. Allow the pan to remain in place over the cake for several minutes. Cake may be served warm or cold (or rewarmed). Makes 9 to 12 servings.

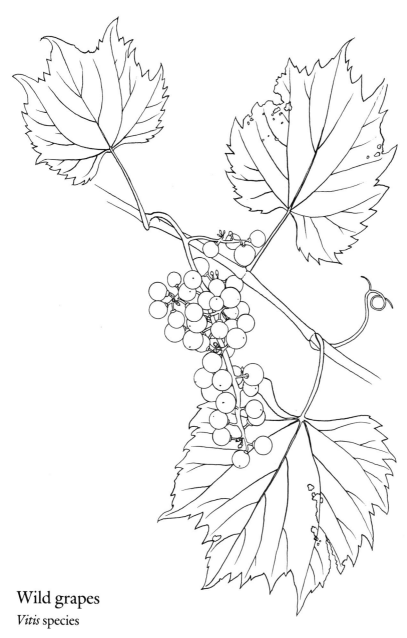

Wild grapes
Vitis species

Grape family: Vitaceae

Description: The wild grapes are woody native vines with papery, shredding bark. Most climb by means of coiling tendrils. The leaves are alternate, often nearly as broad as long, and lobed or unlobed with coarsely toothed margins. The leaves of most species are smooth and medium green above, and lighter, sometimes with cobwebby hairs, below. The flowers are borne in clusters and bloom in late spring. Tiny and pale green, they are easily overlooked, but many have a remarkably pleasant fragrance. Typically, for species in the Great Plains, male and female flowers occur on separate plants. The fruits, which are borne in compact or slightly loose clusters on green to brown stalks, are small and round. When ripe, they are juicy and deep purple to blue black, each with 2 to 4 seeds.

Distribution: Scattered throughout the United States and into Canada; several species in the Great Plains, but only the riverbank grape (*Vitis riparia* Michx.) is found throughout.

Seasons to collect: Mid to late summer, sometimes into autumn.

Edible parts: Ripe fruits, cooked or uncooked; however, slightly underripe fruits are often combined with ripe fruits for jelly and jam because they contain more pectin.

Cautions: Be sure you have the right plant before you pick. Several plants are mistaken for wild grapes. Raccoon grape (*Ampelopsis cordata*) is a vine that often grows in the same habitat. It is not a true grape: its leaves are narrower than those of wild grapes and the flesh of the ripe fruit is at first milky and later dry. As the fruit of the raccoon grape matures, it undergoes several changes of color: beginning with green, it changes to orange, then rosy purple, and finally to turquoise. A single cluster may have fruits of different colors at the same time.

Moonseed (*Menispermum canadensis*) is another vine that often grows in the same habitat as wild grapes and resembles them. However, moonseed leaves do not have teeth along the margins and each fruit contains a single, crescent-shaped seed (like a disk with a notch cut into it). Moonseed fruit is extremely poisonous.

Woodbine (*Parthenocissus vitace*) and Virginia creeper (*Parthenocissus quinquefolia*), two vines closely related to each other, bear grapelike fruits reported to be poisonous, particularly to children. However, the leaves, which are divided into from 3 to 7 leaflets, easily distinguish both plants from wild grapes. Unlike those of wild grapes, the small, branchlike stalks to which the fruits are attached often (not always) become red as the fruits ripen.

If you need assistance in identifying wild grapes, do consult your county agent or other plant authority.

Additional information and recipes: Perhaps with no other wild fruit does the quality vary as much as it does with wild grapes. Some species tend to be better flavored than others, but quality can vary from plant to plant within the same species. Generally, but not always, the better-tasting grapes occur in fairly compact clusters.

When you find a vine bearing particularly tasty fruit, you may wish to plant some of the seeds in your own yard. Wild grapes are easily started from seed. Plant them outdoors in autumn along a fence or other place where they will have support. It is important to mark the spot where you have planted each seed. In spring when the young plants emerge through the soil, the first leaves don't look at all like grape leaves and it's easy to make the mistake of hoeing them out. When the second leaves appear, they will easily be recognized as grapes.

In order to have fruit, you will need at least one vine that bears male flowers and one or more that bear female flowers. It will be several years before the vines flower and bear fruit, but when they do, you will be able to determine which is which—if short of space, you may want to remove all but a few of the male vines.

Wild grapes are most often made into jam or jelly, and there are many recipes and methods. Because the fully ripe fruits rarely contain enough pectin to jell on their own, they are often combined with slightly underripe grapes, tart apples, or commercial pectin. This has another advantage in that the flavor of the fully ripe fruit is generally so concentrated that such combinations generally produce a better-tasting product.

Grape juice, wild or domestic, contains a compound that can cause a harmless but unpleasant grittiness in jelly. Fortunately, if grape juice is allowed to stand at a cool temperature, this material, called tartrate, readily separates and settles to the bottom. It can be removed before the jelly is made by refrigerating the juice in a tall container for at least 8 hours, then slowly pouring the juice out to about 1½ inches from the bottom, leaving the tartrate crystals behind.

For anything you make with grapes, first wash them well and remove them from the small branchlike stalks that hold them in the cluster.

To extract wild grape juice

8 cups ripe grapes

1 cup water

Put the grapes into a large, heavy kettle and crush them slightly with a potato masher. Add the water and stir well. Place the kettle over medium heat until the liquid is simmering; adjust the heat so that it doesn't boil. Cover with a lid and simmer until the grapes are soft—about 10 minutes. Remove from the heat and allow to cool until comfortable to handle. Pour the grapes into a damp jelly cloth and squeeze to extract the juice. Makes about 3 cups of juice.

Wild grape jelly without added pectin

3 cups grape juice

(made from 2 cups ripe grapes and 1 cup slightly underripe grapes)

2½ cups granulated sugar

Read about jelly making, Appendix A.

Stir the juice and sugar together in a heavy kettle and bring to a boil over medium heat, then boil gently until the jelling point is reached. Test for doneness with a jelly thermometer or use the spoon or cold saucer method. (The boiling time will vary with the amount of pectin in the grapes.) When done, remove from the heat and quickly skim off the foam, then pour the jelly into hot, sterile jars leaving ¼ inch headspace. Cap the jars with two-piece screwband lids and process for 5 minutes in a boiling water bath. Makes about 4 cups of jelly.

Wild grape jelly with added pectin

3 cups grape juice

1 package powdered pectin

3½ cups granulated sugar

Read about jelly making, Appendix A.

Measure the sugar and set it aside. Combine the juice and pectin in a large, heavy kettle and stir well. Place over medium high heat and bring to a full boil. Add the sugar all at one time, then, stirring constantly, again bring to a full boil. Begin timing and allow the jelly to boil for 1 minute. Remove from the heat and skim off the foam. Pour into hot, sterile jars, leaving ¼ inch headspace. Cap with two-piece screwband lids and process for 5 minutes in a boiling water bath. Makes about 4 cups of jelly.

Wild grape and elderberry jelly without added pectin

PREPARING THE JUICE

2 cups elderberries
3 cups wild grapes
1 large tart apple
½ cup water

Cut the apple into 8 or more sections, and remove the seeds but do not peel. Put the apple sections, the elderberries, grapes, and water into a large, heavy kettle and bring to a boil over medium-high heat. Reduce the heat to low, cover the kettle with a lid, and allow the fruit to simmer until tender— about 20 minutes. Remove from the heat and allow to cool until comfortable to handle. Put the fruit into a damp jelly cloth and squeeze to extract the juice. Measure the juice; if less than 2½ cups, add enough water to make that amount.

MAKING THE JELLY

2½ cups combination juice
2 cups sugar

Read about jelly making, Appendix A.

Stir the juice and sugar together in a large, heavy kettle and bring to a boil over medium heat, then boil gently until the jelling point is reached. Test for doneness with a jelly thermometer or use the spoon or cold saucer method. (The boiling time will vary with the amount of pectin in the apple.) When done, remove from the heat and quickly skim off the foam, then pour the jelly into hot, sterile jars leaving ¼ inch headspace. Cap with two-piece screwband lids and process for 5 minutes in a boiling water bath. Makes a little more than 2 cups of jelly.

Wild grape and elderberry jelly with added pectin

3 cups wild grape juice
2 cups elderberry juice
1 package powdered pectin
5 cups granulated sugar

See instructions for elderberry juice on page 225. Read about jelly making, Appendix A.

Measure the sugar and set it aside. Stir the juices and pectin together in a large, heavy kettle. Place over high heat and bring to a full boil. Add the sugar all at one time. Stir, and again bring to a full boil. Begin timing and allow to boil for 1 minute. Remove from the heat and quickly skim off the foam, then pour the jelly into hot, sterile jars, leaving ¼ inch headspace. Cap the jars with two-piece screwband lids and process for 5 minutes in a boiling water bath. Makes about 6 cups of jelly. (Note that several weeks may be required for this jelly to set firmly.)

Wild grape jam
EXTRACTING THE PULP

6 cups ripe grapes

2 cups slightly underripe grapes

1 cup water

Put the grapes and water into a large, heavy kettle over medium heat until the liquid is nearly boiling; adjust the heat so that it doesn't boil. Cover with a lid and allow the grapes to simmer until soft—about 10 minutes. Remove the kettle from the heat and allow the grapes to cool until comfortable to handle. Pour the grapes into a cone-shaped colander and press the pulp through with the pestle. Yields vary, depending on the fleshiness of the grapes, but between 4 and 5 cups of pulp is typical.

MAKING THE JAM

Read about jam making, Appendix A.

Measure the pulp and allow ¾ cups granulated sugar for each cup of pulp. Return the pulp to the kettle and stir in the sugar. Using medium heat and stirring constantly, cook the pulp until it is thick enough to hold a slightly rounded shape in a spoon—about 10 minutes. Or check for doneness with the cold-saucer method. When done, pour the jam into hot, sterile jars, leaving ¼ inch headspace. Cap the jars with two-piece screwband lids and process for 5 minutes in a boiling water bath. Makes between 5 and 6 cups of jam.

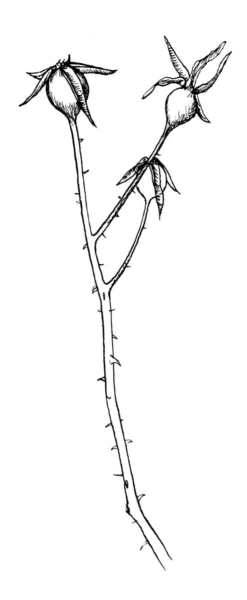

Rose hips

Please read the general information about wild roses on page 64.

Rose fruits, called hips, are valued both for their high content of vitamin C and for their flavor. Often they are used primarily for the vitamin C and combined with other ingredients, because the flavor is not particularly appealing to many persons. However, the flavor of tea brewed from home-dried hips is usually superior to that made with commercially processed hips. This is because the smaller quantities of hips that are dried at home can be managed without artificial heat. Many commercial operations find it necessary to oven-dry the large quantities of rose hips they process.

Ripe rose hips may be used fresh or dried and either cooked or uncooked. When they are ripe, they vary in color from pale orange to bright red and differ considerably in size, shape, and flavor, depending on the species. Once picked, hips must be looked over and those having wormholes, black spots, or signs of fungus should be discarded. An interesting fungus often found on wild roses in the Great Plains is brilliant orange in color, and in some years much of the rose hip crop will be affected.

After sorting, wash the hips well. Although they are most often used for tea, hips can be added to soups and stews and made into a syrup. For most purposes, each hip must first be split open and the seeds and hairs removed. A baby-food spoon (the kind with small bowl) works well for this task. For tea, removing the hairs and seeds is not necessary. Wild rose seeds are not harmful, so for those species having few or very weak hairs, the hips need only be split to promote drying—seeds and hairs can be left in place. For tea, rose hips may be collected either fresh or dry, but for the other recipes they must be picked fresh.

To dry rose hips
Split each hip with a sharp knife and, if necessary, remove the seeds and stiff hairs. Spread the hips in a single layer on a screen or on a kitchen towel laid in a cookie sheet. Place this in a light, airy place away from direct sunlight and cover with a thin towel to protect the hips from dust. Turn the hips each day until they are thoroughly dry. Store the hips in tightly covered containers away from heat and sunlight.

Rose hip tea
Fresh or dry, hips of each species have their own flavor. Depending on the strength of tea desired, use from 1 to 3 teaspoons of hips for each cup of water. Put the hips into a tea ball or have a strainer ready. Put the water into a saucepan and bring it to boiling, add the hips and remove the saucepan from the heat. Cover with a lid and allow the tea to steep about 5 minutes. Re-

move the tea ball or pour the tea through the strainer. If using a teapot, pre-heat it with boiling water before filling it with the tea.

If desired, add honey or lemon. Dried mint, fresh catnip, or other herbs may be brewed with the hips to improve the flavor. Another variation is to simmer a few whole cloves and a stick of cinnamon in the water for about 10 minutes before adding the hips.

Fresh rose hip puree
2 cups fresh rose hips
2½ cups water

Remove and discard the stems and the blossom ends. Split the hips and remove the seeds and hairs—if hairs are few or weak, they may be left in the hips. Put the hips and water into a heavy pot over medium heat. Cover with a lid and simmer until tender—about 15 to 20 minutes. Stir frequently; check the heat and, if necessary, adjust to prevent burning.

Remove the pot from the heat and allow the hips to cool slightly, then crush them with a potato masher. Return the pot to the stove, set the heat on low, and cook for another 5 minutes, stirring frequently. For the last minute of cooking, stir constantly.

Again remove the pot from the heat and allow the hips to cool until comfortable to handle. Either pour the hips into a cone-shaped colander and press the pulp through with the pestle or press it through a sieve using the back of a spoon. The amount of puree (pulp) obtained will vary, depending on the species of rose, but a typical yield is about 1½ cups.

Cream of rose hip soup
For each serving:
2 tablespoons heavy cream
⅓ cup rose hip puree
⅓ cup water
salt and freshly ground black pepper to taste

Put the cream into the soup bowl. Combine the puree and water in a sauce-pan over medium-high heat. Stir well and bring the puree to a full boil, then immediately pour it into the soup bowls, quickly stirring until well blended with the cream. Season with salt and pepper. Serve with hot buttered toast.

Rose hip honey
½ cup rose hip puree
½ cup honey

Combine the puree and honey and stir until well blended. Use on pancakes, toast, or biscuits. To store, this honey must be refrigerated—use it within 2 weeks.

Rose hip dip
1 cup rose hip puree
¼ cup honey
⅛ teaspoon dry mustard
dash of salt
dash each of cinnamon, cloves, and nutmeg
¼ cup lemon juice

Combine all the ingredients except the lemon juice in a saucepan. Place over medium heat and, stirring constantly, cook for 4 minutes. Add the lemon juice and, still stirring, cook for an additional minute. Remove from the heat and allow the dip to cool, then chill. Makes about 1½ cups.

Serve this dip in a small bowl surrounded by chunks of apple, pineapple, orange, or other fruits—provide toothpicks for dipping. Rose hip dip must be refrigerated and used within 10 days.

Prickly-pear cactus fruits

Please read the general information about prickly-pear cactus on page 82.

The flesh of no prickly-pear fruit is harmful to eat, but the quality varies from juicy and very good to dry and inedible. Look for fruits that do not have spines and have few or no glochids. The fruits of the more heavily armed species do not become juicy even when ripe.

If you find a patch of prickly-pear cactus in bloom, begin observing it whenever you can. As the flowers mature and wilt, you will notice round green fruits beginning to form in their place. By late summer many of these fruits will have ripened and you can sample a couple of them (after carefully scraping away any glochids) to determine if the fruit is good tasting. The flesh of good fruit will be pinkish green to deep rose in color, juicy, and pleasantly sweet; the skin may be shades of rose or purple or even green.

Prickly-pear species usually found in the northern portion of the Great Plains have dry, unpalatable fruits, so it is unlikely that persons in North Dakota and surrounding areas will find any fruits worth eating.

Years ago in South Dakota, children showed me a place where prickly-pear fruits could be picked and eaten directly from the plants. Although the green pads were dotted with sharp spines and glochids, the fruits were free of both. We gathered what we could carry and in the shade of a nearby bush ate our fill. Not realizing that prickly-pears with unarmed fruit were unusual for that locality, I neither collected a specimen nor tried to identify the species— oversights that, of course, I now regret.

Although size varies with the species and with such factors as growing conditions, it may be helpful to know that about 40 bigroot prickly-pear fruits will weigh around 1 pound and yield more than 1 cup of juice. Thus, to have enough fruit to make any of the following recipes, collect 120 or more fruits. In the southern portion of the Great Plains, prickly-pear fruits larger than those of bigroot prickly-pear are common; so fewer would be needed.

Collecting is made easier by using simple tools. Often, ripe fruits will fall when touched or may already be on the ground. These are easily retrieved with tongs, but fruits that have been lying on the ground must be inspected for ants. Firmly attached fruits can be skewered with a long two-tined barbecue fork, then cut off with a knife. A metal bucket works well for collecting, but fruits having many glochids are better transported between layers of crumpled newspaper in a disposable cardboard box.

Once you get home, the fruits must be washed and inspected for glochids. Fruits that are free of glochids merely require the removal of the tough disk of skin at the blossom end. When glochids are present, additional steps must be considered. Some wild plant cookbooks claim that glochids will soften with cooking or that they don't matter in jelly making because they simply stick in the jelly cloth and don't come through with the juice. But some glochids seem not to soften much in cooking and, lodged in the jelly cloth, they may get into your hands, sometimes even after the cloth has been washed. So if the fruits have numerous or very stiff glochids, I suggest removing them.

Glochids may be singed off much as pinfeathers are singed from a chicken, but perhaps a better method is to hold a cactus fruit securely with tongs and, with a woven plastic pot scrubber, rub away the glochids, rinsing the fruit in running water as needed. Then, while the cactus fruit is still in the tongs, slice off and discard the tough disk. The prepared fruits may be eaten without cooking, seeds and all. If they are to be cooked, slice them in half. Cactus fruits make good jelly and syrup as well as an unusual salad dressing.

To extract juice from prickly-pear cactus fruit

3 ½ pounds prickly-pear fruits (about 120 to 150)
3 ½ cups water
Prepare the fruit as described above. Place the sliced fruit and water in a large, heavy kettle over high heat and bring to a boil. Stir, then reduce the heat to medium-low and cover the kettle with a lid. Cook until the fruit is tender—10 to 15 minutes. Thoroughly crush the fruit with a potato masher, stir well, then cover again with a lid and cook for another 5 minutes. Remove the kettle from the heat. When cooled enough to be comfortably handled, pour the fruit into a jelly cloth and allow the juice to drip through on its own—don't squeeze or the jelly will be gummy. Makes about 3 cups of juice.

Prickly-pear cactus jelly

3 cups cactus juice
½ cup lemon juice
1 package powdered pectin
4 ½ cups granulated sugar
Read about jelly making, Appendix A.
Measure the sugar and set it aside. In a large, heavy kettle combine the juices and the pectin. Stir well, place over high heat, and bring to a boil. Add the sugar all at one time and again bring to a boil, stirring constantly. Begin timing and allow to boil hard for 1 minute. Remove the kettle from the heat and quickly skim off the foam, then pour the jelly into hot, sterile jars, leaving ¼ inch headspace. Cap the jars with two-piece screwband lids and process for 5 minutes in a boiling water bath. Makes about 5 cups of jelly.

Prickly-pear cactus syrup
cactus juice
lemon juice
granulated sugar
  Read about syrup making, Appendix A.
  For each cup of prickly-pear juice use 1 cup of sugar and 1 tablespoon of
lemon juice. Combine all the ingredients in a heavy kettle and bring to a boil
over high heat. Allow to boil hard for 2 to 3 minutes. Reduce the heat and
allow to boil gently for about 8 minutes. Remove the kettle from the heat
and quickly skim off the foam, then pour the syrup into hot, scalded jars,
leaving ½ inch headspace. Cap the jars with two-piece screwband lids and
process for 10 minutes in a boiling water bath. Yields will vary with the
amount of juice used, but usually the amount of syrup will be about the same
as the amount of juice used.
  Save some prickly-pear syrup for making rosy cactus dressing in autumn.
It is delicious on tossed lettuce and groundcherry salad (page 232).

Rosy cactus dressing
½ cup prickly-pear syrup
1 tablespoon apple cider vinegar
¼ teaspoon dry mustard
few grains of salt
  Combine all the ingredients, stir until blended, then chill thoroughly. Refrigerate to store. Makes ½ cup dressing. Recipe may be doubled, tripled, or
more.

Smooth sumac, sumac, sumach, shumac

Rhus glabra L.

Cashew family: Anacardiaceae

Description: Smooth sumac is a sparsely branched native shrub growing to a height of 10 feet (occasionally taller) and usually occurring in colonies. The leaves are alternate and pinnately compound. The leaflets are lance-shaped with coarsely toothed margins, the upper surface dark green and smooth, and the lower surface pale and also smooth. In autumn the leaves turn shades of brilliant red and orange. The flowers are small, round, and yellow green and are borne in clusters at the ends of the branches, with male and female flowers occurring on separate shrubs. The fruits, which occur in dense, upright clusters, ripen to a deep tawny red. Individual fruits are small, round, dry, and dotted with short hairs. They contain a single seed.

Distribution: Throughout much of the United States and into Canada; common in the eastern and southern portions of the Great Plains, scattered populations north.

Habitat: Prairies, open woodlands and borders, and along roadsides and fence rows.

Edible parts: Ripe fruits as a nibble or as the base for a hot or cold drink.

Season to collect: Autumn.

Cautions: The pleasant, sour taste of sumac is due to malic acid contained in tiny hairs on the surface of the fruit. Pressing or gently bruising the fruit is sufficient to release the acid into the water for flavor, and this small amount is not harmful (malic acid is also present in other fruits, such as green apples). However, the seed within the fruit contains tannin, which, if released, not only will give the drink a strong, raw taste, but is not recommended for routine consumption. Pressing or gently bruising the fruits is safe, but crushing or boiling the seeds releases tannin.

It is important to use pruning shears to remove the fruit clusters, because sumac wood is brittle. Inappropriate collecting practices can seriously damage the shrubs.

Some persons are sensitive to the sap of smooth sumac. Although it is unlikely that ordinary handling would pose a problem, readers are advised to be aware of this possibility.

(Poison sumac, *Toxicodendron vernix,* a plant found in wet areas in the eastern and southeastern United States, *but not in the Great Plains,* is as toxic as poison ivy. Leaves of poison sumac somewhat resemble those of smooth sumac and turn shades of red and orange in autumn. However, poison sumac has loose clusters of pale fruits that are easily distinguished from the red, upright fruit clusters of smooth sumac.)

Additional information and recipes: In areas where it occurs, smooth sumac is a well-known roadside shrub. These shrubs, usually in groups and looking like small trees, are especially noticeable in autumn when their leaves turn brilliant red. Seen against a backdrop of blue sky and buff-colored prairie grasses, sumac can be spectacular.

Years ago Plains Indian people made a lemonade-like drink by bruising ripe sumac fruit in water, sometimes adding sugar syrup made from the sap of certain trees. Some settlers made a similar drink, substituting white sugar or molasses for the tree sugar. Today "wild lemonade," or sumacade, is probably made more often by Scout leaders than by anyone else.

Although the procedure for preparing the drink is fairly simple, there are some details you need to know. If you gather sumac from the wild, choose plants away from roads or other dusty areas—the hairs on the fruits tend to collect dust and grime. Better, of course, is having the shrubs in your own yard. A group of sumacs makes an attractive planting around a house and requires little care or water. Because male and female flowers are borne on separate shrubs, starting out with several plants will increase the likelihood of having both sexes. Be advised that these shrubs do spread; spading will be required to maintain control.

The best time to gather sumac is after the fruits are ripe but before the onset of autumn rains, which may wash away the malic acid. Even when you think you have chosen just the right time, you may find that some of the clusters are quite faded. Probably these are from previous years, so pass them by. Select only the ripe, tawny-red fruit clusters of the current year.

For each glass of sumac drink, collect one fruit cluster. If collecting from a wild area, remember to take clusters here and there, leaving the greater number on the shrubs so that birds and other wildlife will not be short of winter food.

Once home, tear each cluster apart to check for insects. Mobile insects pose no problem—often, by the time you get home they will have left on their own, anyway. What you need to look for are the small, white, cottonlike cocoons often present in sumac clusters. Each cocoon contains a harmless pupa (immature insect), objectionable only because the sumac cluster is to be used for human food. When one of these is found, simply discard the portions of the cluster to which it is attached.

There is no need to strip the fruits from the smaller branches of the cluster itself. When all the clusters are torn apart, wash them in running water, working quickly so that as little acid as possible is washed away. To store them for later use, allow the clusters to dry thoroughly, put them into paper bags with the tops twisted shut to keep out dust, then store them in a dry, airy place.

Sumacade

sumac fruit clusters, inspected, torn apart, and washed
1 ½ cups water for each original cluster
honey or sugar to taste (about 1 tablespoon per original cluster)

Put the sumac fruit into a large pan or bowl and press it against the side with a heavy spoon or gently bruise it with a pestle. Add water and again press or bruise the fruit. Allow the mixture to stand for 5 minutes, then strain it through a cloth to remove debris, or pour it through a strainer into a tall jar and let the liquid stand for a few minutes to allow smaller bits to settle out. Pour the liquid into a pitcher, trying not to stir up material that may have settled to the bottom of the jar, but don't fret if a few flecks remain— they simply add character. Stir in sugar or honey and keep stirring until it has dissolved.

Heated, sumacade has a flavor something like that of Red Zinger herbal tea. Poured over ice, it is more like lemonade. Either way, this drink does not keep well, so it is best to use it the same day it is made.

Highbush cranberry

Viburnum opulus L. var. *americanum* Ait.

Honeysuckle family: Caprifoliaceae

Description: The highbush cranberry is a native shrub that may reach a height of 10 or more feet. The leaves are opposite and deeply 3-lobed, usually with coarsely toothed margins but sometimes with few or no teeth, the upper surface dark green and smooth, and the lower surface paler and either smooth or with scattered hairs along the veins. The flowers are round and white, with 5 lobes and occur in flat or slightly rounded clusters, the center buds opening first. Typically, several flowers on the outer edge of the cluster are larger than the others. The fruits, also in clusters, are small, round to oval in shape, each with a single prominent flat seed called a stone. When ripe, the fruits are glossy and red orange and often pull the branches down with their weight. They may remain on the branches well into winter.

Distribution: North-central United States and into Canada; scattered populations elsewhere; in the Great Plains, eastern and central North Dakota, into western Minnesota, scattered populations where planted.

Habitat: Moist soil on wooded hillsides, in lowlands, and along stream banks and lakeshores.

Season to collect: Autumn.

Edible parts: Ripe fruits, cooked.

Cautions: Use cutters to snip the clusters from the branches—breaking or twisting off clusters can seriously injure the shrubs.

A European species of highbush cranberry, *Viburnum opulus,* was introduced into the United States and Canada and is now widely used in yard plantings. This species is similar to our native species in appearance, but its fruit is bitter and unpalatable.

Additional Information and Recipes: The highbush cranberry is not a true cranberry but was so named because its tart red fruits can be used in much the same way as the familiar low-growing cranberry. In many botanical guides this plant is called by its earlier scientific name, *Viburnum trilobum.*

As a yard planting, the native highbush cranberry not only offers a source of fruit, but is attractive and requires little care. Although these shrubs can be purchased from certain plant nurseries, more often it is the European species that is offered for sale as highbush cranberry. For edible fruit, it is important to buy the American species—the difference in flavor is considerable. Of course, if you already have the European plant, don't do away with it—birds relish the fruits of both species.

Highbush cranberry fruits begin turning red in late summer but are not fully ripe until early autumn. Opinions differ about the best time for picking the fruit. Some persons prefer the flavor of barely ripe fruits that are still firm; others think the fruits are better after frost has softened the flesh. Picked before frost, the fruits usually contain enough pectin to jell on their own; after frost, additional pectin may be needed. Either way, the fruits give off an unpleasant odor during cooking, and the traditional remedy for this is to add fresh orange or lemon.

Highbush cranberries are high in vitamin C and make delicious jelly and sauce, as well as a refreshing drink. However you plan to use them, wash them well and remove any stems or debris.

Highbush cranberry sauce

4 cups highbush cranberries
½ cup water
1 cup granulated sugar
1 package unflavored gelatin or 1 teaspoon powdered (not flaked) agar
½ teaspoon grated orange or lemon rind
¼ cup orange juice

Put the highbush cranberries and water into a large, heavy pot, and place over medium-high heat until the water begins to boil. Reduce the heat, cover with a lid, and allow the fruit to simmer until tender—about 10 minutes. Meanwhile, stir the sugar and gelatin or agar together until well mixed.

Remove the pot from the heat and allow the fruit to cool until comfortable to handle. Pour the fruit into a cone-shaped colander and press the pulp through with the pestle. Return the pulp to the pot. Stir in the sugar-gelatin (or agar) mixture. Add the rind and juice and cook, stirring constantly, for 30 seconds. Allow to cool before serving. Makes about 2 cups of sauce.

This sauce is particularly good as a dip for fresh fruit, or it can be used like regular cranberry sauce and served with meat. Refrigerate to store.

To extract highbush cranberry juice

8 cups highbush cranberries
4 cups water
½ orange, quartered

Put all the ingredients into a large, heavy kettle (or use two kettles) and place over high heat until the water begins to boil. Reduce the heat, cover with a lid, and allow to cook for 3 minutes. Remove the lid, and, using a potato masher, gently crush the fruit. Stir well, loosening any fruit that may have stuck to the bottom. Return the lid and cook for another 5 minutes. Lay a damp jelly cloth inside a cone-shaped colander in such a way that the center of the cloth is in the point of the colander and the ends hang over the rim. Pour the fruit into the jelly cloth and squeeze to extract the juice. This juice may be used to make the jelly recipe below, but for use as a drink, the flavor will be too strong. For drinking, dilute and sweeten to taste, then serve over cracked ice. Makes 4 to 5 cups of juice.

Before-frost highbush cranberry jelly
4 cups highbush cranberry juice
2 cups granulated sugar
      Read about jelly making, Appendix A.
      Stir the juice and sugar together in a large, heavy kettle. Place over medium-high heat and allow to boil until the jelling point is reached. Test for doneness with a jelly thermometer or use the spoon or cold saucer method. When done, remove the kettle from the heat and quickly skim off the foam, then pour the jelly into hot, sterile jars, leaving ¼ inch headspace. Cap the jars with two-piece screwband lids and process for 5 minutes in a boiling water bath. Makes 3 to 4 cups of jelly.
      This makes a tart jelly, good on toast or with cream cheese on whole wheat crackers.

After-frost highbush cranberry jelly
5 cups granulated sugar
4 cups highbush cranberry juice
1 package powdered pectin
      Read about jelly making, Appendix A.
      Measure the sugar and set it aside. Stir the juice and pectin together in a large, heavy kettle and bring to a boil over high heat. Add the sugar all at once. Stir well and again bring to a boil. Begin timing and allow to boil hard for 1 minute. Remove the kettle from the heat and quickly skim off the foam, then pour the jelly into hot, sterile jars, leaving ¼ inch headspace. Cap the jars with two-piece screwband lids and process for 5 minutes in a boiling water bath. Makes about 6 cups of jelly.

Elderberry fruit

Please read the general information about common elderberry on page 105.

As you harvest elderberries, remember that many birds depend on native fruits to survive. Refrain from picking all of the elderberries at any one place, and in those years when wild fruits are scarce, pass elderberries by.

Like the flowers, elderberry fruits are borne in broad, open clusters that are much branched. Elderberries should not be eaten raw, but are delicious when made into jellies, syrups, or desserts. Alone, the flavor is somewhat musky, but in combination with other fruits such as lemon, rhubarb, wild grape, or wild plum, it is unusually good. The ability to blend with and enhance other flavors is only one of the elderberry's outstanding characteristics. Another is its purple-red color, so rich that both the juice and the syrup (recipes follow) can be used as food coloring for drinks, sauces, baked fruit, and desserts.

To harvest elderberries, simply remove the heads from the branches. Some persons are able to snap off the heads cleanly by applying pressure at the point where the first two leaves occur (leaving the leaves attached to the plant), but if this does not work easily for you, use pruning shears or heavy scissors; elderberry branches are brittle and easily damaged. Use a large, shallow cardboard box for collecting your harvest, and to prevent tangling, put each cluster into the box head down. Take only a moderate amount—first-time harvesters often bring home more clusters than they have the time or energy to process.

Elderberry fruits must be removed from the small stems to which they are attached as soon as possible after picking because the stems, if allowed to wilt, tend to break off with the fruit. Although small, these stems are bitter, and if many become mixed in with the fruit, they can ruin an entire batch.

Elderberries can be removed from the stems by hand, but a method that works well involves using a cutting board and either a large fork or a comb with widely spaced teeth. Put the cutting board in a large pan, resting one end on the rim so that the board slants into the pan. Hold the cluster, head down, against the board, then with your other hand, "comb" the elderberries from the cluster. A few small stems won't matter, but once the fruit is combed off, pick out as many broken stem pieces as you can.

Although most persons can consume cooked elderberry fruit perfectly well, some (I am one of them) experience nausea after eating cooked elderberry products containing the seeds. I have never known anyone to experience discomfort from the cooked pulp or juice. By following the directions below, the seeds can easily be removed. However, if you make the pie recipe calling for whole elderberries, serve very small pieces at first so that each person can determine whether he or she can tolerate the seeds. Purple passion pie is made with elderberry juice and therefore should present no problem.

To extract elderberry juice

4 cups elderberries
1 cup water

Place the elderberries and water in a heavy kettle. Cover with a lid and allow to simmer over medium-low heat for about 15 minutes. Remove from the heat and allow the fruit to cool until comfortable to handle. To extract the juice, place the fruit in a damp jelly cloth and squeeze gently. Makes about 2 cups of juice (sometimes more, depending on the juiciness of the fruit).

Elderberry juice does not contain enough acid to can safely. However, when the fruit is mixed half and half with rhubarb, the resulting juice may be canned.

Elderberry-rhubarb juice

4 cups elderberries
4 cups diced rhubarb stalk
4 cups water

Place all the ingredients in a heavy kettle and heat to boiling. Reduce the heat to medium-low, cover a with a lid, and allow the mixture to cook gently for about 15 minutes. Remove the kettle from the heat and let the contents cool until comfortable to handle.

To extract the juice, pour the mixture into a damp jelly cloth and squeeze. Makes about 3 cups of juice.

For a pleasant drink, stir a little more water into the pulp that is left after squeezing the juice from the cooked fruit, then squeeze or strain again. Sweeten to taste with honey or sugar and serve over ice. (To use canned or frozen juice for drinking, dilute with one third as much water.)

To can elderberry-rhubarb juice

Read about canning, Appendix A.

Reheat the juice to boiling and allow it to boil gently for 1 minute, then pour it into hot, sterile jars, leaving ½ inch space at the top. Cap the jars with two-piece screwband lids and process in a boiling water bath—10 minutes for either pints or quarts.

To freeze elderberry-rhubarb juice

Pour the cooled juice into ice cube trays and freeze, then transfer the cubes to tightly covered containers and keep them frozen. Remove 1 or more cubes as needed for coloring or flavoring.

Elderberry syrup

4 cups elderberry juice or elderberry-rhubarb juice
3 cups granulated sugar
   Read about syrup making, Appendix A.
   Stir the juice and sugar together in a large kettle. Place over high heat and bring to a boil. Reduce the heat and allow the liquid to boil gently, stirring occasionally, until it becomes syrupy—about 15 minutes. Remove the kettle from the heat and immediately skim off the foam, then pour the syrup into hot, scalded jars, leaving ½ inch headspace. Cap the jars with two-piece screwband lids and process for 10 minutes in a boiling water bath. Makes about 3¾ cups of syrup.
   A tablespoonful of elderberry syrup added to a vanilla shake makes a purple cow. The same added to a glass of lemonade turns it deep pink. Of course, the syrup is also good on pancakes, ice cream, and yogurt.

Elderberry-plum jelly

1 cup elderberry juice
1 cup plum juice
2 cups granulated sugar
   Read about plum juice, page 197. Read about jelly making, Appendix A.
   Stir ingredients together in a heavy kettle. Place over high heat and bring to a boil. Reduce the heat and, stirring occasionally, allow to boil gently until it reaches the jelling point. Test for doneness by using a jelly thermometer or use the spoon or cold saucer method. When done, remove the kettle from the heat and quickly skim off the foam, then pour the jelly into hot, sterile jars, leaving ¼-inch headspace. Cap the jars with two-piece screwband lids and process for 5 minutes in a boiling water bath. Makes 2 cups of jelly.

Elderberry-grape jelly

(See page 205 under Wild Grapes.)

Purple passion pie

crumb crust for a 9-inch pie
1 envelope unflavored gelatin or ½ teaspoon powdered (not flaked) agar
1 cup elderberry juice
2 eight-ounce packages cream cheese, softened to room temperature

½ cup sugar or honey

2 tablespoons lemon juice

    Press the crust into the pie pan and refrigerate or freeze it until ready to add the filling.

    Sprinkle the gelatin or agar over ¼ cup of the elderberry juice in a medium bowl and stir until thoroughly moistened. Heat the remaining elderberry juice to the boiling point. If you are using gelatin, pour the hot juice into the gelatin mixture and stir until the gelatin is dissolved. Set aside to cool. (To hasten cooling, place the bowl in a shallow pan of cold water; stir frequently.) If you are using agar, stir the agar mixture into the hot juice in the pot, then stir and cook until the agar has dissolved. Allow to cool only slightly.

    In a large bowl, combine the cream cheese, sugar or honey, and lemon juice. Beat with an electric mixer until smooth. With the mixer running at medium speed, gradually add the cooled gelatin mixture or the hot agar mixture to the cream cheese and continue beating until well blended. Pour this into the crust and refrigerate until firmly set (about 2 hours). Serve plain or spread with sour cream topping (below). Makes 6 to 8 servings.

    This recipe can be multiplied, and because it can be made ahead of time and is easy to serve, it works well as a dessert for a crowd. A camp cook who made it for sixty persons used large, rectangular pans instead of pie pans and simply sprinkled graham cracker crumbs into the bottom of the pans after generously greasing them with margarine. She cut the dessert into squares and added a dollop of sour cream topping to each square.

SOUR CREAM TOPPING

1 cup dairy sour cream

2 tablespoons sugar

1 teaspoon vanilla

few grains of salt

    Combine all the ingredients and stir until the sugar is dissolved. Spread topping over chilled pie.

Elderberry pie

(Read about elderberry seeds above.)

425 degree oven to start

pastry for a 2-crust 8-inch pie

3 cups elderberries

1 cup dairy sour cream

¼ cup flour

¾ cup granulated sugar

dash each of salt, cinnamon, and nutmeg

1 tablespoon butter

1 tablespoon sugar with a dash of cinnamon

    Roll out the pastry, arrange the bottom crust in the pie pan, and set aside. In a large bowl, combine the elderberries and sour cream. Sift together the flour, sugar, and seasonings, then add them to the elderberry mixture. Stir gently to combine. Ladle the mixture into the pastry-lined pan. Cut the butter into pieces and scatter them over the filling. Put the top crust in place and seal the edge. Make a 2-inch slash in the top crust to allow steam to escape while baking; sprinkle with the sugar and cinnamon. Bake at 425 degrees for 10 minutes, then reduce the heat to 350 and bake for another 25 minutes. Remove the pie from the oven and allow it to cool on a rack. Makes 6 servings.

Groundcherries

Physalis species

Nightshade family: Solanaceae

Description: Groundcherries are herbs, and several native species are found in the Great Plains. The plants may reach a height of 3 feet but usually are less than half that tall. Some are annuals, some perennials; some reproduce by seed, some by lateral roots or underground stems. Aboveground stems range from erect to sprawling, but usually are widely branched. The leaves may be smooth or covered with soft hairs and may be toothed or not. The flowers are bell-shaped and drooping and may be cream, yellow, or yellow-green, often with a dark center. Like the flowers, the fruits, which are berries with numerous seeds, hang singly from the axils of the leaves. Each is covered by a papery, inflated husk having 5 segments. The berry is green at first but ripens to a yellow or yellow green or reddish brown. The husk changes from green and moist to light green and finally dries to a light tan.

Distribution: Clammy groundcherry: in the eastern and central United States, some western states, and into Canada; scattered throughout the Great Plains (other species, scattered throughout the United States and into Canada).

Habitat: Open areas, along roadsides and fence rows, in prairies and pastures.

Edible parts: Ripe fruits only, cooked or uncooked. Ripe fruits will be yellow, yellow slightly tinged with green, or reddish. Ripe fruits of clammy ground cherry are yellow.

Season to collect: Autumn.

Cautions: Use the ripe fruits only. The groundcherry plant itself, as well as the green, *unripe* fruits, contains chemicals that are poisonous if eaten. Be aware that there are plants that have small, round yellow fruits *without papery husks*. These are not groundcherries and may be poisonous.

Additional information and recipes: All of the native groundcherries have edible fruit, but those with hairy leaves and stems usually have tastier fruits than those with smooth leaves and stems. An especially good tasting species is the clammy groundcherry, *Physalis heterophylla* Nees, which not only has soft hairs but is slightly sticky to the touch, leading to the name "clammy." It is a perennial, spreading by rootstocks, and its fruit ripens to a clear yellow.

In interviews with Plains Indian people in the early 1900s, the botanist and ethnographer Melvin Gilmore found that they readily distinguished one kind of groundcherry from another. "The fruits of the edible species, *P. heterophylla,* are made into a sauce for food by all these tribes," Gilmore wrote, adding that if a sufficient supply was found, fruits were dried for winter. Gilmore translated the Omaha-Ponca name for groundcherry as "forehead to pop," explaining that the name referred to the use children made of the inflated husks, "which they pop on the forehead in play."

Settler children played with groundcherries in the same way, popping them between their fingers or on their foreheads and calling them simply "poppers." Some settlers believed that groundcherries were poisonous, but for many settler families, groundcherries became an important dietary item, at times serving as the major source of fruit for sauce, jam, or pie. A woman from South Dakota, who remembered her mother's stories about early days on the prairie, said that at first, groundcherries were gathered from the wild, but it was soon learned that the plants could be grown near one's home. So when the fruits were ripe in autumn, her mother took some of the "best-tasting kind" and scattered them in the yard, crushing each under her shoe to press the seeds into the soil. The plants came up the following spring and later produced a crop of fruit only a few steps from the kitchen.

It is not possible to know which groundcherry the settlers considered to be the best-tasting kind, or whether that category included more than one species, but if you find a good groundcherry, you can use the method the settler woman used and plant the seeds in your own yard. Garden nurseries sell groundcherry seed under such names as husk tomato, strawberry tomato, and cape gooseberry. These, too, are easily grown from seed, but although often more prolific than the clammy groundcherry, they are not quite as tasty.

Sometimes in autumn, a cold snap will hit before the groundcherries are fully ripe. A hard freeze may ruin the fruit, but a light frost won't hurt them, and some persons believe a nip of cold may even hasten ripening. If a hard freeze is predicted and the groundcherries are not yet fully ripe but are already tinged with yellow, pick them and, leaving the husks on, shake them out in a single layer on a cookie sheet. Set them away in a dry dark place at room temperature. Sometimes they will continue to ripen; sometimes they won't. It may have to do with the species—readers may want to experiment.

To prepare ripe groundcherries, simply husk and wash them, refrigerating any that won't be used right away. Groundcherries are good eaten fresh as a nibble or added to salads, but they are more often served cooked in the form of jam, marmalade, or pie. Groundcherry sauce, like other fruit sauces, seems to be a thing of the past, but it is flavorful and makes an excellent, not-too-sweet dessert.

Least known is the groundcherry's talent for blending with meat, particularly fowl. The groundcherry-chicken soup recipe, below, is similar to Greek lemon soup, but the flavor is uniquely groundcherry and very good. If you are just beginning with groundcherries and wonder what to try first, I recommend the soup.

Groundcherry soup

1 ⅓ cups ripe groundcherries (husked)

1 quart chicken broth

⅔ cup cooked rice

2 eggs, separated

salt and freshly ground black pepper to taste

   Place the groundcherries and 1 cup of the broth in a saucepan and cook over medium heat until the fruit becomes soft—about 5 minutes. (Groundcherries burn easily, so check and stir often.) Remove from the heat and, using a blender or an egg beater, puree the groundcherries.

   Heat the remaining broth in a kettle, then add the groundcherries and the rice and stir well. Season with salt and pepper. Allow the broth to simmer, but turn off the heat before it begins to boil. Meanwhile, beat the egg whites until stiff, add the yolks, and continue beating until light and fluffy.

   The next step is especially important: slowly pour about 1 cup of the hot broth mixture into the beaten eggs, stirring only until blended, then slowly pour this mixture back into the remaining broth and stir well. Allow it to simmer for about 1 minute, then serve immediately. Note that once the soup is put together, high temperatures or reheating will cause it to curdle. (If it does curdle, the texture will be something like egg-drop soup—which you can say it is—the flavor will still be delicious.) Makes 4 servings.

   This soup is particularly good served with crusty bread and a fresh salad.

Groundcherry and lettuce salad with rosy cactus dressing

small head of iceberg lettuce or equivalent amount of other salad greens

small purple onion or other mild onion

1 cup groundcherries

freshly ground black pepper to taste

½ cup or more rosy cactus dressing (see page 214)

   Cut the base out of the lettuce and wash the head upside down under cold running water so that the water will run through the head, then tear the lettuce apart, still washing it in the water as you work. Allow the lettuce to drain. Tear the leaves into bite-size portions—somehow this makes lettuce taste better than if it is cut. Again set the lettuce aside to drain.

Meanwhile, cut the onion into very thin slices, then with your fingers, gently separate the rings. Check the lettuce pieces to make sure they have drained thoroughly, then combine the lettuce with the rings of onion and the groundcherries in a bowl. Cover the bowl and refrigerate for 1 hour or more until thoroughly chilled. Also chill the cactus dressing and, if you will use a different bowl or individual salad bowls for serving, chill these also.

To serve, reserve a few onion rings for decorating the top, then toss the lettuce, groundcherries, and remaining onion slices with the dressing and season with black pepper. Arrange onion rings on top. Or serve the salad, dressing, and pepper separately, to be combined at the table. Makes 4 to 6 servings.

Groundcherry sauce

4 cups groundcherries
¼ cup water
½ cup granulated sugar or honey, or sweeten to taste

Combine the fruit and water in a kettle. Cover with a lid and cook over medium heat for about 3 minutes. Stir in the sugar or honey and cook for about 4 minutes more. Serve chilled. Makes 4 to 6 servings.

Groundcherry-honey drizzle

1 ½ cups groundcherries
½ cup honey

Combine the groundcherries and honey in a saucepan and allow to boil gently for about 3 minutes. Remove from the heat and cool. Makes a little more than 1 cup. Store in a refrigerator.

This is good on yogurt and, although a bit runny, is wonderful on light rye or whole wheat toast. For variation, add 1 tablespoon lemon juice or a few drops of freshly squeezed ginger root juice to the mixture after it has cooled. (Buy ginger root in the produce section of a grocery store—peel and cut off a ½-inch piece, then use a garlic press to extract the juice.)

Groundcherry jam

4 cups groundcherries
2 tablespoons water
4 cups granulated sugar
3 tablespoons lemon juice

Read about jam making, Appendix A.

Put groundcherries and water into a large, heavy kettle. With a large spoon, crush some of the groundcherries to release the juice. Place over medium-high heat and stir several times until the mixture reaches the boiling point. Reduce the heat to medium, cover with a lid, and allow to boil gently for 5 minutes. Remove the lid and stir in the sugar and lemon juice. Boil gently, uncovered, for about 30 minutes or until clear and thick. To prevent burning, stir frequently as the mixture cooks and stir constantly after it begins to thicken. Remove from the heat and stir well, then ladle the jam into hot, sterile jars, leaving ¼ inch headspace. Cap the jars with two-piece screwband lids and process for 5 minutes in a boiling water bath. Makes a little more than 4 cups of jam.

Groundcherry marmalade

6 cups groundcherries

1 medium lemon

½ medium orange

3 cups sugar

½ teaspoon whole cloves

3-inch stick of cinnamon

Read about jam making, Appendix A.

Break the cinnamon and tie the pieces with the cloves in a square of cheesecloth or put them into a tea ball. Cut the lemon and orange into thin slices, then cut the slices into fourths. Set all of this aside.

Put the groundcherries into a large, heavy kettle and crush them with a potato masher. Place this over high heat and cook uncovered for about 5 minutes, stirring frequently. Add the sugar and stir and cook until the sugar dissolves. Allow to cook for another 5 minutes, stirring 2 or 3 times during this period. Add the pieces of lemon and orange and the spices. Cook for about 20 minutes or until the marmalade thickens and clears. To prevent burning, stir frequently as the mixture cooks, and stir constantly as the mixture thickens toward the end of cooking. Remove the kettle from the heat.

Remove and discard the bag of spices. Stir the marmalade and ladle it into hot, sterile jars, leaving ¼ inch headspace. Cap the jars with two-piece screwband lids and process for 5 minutes in boiling a water bath. Makes about 4 cups of marmalade.

Groundcherry pie

400 degree oven

pastry for a two-crust 8-inch pie

4 cups groundcherries

1 cup sugar

⅓ cup flour

dash of salt

2 teaspoons grated lemon rind (optional)

2 tablespoons margarine or butter

1 tablespoon sugar mixed with a dash of cinnamon and nutmeg

Roll out the pastry, place the bottom crust in the pan, and set it aside. Put the groundcherries into a mixing bowl. Combine the first amount of sugar with the flour and salt, then sift this over the groundcherries. If using lemon rind, add that also. Stir gently to mix. Pour the filling into the pie pan. Cut the margarine or butter into several pieces and scatter it over the fruit. Put the top crust into place and seal the edge. Cut a 2-inch slit in the top crust to allow steam to escape during baking. Sprinkle the top with the sugar and spices. Note that groundcherry pie is quite juicy—a cookie sheet under the pie pan may save having to clean the oven. Bake for 35 to 45 minutes. Cool before serving. Makes 6 servings.

Bite-size popper pies

350 degree oven

CRUST

1 cup unsalted butter, chilled

½ cup powdered sugar

2 cups all-purpose flour

dash of salt

Grease a 9 x 13–inch baking pan with butter and set it aside. Combine all of the ingredients in a medium bowl. With a pastry blender or two knives, cut the butter into the flour, sugar, and salt until the mixture is well blended. To form the crust, press the mixture into the baking pan, making a rim around the edges so that the fruit and juice will not run out when they are added later. Bake the crust until lightly browned—about 15 minutes.

FILLING

½ cup water

3 tablespoons minute tapioca

4 cups groundcherries

1 cup water

⅔ cup granulated sugar

1 tablespoon grated lemon rind

2 tablespoons fresh lemon juice

Stir the tapioca into the first amount of water and set it aside to soften for at least 10 minutes.

Put the groundcherries and the second amount of water into a kettle over high heat and bring it to a boil. Reduce the heat to medium-low, cover the kettle with a lid, and allow the mixture to simmer for about 12 minutes. Add the sugar and softened tapioca to the hot groundcherry mixture and, stirring constantly, cook until the tapioca becomes clear—about 3 minutes. Remove from the heat and stir in the lemon rind and juice. (The mixture will be thin, but will thicken during baking.)

Pour the hot mixture evenly over the crust and return the pan to the oven. Bake until the filling is thick but not browned—about 10 minutes. Remove from the oven and allow the crust to cool before cutting. Makes about 48 squares or "pies."

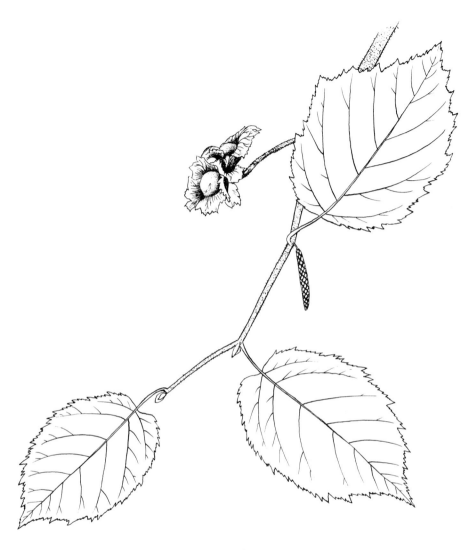

Hazelnut, American hazelnut, filbert
Corylus americana Walt.

Hazelnut, beaked hazelnut, filbert
Corylus cornuta Marsh.

Birch family: Betulaceae

Description: The hazelnuts are native shrubs often forming thickets, but sometimes occurring in scattered patterns or even alone. They may attain a height of up to 12 feet. The leaves of both species are alternate and oval with a pointed tip; the margins are doubly serrate, often irregularly so. Male and female flowers occur separately but on the same plant; both are small and lack petals. Male flowers develop in catkins that hang from the axils of leaves; female flowers develop in small clusters that resemble a single leaf bud. Both male and female flower buds form in late summer, wintering over to open in early spring. Hazelnuts may occur singly or in clusters, but each nut is enclosed in a leafy husk with a ragged opening. The husk of the American hazelnut encloses the nut but opens with what looks like a short ruffle to reveal the nut inside. The husk of the beaked hazelnut not only encloses the nut but extends, beaklike, 1 to 2 inches beyond.

Distribution: American hazelnut: eastern and north-central United States and into Canada; eastern and northern portions of the Great Plains, from Minnesota south to Oklahoma and east to parts of Iowa and Missouri. Beaked hazelnut: scattered in the northern United States and into Canada; northern Great Plains, including Minnesota and North Dakota, and the Black Hills of South Dakota.

Habitat: Rocky hillsides, borders of woods, creek banks, ravines, and fence rows.

Seasons to collect: American hazelnuts in early autumn; beaked hazelnuts in late summer or early autumn.

Edible parts: Nutmeats, cooked or uncooked.

Cautions: Wear gloves for picking. The hairs on the leafy husks covering the nuts are irritating to the skin—those on the beaked hazelnut particularly so.

Additional information and recipes: Hazelnuts were once so numerous along the bluffs of the Missouri River that in autumn, families would go nutting and bring back basketsful to store for winter. Now, in many of these areas, few hazelnut shrubs can be found. Squirrels and certain birds are quick to harvest any nuts that are produced, and deer take a heavy toll on the shrubs, but you might consider planting hazelnuts in your own yard. They are attractive and require little care, and by having them close at hand, you are more likely to get a share of the crop.

Although the mature nuts and husks appear dry, they contain enough moisture to foster the growth of mold, so as soon as you can, spread your harvest out to dry, preferably in a single layer on a screen or in a large cardboard box. Place this where squirrels and birds will not have access. In a week or so, with gloves on, remove the husks and store the nuts in a mesh bag or other container that will allow for circulation of air—nuts stored in closed containers may still be subject to mold. However you bundle them, they must be stored in a cool, dry place. Hazelnuts need time to cure—they are ready to use when the nutmeats become crisp. After the nuts have cured, some persons remove the shells. If you do that, the shelled nutmeats must be stored in a tightly covered container in a cold place, such as a refrigerator.

Hazelnuts can be used in numerous ways. Long treasured for baked goods, they are also delicious in salads or cooked with vegetables or meat. For some recipes it is best to first toast the hazelnuts and rub off the skins, but for others, such as hazelnut cake (below), the skins add a desired flavor.

To toast hazelnuts

If the hazelnuts are not shelled, do that first. Then place the nutmeats in a shallow pan and bake them at 350 degrees for 10 to 15 minutes or until the skins begin to crack. Remove the pan from the oven and shake the nutmeats out onto a kitchen towel—one with a rough surface works best. When they are cool enough to handle, slip your hands under the towel and, bringing up the sides, shake the nutmeats toward the center, then rub them with the towel to remove the skins. Shake and pick out the nutmeats and discard the skins. If not to be used within a few days, toasted nutmeats must be refrigerated or frozen in a tightly covered container.

Spiced chicken with hazelnuts

350 degree oven

PREPARING THE RICE

1 cup short-grain brown rice

2 ¼ cups water

Use a medium pot (about 3 quarts) with a tightly fitting lid. Wash the rice well, then put it and the water into the pot, but do not cover. Place over high heat until the water reaches a full boil, then turn the heat to very low, cover with a lid, and allow the rice to cook for 35 minutes *without lifting the lid.*

Turn off the heat and allow the rice to remain in the pot until you are ready to add it to the other ingredients.

PREPARING THE CHICKEN

2 chicken breasts, cut in half
cooking oil
¼ teaspoon ground cinnamon
¼ teaspoon ground cloves
¼ teaspoon ground nutmeg
salt and freshly ground black pepper to taste
½ cup thinly sliced green onion, including tops
2 tablespoons grated orange rind
⅓ cup fresh orange juice
½ dried currants (from a grocery store)
1 inch piece fresh ginger root, peeled and cut into fourths
2 to 3 cloves garlic
1 cup toasted hazelnut kernels, skins removed

   Have ready a 2- to 3-quart baking dish with a cover. Also, have all of the ingredients prepared and ready to work with—the chicken washed, the onion sliced (cut diagonally for the best flavor), the orange peel grated, the garlic cloves and ginger root peeled, and the hazelnuts toasted—or toast the hazelnuts while the chicken bakes.

   Pat the chicken dry with a paper towel and, if desired, remove the skin and bones. Place a skillet over medium-high heat and pour in a small amount of oil. Add the chicken and brown it for a few minutes on each side. While the chicken is browning, sprinkle it lightly with the spices, salt, and pepper. (I confess I don't measure the spices; I simply sprinkle lightly). When the chicken has browned, move it from the skillet to the baking dish.

   Set the heat at medium. Put the green onion slices into the drippings in the skillet and cook them, stirring frequently, until they are tender but not browned. Add the orange peel and the currants; stir and cook for about 30 seconds. Use a garlic press to squeeze the garlic cloves and ginger root, allowing the juices from each to drip directly into the skillet. Add the orange juice and stir well. Cook for about 30 seconds, then remove from the heat.

   Spoon the mixture from the skillet over the chicken. Cover the dish with the lid and bake for 1 hour. Remove from the oven and carefully lift the pieces of chicken over onto another dish. Add the cooked rice to the mixture in the bottom of the dish the chicken was baked in and stir to combine. Taste the mixture and add salt if needed. Return the chicken to the baking dish and partially bury each piece in the rice mixture. Cover with a lid and bake for another 15 minutes to blend the flavors. Just before serving, scatter the hazelnuts over the top. Makes 4 generous servings.

This recipe can also be used with wild fowl, such as pheasant or quail.

Hazelnut cake

350 degree oven

4 cups hazelnut kernels (about 20 ounces)
3 tablespoons all-purpose flour
1 teaspoon baking powder
8 eggs, separated and at room temperature
1¼ cups sugar
¼ teaspoon salt
1 teaspoon vanilla extract

Heavily grease a bundt cake pan or two 5 x 9 x 3–inch loaf pans with margarine or butter, then dust with flour and set aside. (Be careful not to miss even a small space, or the cake will stick to the pan.)

Put the hazelnuts into a blender, about ¾ cup at a time, and process until finely chopped. This should make about 5 cups of hazelnut meal; set this aside also.

Stir the flour and baking powder together, then sift this mixture onto a piece of waxed paper. Separate the eggs, using a large bowl for the whites and a large bowl for the yolks. With an electric mixer, beat the whites until stiff—about 4 minutes. Beat the yolks until foamy, then gradually add the sugar and salt, continuing to beat for about 4 minutes or until the mixture is very thick and light.

Mix the flour into the ground nuts and gently stir this into the beaten yolks. Add the vanilla, then gently work the beaten whites into the beaten yolk mixture. Pour the batter into the greased pan (or pans) and bake until the surface springs back when lightly touched at the center—about 45 minutes.

Remove the cake from the oven and allow it to cool for 10 minutes, then remove it from the pan by loosening the edges with a table knife and turning it out onto a wire rack. (If you used a bundt pan, don't forget to loosen the edge around the center as well.) Cover with a kitchen towel until cooled, then place it in a tightly covered container.

With so little flour, this is a rich cake, better sprinkled lightly with powdered sugar than frosted. It freezes well and actually slices better when cold. Makes 12 to 16 servings.

Shagbark hickory, shellbark hickory
Carya ovata (P. Mill.) K. Koch

Kingnut, big shellbark hickory
Carya laciniosa (Michx. f.) Loud.

Walnut family: Juglandaceae

Description: These are tall native trees reaching a height of 60 or more feet. Their trunks are distinctive, with gray bark that separates into long strips. Often loosening from one or both ends, these strips give the trees a shaggy appearance and, as its name implies, the shagbark hickory is the shaggier of the two. The leaves of both are alternate and pinnately compound with the terminal leaflet usually larger that the rest. Typically, the shagbark hickory has 5 leaflets, the kingnut hickory 7 to 9 leaflets. The surface of the leaflets is green and smooth above, paler and with some hairs below. The margins of the leaflets are serrate and have very small hairs, which occur fairly regularly all along the edge on the kingnut, but occur in tufts on the shagbark hickory. Male and female flowers are borne on the same tree and are small. The male flowers hang in catkins on the previous year's branches or on new growth. The female flowers occur in clusters on new branches. Nuts may be solitary or occur in clusters of 2 or 3. Each is encased in a thick husk that splits into four quarters—often as soon as the nut falls from the tree. The nut itself is round, light tan, and very hard, with several ridges running lengthwise and terminating in a point.

Distribution: Scattered throughout much of the eastern United States and into Canada; along the eastern edge of the Great Plains as far north as eastern Kansas—shagbark hickory extends into southeastern Nebraska and western Iowa.

Habitat: Woods, especially wooded hillsides and river banks.

Edible parts: Cooked or uncooked nutmeats.

Season to collect: Early autumn to midautumn.

Cautions: Hickory nuts are so delicious that it is tempting to take all that can be found, but leave some for squirrels who rely heavily on native nuts for winter survival.

Additional information and recipes: The mockernut hickory, *Carya tomentosa* Nutt., occurs in much the same area as the species described above. It bears edible nuts but is less desirable due to its extremely hard shell. The black hickory, *Carya texana* Buckl., has good-tasting nuts but is less common in the Great Plains. Neither of these latter species has the characteristic shaggy bark of the kingnut or shagbark. The nuts of the bitternut hickory,

Carya cordiformis (Wang.) K. Koch, are strongly bitter (but not harmful if tasted). They resemble those of the edible hickories, but have much thinner husks. Bitternut hickory trees do not have shaggy bark and the winter leaf buds at the tips of the branches are golden yellow.

Although the enjoyment of hickory nuts is mostly in the eating, a good share of it is in the gathering. There is something about hiking through the trees and searching for the nuts that adds to the pleasure of eating the foods made from them.

The flavor of a hickory nut soon after it falls is not the same as after it has had time to cure. When ready to eat, the nutmeats should be crisp and flavorful—uncured nutmeats are pliable and lack flavor. To cure, shake the nuts out onto a screen or into a large open box. Hickory nuts may be stored in the shell in a cool, dry place or cracked and then stored in a refrigerator or freezer.

From time to time as you inspect your harvest, you may notice that some of the nuts have small holes. Likely these were made by insects who chewed their way out, rather than in. Larvae of this insect may still be present in other nuts. For this reason, hickory nuts are often cracked and picked over as soon as possible after the nuts have cured. Nutmeats must be refrigerated or frozen in tightly covered containers.

Because the shells are very hard, the nuts are best cracked with a hammer or nut-cracking machine; an ordinary nutcracker is not adequate. Use a nut-pick or toothpick to remove the meats from the shells, then inspect them carefully, picking out any pieces of shell.

Hickory nuts are versatile and taste wonderful in anything to which they are added. Theirs is a unique mellow flavor unlike any other, and some recipes, such as persimmon pudding, are simply not the same when made with other nutmeats. They are good baked with squash or yams or added to salads, but perhaps hickory nuts are most loved for their use in cakes.

Mother's favorite hickory cake

375 degree oven

7 egg whites

2 ¼ cups granulated sugar

1 cup margarine or butter

1 teaspoon salt

3 ¾ cups all-purpose flour

4 teaspoons baking powder

1 ⅓ cups water

2 teaspoons vanilla extract

½ to 1 cup hickory nutmeats, chopped

Grease a 9 x 13–inch cake pan, or prepare three 9-inch layer pans by placing two circles of waxed paper, cut to fit, into the bottom of each and greasing the sides with margarine or butter; set aside. Reserve 2 tablespoons of the nutmeats to sprinkle over the frosting.

In a large bowl, beat the egg whites with an electric mixer until foamy, then gradually beat in ½ cup of the sugar and continue beating until very stiff. In another large bowl, again using the mixer, cream the margarine or butter with the salt and the remainder of the sugar.

Sift the flour and baking powder together three times (sifting onto waxed paper works well), then add this and the water alternately in halves to the margarine or butter mixture, beating well with the mixer after each addition. (The batter will be thick.) Stir in the vanilla and chopped nutmeats, then slowly fold in the beaten whites. Pour into the prepared pan or pans and bake until the surface springs back when touched lightly at the center— about 40 minutes for a rectangular cake, 25 to 30 minutes for layers.

Remove the cake or cakes from the oven and place on wire racks to cool. With layers, wait only 15 to 20 minutes and, while the cakes are still warm, loosen them around the edges with a knife and turn them out onto the racks. Peel off the waxed paper but lay it back onto the cakes to prevent drying. When thoroughly cooled, frost the cake with fluffy frosting. Hickory cake freezes well, frosted or unfrosted. Makes about 18 servings.

FLUFFY FROSTING

1 cup milk

4 tablespoons all-purpose flour

½ cup margarine or butter

1 cup granulated sugar (or use half granulated, half brown sugar)

1 teaspoon vanilla

Combine the milk and flour in a small saucepan and stir with a whisk or fork until well blended. Place over medium heat and stir constantly until the mixture bubbles and thickens. Remove the saucepan from the heat and set it aside until thoroughly cooled.

Place the margarine or butter in a medium bowl and, with an electric mixer, beat until light. Gradually add the sugar and continue beating until very light and fluffy. Add the vanilla and the cooled milk-flour mixture and beat until well blended. Spread on the cake and sprinkle with chopped nutmeats. This frosting freezes well either spread on a cake or in a tightly closed container.

The following recipe calls for whole wheat flour. Whole wheat flour available in grocery stores is usually a mixture of hard whole wheat and all-purpose flour. It will work for this recipe, but better results can be obtained by using pure whole wheat pastry flour, which is milled from low-gluten, soft wheat. If you don't find whole wheat pastry flour in a regular grocery store, look for it at health food stores or food co-ops.

Hickory-carrot cake

325 degree oven

2 cups whole wheat flour
1 ½ teaspoons baking soda
½ teaspoon salt
1 ½ teaspoons ground cinnamon
1 teaspoon ground nutmeg or allspice
1 cup vegetable oil
1 cup granulated sugar
4 eggs
2 teaspoons vanilla extract
1 cup minus 2 tablespoons plain yogurt
4 cups finely grated carrots (about ¾ pound)
½ cup coarsely chopped hickory nutmeats

Grease a 9 x 13–inch cake pan with margarine or butter and set it aside. Grate and set aside the carrots also.

Sift the flour, soda, salt, and spices together onto a sheet of waxed paper. In a large bowl, stir the oil and sugar together and beat until smooth with an electric mixer. Add the eggs, one at a time, beating well after each. Add the vanilla with the last egg, then add the flour mixture and beat again. Add the yogurt and beat until smooth and well blended. Gently fold in the grated carrots and nutmeats, then pour the batter into the greased pan. Bake for 40 minutes or until the surface springs back when touched lightly at the center. When done, allow the cake to cool on a rack and when completely cooled, frost with the cream cheese frosting. Makes 12 to 15 servings.

CREAM CHEESE FROSTING

1 eight-ounce package cream cheese
2 tablespoons margarine or butter
2 tablespoons plain yogurt
¼ cup honey or sifted powdered sugar
½ teaspoon vanilla extract

Remove the cream cheese and the margarine or butter from the refrigerator and allow them to soften to room temperature. When soft, place both in a medium mixing bowl and beat with an electric mixer until blended. Add the remaining ingredients and beat until smooth and creamy, then spread on the cooled cake. If not to be served directly, the cake must be covered and refrigerated.

Hickory-carrot cake is even better the second day, after the frosting and cake have had time to mellow. The frosted cake may be frozen for serving later; the frosting freezes well either spread on the cake or in a tightly closed container.

Hickory-apple cake

350 degree oven

⅓ cup flour

1 teaspoon baking powder

¼ teaspoon salt

1 egg

⅔ cup granulated sugar

1 teaspoon vanilla extract

1 cup peeled and chopped apple

½ cup hickory nutmeats

Grease an 8 x 8–inch square cake pan with margarine and set it aside.

Sift the flour, baking powder, and salt together onto a piece of waxed paper. Put the egg, sugar, and vanilla into a medium bowl and beat with an electric mixer until thick and creamy. To this add the chopped apple and nutmeats; stir well. Add the flour mixture and stir until all the ingredients are well mixed. Pour into the prepared pan and bake for 45 minutes or until the surface springs back when touched lightly at the center. No frosting is needed. Makes 9 to 12 servings.

Black walnut

Juglans nigra L.

Walnut family: Juglandaceae

Description: The black walnut is a large native tree sometimes attaining a height of more than 100 feet. The bark is dark gray brown and rough, with deep fissures. The leaves are alternate and pinnately compound. The leaflets are narrow and tapering, the upper surface dull green and smooth, and the lower surface lighter and with fine hairs. The leaflets occur in opposite pairs with a terminal leaflet; the margins are toothed. The inconspicuous male and female flowers occur on the same tree. Male flowers are borne in catkins that hang from branches of the previous year; the female flowers occur on new growth near the ends of branches. The nuts may develop singly or in groups of 2 or 3, occasionally 4, at the ends of branches. Each nut is covered by a thick light-green husk, which becomes black later in the season. The nut itself is round and black with a rough, fissured surface. The nutmeat inside is soft and somewhat oily.

Distribution: Throughout much of the eastern United States, north to Massachusetts, south to northern Florida; in the Great Plains, through much of Oklahoma and Kansas, along the Missouri River though Nebraska and into South Dakota; rare in southeastern North Dakota.

Habitat: Rich soil in woods and bottom lands, along streams and roadsides; often planted near homes and on farms.

Edible parts: Nutmeats, cooked or uncooked.

Season to collect: Autumn.

Cautions: Be aware that the juice from walnut husks is one of nature's most permanent dyes. It will stain cloth, skin, and even concrete. When husking walnuts, wear old clothes and gloves, and work where dark brown stains won't matter.

Additional information and recipes: Success with black walnuts begins at the tree. As soon as a few nuts fall to the ground on their own and you can dent the husk with your thumb, the nuts on that tree are ready to harvest. At this time, the husks will still be light green and fairly firm. If allowed to remain on the nuts, the husks will become black and soften to a moist mush, then eventually shrivel and dry.

It is understandable that many persons remove the husks at the shriveled-and-dry stage, because earlier they would have to contend with the juice and the prospect of stained hands. However, the strong juice that stains hands also penetrates the nutshell and alters the flavor of the nutmeats inside. For this reason, it is best to remove the walnut husks when the nuts first become ripe and the husks are still green.

There are numerous methods and machines for removing walnut husks, but the following method is simple and works well. Put on old rubber-soled shoes, find a flat rock or piece of concrete, and roll each walnut back and forth under your foot. Wear heavy plastic gloves (such as the kind sold for re-finishing furniture) and after you've broken open the husks, remove the nuts by hand, tossing them into a 5-gallon bucket as you work. (In the wild, the husks decompose, enriching the soil around the walnut tree, but walnut husks contain chemicals that can inhibit the growth of other plants, so it is best to discard them.)

When the bucket is about half full, pour in enough water to cover the nuts. Using a stout stick, a broom handle, or a large drain plunger, pound the nuts vigorously for several minutes, then holding them back with whatever tool you are using, pour off as much water as possible. Add fresh water and again vigor-ously work the nuts up and down, draining when the water becomes stained. Repeat one more time, draining well. Shake the nuts into a large shallow con-tainer such as a cardboard box—if necessary, use more than one box so all of the nuts are spread out in a single layer. Repeat this process with the remainder of the unhusked nuts (setting the boxes out of the reach of squirrels).

If you do get a stain where it will be a problem, try a liquid stain remover. If applied soon after the stain occurs, this product will help. (Years ago, black walnut husks were boiled to make a rich brown dye for dyeing cloth and the tendency of the stain to be permanent was considered one of the black wal-nut's greatest virtues.)

About 2 weeks are required for the nuts to dry and another 2 weeks for them to cure. Nutmeats are ready to use when they are crisp and slightly oily, but opinions differ about when and how the nuts should be cracked. Some persons crack all of the nuts early in the season, storing the nutmeats in glass jars in a cool place. Others prefer to wait months, some even a year or two. If I have time, I crack most of my harvest about Thanksgiving of the same year they grew, but you may wish to sample walnuts at various times to determine when you think they are at their best. Walnut cracking devices are available through catalogs and stores and although some are expensive, if you have a lot of walnuts to process, are well worth the money. Most often, black wal-nuts are simply cracked with a hammer on a hard surface. There are various theories about how to position a walnut for cracking so that the nutmeats inside will remain as whole as possible, but standing a nut on end, then tilting it slightly and delivering one or more good blows with the hammer will usually open it satisfactorily. Also, walnuts that have been out of their husks for more than 3 months will crack better if covered with boiling water the night before and allowed to soak until morning. Finally, it may be helpful to know that 1 pound of walnuts in the shell will produce about 1 cup of nutmeats.

After the nuts are cracked, use a nutpick or toothpick to remove the meats. Work carefully, trying to avoid getting pieces of broken shell in with the meats. Of course, it is impossible not to get a few fragments mixed in, so the next step is to look over the nutmeats and remove even the smallest bit of shell. Do this by examining only a small portion at a time—a magnifying glass is a great help. To store, allow the nutmeats to dry overnight in an open container, then shake them into jars, cover with lids, and store in a refrigerator or freezer.

Traditionally, black walnuts have been used in candies, baked goods, and ice cream, but the flavor also complements baked squash and yams, as well as fresh or cooked fruit. In combination with yogurt, black walnuts make a delicious dressing for salads.

Black walnut caramels, toffee, and fudge are delicious and easy to make, but if not stored properly, their quality quickly deteriorates. If stored in tightly covered containers, fudge and toffee may be refrigerated or frozen. Caramels that will be eaten soon after cooking may be dusted with powdered sugar and arranged in a single layer on a plate, but caramels that will be stored will stick together if not individually wrapped in waxed paper or cellophane. If kept more than 2 weeks, caramels should be frozen.

For caramels that will be wrapped, it is necessary to give thought to the wrappers before making the candy. Although waxed paper will do, cellophane, such as that used to wrap baskets of fruit, provides better protection and is more attractive. Clear or colored cellophane may be purchased at craft and hobby shops year-round and at grocery stores before major holidays. It may help to know that cellophane usually measures 20 inches wide, this recipe makes about 90 pieces of candy, and a good size for a wrapper is 3 x 5 inches.

Black walnut caramels

1 ½ cups heavy cream
2 cups granulated sugar
1 cup light corn syrup
1 cup (2 sticks) butter

1 teaspoon vanilla extract

½ cup black walnut meats

Grease a 9 x 13 x 2–inch pan with butter and set it aside.

Use a large kettle and a long-handled spoon. If possible, use a candy thermometer, and note that when reading a thermometer, it is important to
bend over and read it straight on. When read from above, incorrect readings
can easily occur. If you don't have a candy thermometer, set out a cup of ice
water. You can test for doneness by dripping a few drops of hot candy into
the ice water—when the drops hold together and are firm yet chewy, the
candy is done.

In the kettle, combine ½ cup of the cream with the sugar, syrup, and butter.
Cook uncovered over low heat for 30 minutes, then stir in the remaining cup of
cream. Cook over medium-low heat until the mixture reaches 248 degrees on a
candy thermometer or proves done with the ice water test. Cooking time will
vary with the size and shape of the kettle, but 45 to 60 minutes is typical.

Remove the kettle from the heat and allow it to cool for about 10 minutes,
then stir in the vanilla and nuts and pour the candy into the greased pan.
While still slightly warm, cut the caramel into bite-sized pieces, or shape it
with your hands into a long rope about 1 inch thick and cut off ¼-inch slices
(this goes fast with kitchen shears). Wrap each piece, twisting the ends of the
wrapper securely. Makes about 90 pieces of caramel. To store, freeze or refrigerate in a tightly closed container.

Many persons have never tasted old-fashioned fudge made without marshmallow creme. The following recipe predates the marshmallow versions and
is delicious. It is surprisingly simple and quick to make, but do pay attention
to timing.

Black walnut fudge

4 cups granulated sugar

⅔ cup cocoa

1 cup evaporated milk

½ cup light corn syrup

1 cup (2 sticks) butter or margarine

2 teaspoons vanilla extract

½ cup coarsely broken black walnut meats

Have ready a clock or watch with a second hand. Grease a pan such as a 7 x
11 x 2–inch glass baking dish, then set it aside.

To avoid boiling over, use a large kettle—one having a capacity of 4 quarts is ideal. If you don't have a kettle that large, halve the recipe and use a 2-quart pot. (Also, use a smaller baking dish.) In either case, use a long-handled spoon.

In a large bowl, stir the sugar and cocoa together until well mixed. Put the milk, syrup, and margarine or butter into the kettle, then add the sugar-cocoa mixture. Stir carefully so that grains of sugar are not cast onto the side of the kettle above the surface of the liquid—this can cause the fudge to be grainy. Place the kettle over medium-low heat; stir until the sugar has dissolved, then turn the heat to medium-high. When the mixture reaches a full rolling boil, begin timing. Stir and boil for 1½ minutes. Remove the kettle from the heat. Allow the fudge to cool until the kettle is still quite warm but not too hot to touch—usually from 20 to 40 minutes, depending on the size and shape of the kettle. Add the vanilla and nutmeats. Beat vigorously with the spoon until the fudge begins to thicken, then beat only a few more strokes before pouring it into the greased pan and spreading it into the corners with the spoon. When the fudge is cool, use a sharp knife to cut it into squares. Store in a tightly covered container—do not wrap in aluminum foil or plastic wrap because these products may cause the fudge to mold.

This fudge is greatly improved if allowed to mellow for 24 hours. For use within a few days, simply keep it in a cool place; for longer storage, it must be refrigerated or frozen. Makes about 3 dozen large pieces of fudge.

Black walnut toffee
¾ cup black walnut meats
½ cup (1 stick) butter
½ cup granulated sugar
1 tablespoon light or dark corn syrup
1 teaspoon vanilla extract

You will need a clock or watch with a second hand. Close timing and the color of the toffee will tell when it is done.

Have ready a shallow heat-resistant pan or cookie sheet (greasing is not necessary). Combine all the ingredients except the vanilla in a heavy 10-inch skillet over medium-high heat. Bring to a boil, stirring constantly so that the oil in the butter does not separate from the other ingredients. Continuing to stir, boil for 2 to 3 minutes—it is done when it turns a light caramel color. Be careful not to cook too long. When the color is right, remove the skillet from the heat and stir in the vanilla. Immediately pour the toffee into the shallow pan and spread it out with the back of the spoon. When the toffee is cool, break it into about 50 bite-sized pieces and put it into a container with a tightly fitting cover. Both texture and flavor are improved by allowing the toffee to mellow overnight at room temperature, but for longer storage it must be refrigerated or frozen.

Mom's black walnut bread pudding

3 5 0 degree oven

3 slices white bread (about 3 cups when torn into pieces)

1 ½ cup milk

2 eggs

⅓ cup granulated sugar

1 teaspoon vanilla extract

dash each of cinnamon and nutmeg

¼ cup black walnut meats

For bread pudding, slightly stale (but not moldy) bread is preferred because it retains its texture better than fresh bread. If you have fresh bread, the tendency to become gummy can be lessened by toasting it and allowing the slices to cool uncovered.

Grease an 8 x 8–inch baking dish or 1 ½ quart casserole and set it aside. In a mixing bowl, combine all of the ingredients except the bread and nutmeats. Beat with a whisk or egg beater until the sugar has dissolved.

Tear each slice of bread into several pieces. Add the bread to the milk mixture and stir well, then wait for about 5 minutes so that the bread will become thoroughly moistened. Using two forks, tear the pieces of bread into even smaller pieces. Add the nutmeats and stir well. Pour the mixture into the greased dish.

Bake until the pudding is set and slightly puffed—45 to 60 minutes, depending on the shape of the dish, then remove it from the oven and allow it to cool for 10 to 15 minutes. Bread pudding is best if served slightly warm with very cold unsweetened cream. If you can't use cream, try the berry milk, Appendix B. Makes 5 to 6 servings. (The recipe may be doubled, but use a larger dish and increase the baking time.)

The next recipe came out of the hard times of the 1930s—at least that is a story handed down in my family. In farming areas when grain was ready to be threshed, neighbors would arrange to work together to harvest one family's fields, then another family's, and so on. The men worked in the fields; the women cooked and served the meals. It was hard work and threshers were known for their hearty appetites. Sometimes it was difficult to have enough eggs for the baked goods needed to feed these hungry crews, because during the extremely hot, dry summers there were times when the hens quit laying. Even if eggs were available at a store, few families had money to buy them. One of our aunts came up with this recipe for eggless cookies to help solve that problem. The cookies were served so often during threshing that they came to be known as "Threshermen's Cookies," and they were so good that they are still made today.

Threshermen's cookies

350 degree oven
2½ cups all-purpose flour
1 teaspoon soda
1 teaspoon baking powder
½ teaspoon salt
1 teaspoon cinnamon
1 cup water
1 cup sugar
½ cup (1 stick) margarine or butter
1 cup raisins
1 teaspoon vanilla extract
½ to 1 cup black walnut meats

Lightly grease two cookie sheets with margarine or butter and set them aside. Sift the flour, soda, baking powder, salt, and cinnamon together; set this aside also.

Cut the margarine or butter into pieces and put these and the water, sugar, and raisins into a medium-sized pot over high heat. When the mixture comes to a full boil, remove it from the heat and immediately add the sifted dry ingredients all at one time. Stir until well blended. Add the vanilla and nutmeats and stir again. Drop by teaspoonsful onto the cookie sheets. Bake for 15 minutes or until nicely browned. Remove the cookies from the oven and allow them to cool for about 5 minutes, then while still warm, frost with powdered sugar frosting (below). Makes about 3 dozen cookies.

To store, frost first, then refrigerate or freeze in a tightly covered container.

POWDERED SUGAR FROSTING
1½ cups powdered sugar
3 tablespoons margarine or butter, softened
1 tablespoon boiling water
½ teaspoon vanilla extract

In a medium bowl, combine all ingredients and beat with a large spoon or with an electric mixer until smooth and creamy.

Black walnut wafers

325 degree oven
1 cup powdered sugar
¼ cup all-purpose flour
¼ teaspoon baking powder
¼ teaspoon salt
¼ cup egg white (whites of 2 medium eggs)
½ teaspoon vanilla
½ to ¾ cup coarsely chopped black walnut meats

Note that these cookies are somewhat difficult to remove from the cookie sheet, especially if they are not baked long enough. In removing them it is helpful to have ready more than one pancake turner because a small ridge of cookie dough soon adheres to the front of the turner and you may need to reach for a clean one to finish the job. Also, it is important to measure the egg white in order to use the exact amount called for.

Grease two cookie sheets with margarine or butter and set them aside.

Sift the dry ingredients together into a medium-sized bowl, then add the egg whites and vanilla; stir until well blended. Add the nutmeats and stir again. Drop by half teaspoonsful onto the cookie sheets. Place one cookie sheet into the oven, but wait about 10 minutes before putting the second one in. This way you will have time to remove the cookies from one pan before the other one is ready. Bake the cookies until lightly browned all over—about 20 minutes.

Take the cookie sheet from the oven and remove the cookies immediately. If the last few cookies stick, put the sheet back into the oven for about a minute and try again. Makes about 36 cookies.

Although their tendency to stick is a bother, these cookies are unusually crisp and tasty—well worth the trouble.

Black walnut loaf cake

350 degree oven
⅓ cup butter (softened to room temperature)
1 cup brown sugar
2 eggs, separated
½ cup milk
1⅓ cups all-purpose flour
2 teaspoons baking powder

¼ teaspoon salt

1 teaspoon vanilla

½ cup chopped black walnut meats

Grease and flour a 5 x 9–inch loaf pan and set it aside. In a medium-sized bowl, beat the egg whites with an electric mixer until stiff; set this aside also.

In a large bowl, combine the butter and sugar and beat until fluffy. Add the egg yolks and milk and beat again—the mixture will have a creamy, curdled appearance. Sift the flour, baking powder, and salt together and add to the creamy mixture. Beat well, then stir in the vanilla and nutmeats. Gently fold in the beaten egg whites. Pour the batter into the prepared pan and bake for about 45 minutes. Remove the cake from the pan and allow it to cool on a wire rack. No frosting is needed. Makes 8 servings.

Black walnut and yogurt dressing

1 cup vanilla-flavored yogurt

1 tablespoon coarsely chopped black walnut meats

1 tablespoon powdered sugar or honey

Toast the nutmeats in a 350 degree oven for 10 to 12 minutes. Remove and allow to cool. Place the nutmeats on a paper towel, bring up the edges and rub the nutmeats with the towel to remove the loose skins. Remove the nutmeats from the towel, leaving the skins behind. Discard the towel and skins.

Stir the nutmeats and other ingredients together in a small bowl. Cover and chill for at least 1 hour before serving. This dressing is good spooned over fruit or mixed into fruit salad. It is particularly good drizzled over chilled slices of banana or canned spiced apple rings.

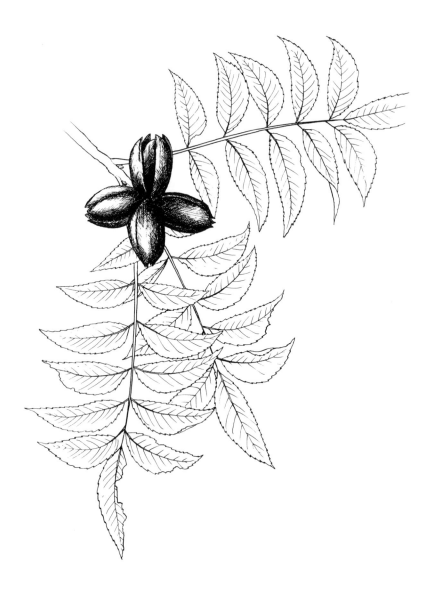

Pecan, wild pecan

Carya illinoensis (Wang.) K. Koch

Walnut family: Juglandaceae

Description: The wild pecan is a large native tree sometimes reaching a height of 80 feet or more. The leaves are alternate and pinnately compound. The leaflets are narrow and pointed with serrate margins; the upper surface is dull green and smooth, the lower surface paler and mostly smooth but with tufts of hair in the axils of the veins. The male flowers are borne in loose, slender catkins hanging in groups of three; the female flowers occur singly or in short spikes at the end of new growth. The nuts are oblong and light brown, often with irregular black spots or streaks. Each nut is encased in a 4-part leathery husk, which usually splits open while still attached to the branch, allowing the nut to fall free.

Distribution: Central portion of the eastern United States, range extended south and east by cultivation; southeastern portion of the Great Plains, scattered in Iowa and eastern Nebraska where planted.

Habitat: Woods, hillsides, rich bottom lands; sometimes in yards and planted commercially in groves.

Edible parts: Nutmeats, cooked or uncooked.

Season to collect: Mid to late autumn.

Cautions: No particular cautions.

Additional information and recipes: Unlike black walnuts, pecans are relatively easy to harvest, and their shells are not difficult to crack. When mature, the nuts usually fall on their own, and as soon as a few fall, it is a sign that others will also come down easily. A long stick can be used to reach and shake the branches (which are often high above the ground), but take care not to injure the tree. With pecans, it is best to collect only the nuts that fall free of their husks or have loose husks—an unloosened husk usually means that the nutmeat inside did not mature or is otherwise defective.

Before being stored, pecans must be allowed to dry. Shake them out onto a screen or into a large cardboard box and put them where they will not be found by squirrels. About 3 weeks after they fall from the tree, the nuts will be cured and ready to eat, but you can test their readiness by cracking and tasting a few nutmeats. They should be flavorful and crisp.

After the pecans have dried and cured, store them in mesh bags in a cool, dry place. For long storage, they must be kept cold—if kept frozen they can be stored for more than a year. Once shelled, pecan nutmeats have a short shelf life—refrigerate or freeze them in tightly covered containers for extended storage.

Pecans are so often used in baked goods and sweets that their compatibility with other foods is sometimes overlooked. The flavor of pecans, particularly when toasted, is delicious with rice, fruits, vegetables, and meats.

To toast pecan meats:

Toasting pecans can be tricky—if not baked enough, they will lack flavor, if overdone, they will have a strong aftertaste. The number of minutes required to toast pecans depends on the age of the nuts, their moisture content, and even on the particular oven used. A good method for determining the correct time for your oven is to put a few pecan meats into a shallow pan at 350 degrees and check the flavor after about 5 minutes, then again in another 2 or 3 minutes, and so on until the optimal number of minutes is reached (8 to 10 minutes is usually adequate). Once the baking time has been established, a larger quantity can be toasted. Shake the meats out in a single layer into the pan—deeper layers toast unevenly. To keep pecan meats after they have been toasted, refrigerate or freeze them in tightly covered containers.

Rice medley with toasted pecans

1 cup short-grain brown rice
2 ¼ cups cold water
½ cup wild rice
1 ½ cups cold water
¾ cup broken pecan meats
salt and freshly ground black pepper to taste
butter or margarine to taste

Wash each kind of rice separately and put each into a medium-sized pot that has a tightly-fitting lid, but do not cover. Add the first amount of water to the brown rice and the second amount of water to the wild rice. Place the pots over high heat and, when the water reaches a full boil, reduce the heat to very low. Cover the pots with lids and allow the rice to cook—no peeking—for 35 minutes. (Lifting the lid allows the steam to escape, resulting in less flavorful, less fluffy rice.)

After the 35 minutes, turn off the heat, but allow the pots to remain with the lids in place for another 5 minutes. Then spoon both kinds of rice into a large bowl and add the pecans, butter or margarine, and the salt and pepper.

Stir gently until combined, then cover the bowl to keep the rice warm until it is served. Makes 4 generous servings.

Coleslaw with toasted pecans and dates

DRESSING

2 tablespoons salad dressing or mayonnaise
2 tablespoons milk
½ teaspoon granulated sugar
½ teaspoon apple cider vinegar
freshly ground black pepper to taste
  Combine the ingredients in a bowl and stir until blended.

COLESLAW

1 cup shredded cabbage
¼ cup toasted pecan meats, coarsely broken
¼ cup pitted, chopped dates (or other dried fruit)
  Combine the ingredients in a bowl, add the dressing and toss lightly. Cover the bowl and refrigerate for about ½ hour to allow the flavors to blend. Makes 2 servings. Recipe may be doubled or more.

Crispy oatmeal-pecan cookies

350 degree oven
1 ½ cups flour
1 teaspoon baking soda
1 cup (2 sticks) margarine or butter
1 cup firmly packed brown sugar
1 cup granulated sugar
½ to 1 teaspoon salt
2 eggs
1 teaspoon vanilla extract
3 cups quick-cooking oatmeal
1 cup pecan meats
  Sift the flour and soda together and set them aside. Put the margarine or butter, sugars, and salt into a large bowl and beat with an electric mixer until well blended. Add the eggs and vanilla and beat until thick and creamy. Add the flour and soda mixture and beat again. Use a large spoon to stir in the oatmeal and pecan meats.
  Lay out 4 pieces of waxed paper, each about 18 inches long. Divide the dough into 4 portions, placing a portion on each piece of waxed paper. Shape each portion of dough into a roll about 14 to 16 inches long, then roll

the dough up in the waxed paper and freeze it for several hours until firm. (If well covered, the dough can be kept frozen for up to 6 months.)

When the dough is firm, cut it into slices about ¼ inch thick. Bake these on an ungreased cookie sheet until lightly browned—10 to 12 minutes. Makes about 5 dozen cookies.

These cookies can be crushed into crumbs that are delicious sprinkled over vanilla ice cream or yogurt.

There are many versions of pecan pie, and I've never tasted a bad one. The following recipe is not as sweet as most. This, I believe, allows the pecan flavor to be more prominent.

Not-too-sweet pecan pie

300 degree oven
pastry for a single-crust 8-inch pie
3 eggs
¾ cup firmly packed brown sugar
¾ cup light corn syrup
1 tablespoon melted margarine or butter
1 teaspoon vanilla extract
1 cup pecan meats (halves or pieces)

Roll out the pastry, arrange it in the pie pan, and set it aside.

Break the eggs into a large bowl and beat with an egg beater or whisk only until blended. Add the sugar, syrup, margarine or butter, and vanilla and stir well. Scatter the pecan meats in the crust and pour the pie filling over them. Bake until a knife inserted in the middle comes out clean—50 to 60 minutes. Remove the pie from the oven and allow to cool before cutting. Makes 6 servings.

Individual pecan pies

1 recipe cream cheese pastry
1 egg
¾ cup firmly packed brown sugar
1 tablespoon soft margarine or butter
1 teaspoon vanilla extract
¾ cup pecan meats

Prepare cream cheese pastry according to the recipe in Appendix B, using a muffin pan as instructed for individual pie shells.

In a medium bowl combine the egg, sugar, margarine or butter, and vanilla. Beat with an egg beater or whisk only until well blended.

Reserve 12 whole pecan meats. Break the remaining meats into coarse pieces, put them into the individual shells, and pour the filling over them. Center a whole pecan meat on the surface of each pie. Bake until the filling is browned and the rim of the crust is lightly browned—about 25 minutes. Remove the pies from the oven and allow them to cool for 15 minutes, then loosen the edges of each pie with a table knife and carefully turn the pan over, shaking it slightly to free the pies. Turn the pies upright and cool them on a wire rack. Makes 12 individual pies.

Butterscotch pie with pecans
1 eight-inch pie shell, baked
3 tablespoons butter
1 ¼ cups firmly packed brown sugar
⅓ cup flour
⅛ teaspoon salt
2 cups milk
2 egg yolks
1 teaspoon vanilla
¼ cup pecan meats, toasted and chopped

Prepare and bake the pie shell according to the directions in Appendix B.

In a saucepan, stir together the butter and half of the sugar. Place over medium heat and bring to a boil, then stir and cook for 1 minute. Remove the saucepan from the heat and set it aside.

In the top of a double boiler stir together the remainder of the sugar, the flour, and the salt. In another saucepan, heat the milk to the boiling point and add it gradually to the dry ingredients in the top of the double boiler, stirring until well blended. Next, add the cooked sugar and butter mixture and stir until blended.

Heat the water in the bottom of the double boiler to boiling and set the top in place. Cook, stirring constantly, until the mixture becomes thick and smooth. Cover with a lid and cook for another 10 minutes.

In a medium-sized bowl beat the egg yolks. Then gradually add 1 cup of the hot mixture to the yolks, stirring as you pour to blend well. Pour this back into the mixture in the top of the double boiler, again stirring as you pour. Cover and cook for 3 minutes. Remove the top of the double boiler from the bottom and stir the vanilla extract into the filling. Cover with the lid and allow to cool to room temperature.

While the filling cools, make the meringue.

MERINGUE
350 degree oven
3 egg whites, at room temperature
¼ teaspoon cream of tartar
½ teaspoon vanilla extract
6 tablespoons granulated sugar
Beat the egg whites with the cream of tartar and vanilla until soft peaks form. Gradually add the sugar, beating until all of the sugar has dissolved and the meringue is stiff and glossy.

Pour the cooled filling into the pie shell and spread the meringue over it, pushing it with a spoon to the edge of the pastry—this seals in the filling and prevents the meringue from shrinking.

Bake for 12 to 15 minutes or until the peaks of the meringue are lightly browned. Remove the pie from the oven and place it on a rack to cool. Just before serving, sprinkle with toasted pecans. Makes 6 servings.

The following recipe is for an unusually delicious dessert, but not one to be served often. Made by stacking alternate layers of chocolate cake, nut meringue, butter cream frosting, and crushed praline and allowing them to mellow at least 24 hours in a freezer, the celebration cake takes several hours to make and is high in both calories and cholesterol. For a special celebration, however, it is truly outstanding.

I first heard about this cake from a Nebraska woman who said she found it in a magazine long ago. She reported it was remarkably good but took a long time to prepare; also, she thought the proportions seemed a bit off. So I made it, experimented, and came up with a recipe that has become a family favorite for special occasions. I should say also that I experimented by using ordinary butter in place of unsalted butter in the frosting. It was a mistake. Surprisingly, that small amount of salt in the frosting made a big difference in the overall flavor of the finished dessert. Although most grocery stores carry unsalted butter, you may need to look for it in the frozen food section, but it is worth the search—the difference is considerable.

Even with the improved recipe, the celebration cake still takes longer to prepare than most deserts. It often works best to make the cake and praline powder one day and the meringue and frosting the next. Also, making two cakes is nearly as easy as making one, so I sometimes double the recipe and store one in the freezer.

None of the parts of the celebration cake is difficult to make, but it is important to follow the directions carefully. This is especially true for the butter cream frosting, where hot and cold temperatures matter a lot, and for the meringue, where oil-free utensils are essential for success. A final word: note that although the finished dessert has two layers of cake, you need bake only one layer for each dessert. After the cake layer has cooled, it is split horizontally to form two thinner layers.

Celebration cake

CHOCOLATE CAKE

350 degree oven

1 egg, separated

¾ cup granulated sugar

1 cup plus 2 tablespoons sifted cake flour

¼ cup cocoa powder

½ teaspoon soda

¼ teaspoon salt

¼ cup vegetable oil

½ cup milk

1 teaspoon vanilla extract

Make 2 waxed paper liners by setting an 8-inch cake pan on two folds of waxed paper, marking around the base with scissors, then cutting them out. Place the liners, one on top of the other, in the pan and set it aside.

With an electric mixer, beat the egg white until frothy. Still beating, gradually add ¼ cup of the sugar and continue beating until the whites are stiff and glossy. Set this aside also.

Sift the flour, cocoa, soda, salt, and remaining sugar together into a large mixing bowl. Add the oil, egg yolk, milk, and vanilla. Stir well, then beat for 2 minutes with the electric mixer, scraping the sides and bottom of the bowl frequently. Gently fold in the beaten egg white. Pour the batter into the cake pan and bake until the surface springs back when lightly touched at the center—about 40 to 50 minutes.

Take the cake from the oven and allow it to cool on a rack for 15 minutes (no longer). Remove the cake by carefully running a knife around the rim of the pan, then turning the pan over and shaking it lightly until the cake falls free. Peel the waxed paper from the bottom of the cake, but lay it back onto the cake to prevent drying as the cake cools.

When cool, cut the cake across horizontally to form the 2 thinner layers. (For evenly sliced layers, insert several toothpicks into the side of the cake to serve as guides, then using a long knife, such as a bread knife, slowly cut through with a sawing motion.) Store the layers in a tightly covered container; freeze, if not to be used within 24 hours.

PRALINE POWDER

¼ cup granulated sugar

1 tablespoon water

¼ cup coarsely chopped pecan meats

Heavily grease a shallow, heat-resistant pan, such as a cake pan, and set it aside.

Combine the sugar and water in a small, heavy skillet. Heat slowly until the sugar dissolves and becomes light brown. Stir in the pecans and cook only enough to heat through (less than a minute). Remove the skillet from the heat and immediately pour the mixture into the greased pan, spreading it out with the back of a spoon to form a thin layer. When the praline has cooled, break it into pieces, then pulverize it into a coarse powder with a mortar and pestle (or put it into a heavy plastic bag and crush it with a hammer, or use a food processor). Praline powder keeps well if refrigerated or frozen in a tightly covered container.

MERINGUE

275 degree oven

2 egg whites

⅛ teaspoon cream of tartar

½ cup granulated sugar

½ cup coarsely chopped pecan meats

Note that the two meringue layers will each bake on waxed paper laid over a cake pan turned upside down. To make the meringue layers the same size and shape as the cake layers, use the pan in which you baked the cake and another one just like it.

To prepare the pans, turn them upside down and cover each with two sheets of waxed paper slightly larger than the bottoms of the pans. (Spreading a little grease on the center of each pan and the first sheet of paper laid on top of it will help to hold the sheets in place. Do not cut the sheets to fit—the corners of the paper make good handles for lifting and moving the meringue. If you don't have two pans the same size, you can spread a meringue layer on one waxed-paper-covered pan to the desired size and shape, and then carefully slide it off, waxed paper and all, onto a cookie sheet.

It is important to use a glass or metal bowl for beating the egg white—plastic is not recommended because it tends to harbor oil. To ensure that the bowl and the beaters are completely free of oil, wash them with detergent in very hot water, dry, and let cool.

Put the egg whites and cream of tartar into the bowl and beat them with the electric mixer until foamy. Gradually add the sugar as you beat and continue beating until the meringue is stiff and glossy. Gently fold in the nutmeats. Spoon equal portions of the meringue onto the waxed-paper-covered pans. Pick up a pan and, holding it and the paper together to prevent slipping, spread the meringue to the rim with the back of a spoon. Also use the spoon to shape the layer, smoothing the edges and surface and making the thickness as even as possible. Repeat with the second pan. Bake for 65 minutes.

Remove the pans from the oven and allow the meringue to cool for 5 to 10 minutes. While still quite warm, slip a spatula between the pan and the waxed paper and lift the paper and meringue layer from each pan. Place the layers on a wire rack to cool, but do not cover them. When they are cool, peel away and discard the waxed paper. If not to be used right away, the meringue layers may be placed in a tightly covered container and stored in a freezer for up to 2 months.

BUTTERCREAM FROSTING

4 egg yolks

½ cup granulated sugar

3 tablespoons water

½ cup (1 stick) unsalted butter

1 teaspoon vanilla extract

Allow the butter to warm to room temperature. In a shallow pan, such as a dishpan, pour cold water to a depth of 2 or 3 inches. Add a dozen or so ice cubes; set this aside.

Put the egg yolks into a medium bowl and beat them with an electric mixer until light colored and very thick—the beating may take as long as 10 minutes. Set this aside but allow the mixer to remain in the bowl.

Combine the sugar and water in a medium saucepan over high heat. As soon as a full boil is reached, reduce the heat so that the syrup boils only gently. Cover with a lid and cook for 2 minutes. Remove the lid and boil gently until the syrup reaches 250 degrees on a candy thermometer—this will take only about another 2 minutes. If you don't have a thermometer, allow a few drops of syrup to fall into very cold water—when ready, the syrup will form a firm, but *not brittle,* ball in the water. It is important to check the syrup frequently so that it does not overcook. Should this happen, discard the syrup and begin again.

When the syrup is done, start the mixer and slowly pour the syrup into the yolks as you beat. Continue beating for about a minute after all of the syrup has been added. Stir in the vanilla.

Place the bowl in the pan of ice water and continue to beat until the mixture is thoroughly cooled (if the butter is added when the mixture is warm, the consistency of the finished frosting will not be right). Then, still beating, add the soft butter, 1 tablespoon at a time, and continue beating until the frosting is thick. Cover and allow to remain cool until ready to use. To store, place the frosting in a tightly covered container and refrigerate or freeze. If frozen, it will keep for several months.

ASSEMBLING THE CAKE

When you have made all 4 parts of the recipe, you are ready to assemble the cake. Make certain that none of the parts is even the slightest bit warm, then place one layer of the cake on a plate and frost it with one fourth of the buttercream frosting. Add a layer of meringue and frost it with another fourth of the frosting, filling in any depressions in the surface, then sprinkle it with half of the crushed praline. Add the other layer of cake, frost it with a fourth of the frosting, and top with the remaining meringue layer. Frost this top layer of meringue with the remaining frosting and sprinkle it with the rest of the praline powder. Place the cake in a tightly covered container and freeze it for at least 24 hours. (It can be kept frozen up to 3 months.)

When ready to serve the celebration cake, take it directly from the freezer, slice it, and serve immediately. It will not seem frozen and is best served that way—very cold. Makes about 12 servings.

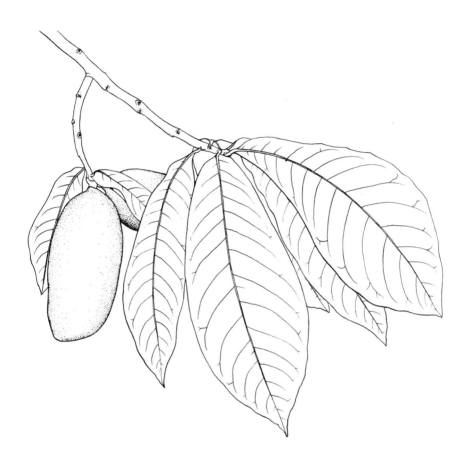

Pawpaw, custard apple

Asimina triloba (L.) Dun.

Custard apple family: Annonaceae

Description: The pawpaw is a native tree growing to about 25 feet tall. Pawpaws usually grow in colonies and often are found among other, taller trees. The leaves are alternate and very large (sometimes up to 12 inches long) and are not toothed. The upper surface is medium green and mostly smooth; the lower surface is paler with some hairs early in the season but becoming smooth as the leaf matures. In autumn, the leaves turn a beautiful lemon yellow. The striking flowers appear along with the leaves in April or May. The 6 purple to maroon petals are arranged in two whorls—3 smaller petals inside 3 larger ones. The fruits are sometimes compared to short, stubby bananas, but are thicker and more rounded. The skin of the ripe fruits is light green or yellow green, often with purple-brown mottling; the flesh is custardlike. The seeds, from 2 to several, are flat, dark brown, and fairly large.

Distribution: Scattered populations in the eastern United States from Michigan to northern Florida; southeastern portion of the Great Plains.

Habitat: Open woods, especially wooded hills and ravines, flood plains, and along streams; usually in good soil and in partial shade.

Edible parts: The cooked or uncooked flesh of the ripe fruits, after the skin, the greenish layer lining the skin, and the seeds have been removed.

Season to collect: Mid to late autumn; fruits usually ripe before frost.

Cautions: Underripe or overripe pawpaws can cause indigestion and abdominal cramps. The seeds, as well as the skin and the greenish layer between the skin and flesh, are not edible. Handling pawpaw fruit causes some persons to develop a skin rash.

Additional information and recipes: Pawpaw trees are attractive and do well in partial shade. They require little care other than hoeing to keep them from spreading, and the tendency to spread lessens as the trees grow older. Pawpaws have a long taproot and frequently do not survive transplanting, but they can be started from seed if planted in autumn—just be certain to plant them where you will want the trees to remain permanently. If you try this, plant seeeds from fruits of various trees and be selective about the quality of the fruit from which you get the seeds. Although the foliage of all pawpaws is attractive, the flavor of the fruit is less consistent. Your chances for success are better if you plant seeds from good fruit.

When gathering pawpaws, use a shallow box or basket. If they are stacked too deeply, the weight of those on top will bruise those below. Also, set them out in a single layer as soon as you are home. Pawpaws are easy to prepare: simply cut the fruits in half, then remove the seeds and scoop out the flesh with a spoon, being careful not to scrape into the greenish layer that lines the skin. Another method (often used when eating pawpaws directly from the tree) is to split the skin and squeeze out the flesh—the bitter layer remains in the skin.

The flesh of ripe pawpaws varies from white to yellow, and fruits having yellow flesh are usually more rounded in shape and superior in flavor. The flesh should have a pleasant fragrance and be soft but not mushy (fully ripe but not overripe). Persons who have waited for this stage only to find that wild animals have beaten them to the harvest often collect slightly underripe fruits and try to ripen them at home. This doesn't always work. The fruits may soften and appear to ripen, yet fail to develop the full flavor of those left on the tree; fruit flies may become a problem; sometimes the fruits spoil. But it's worth a try. Burying the fruits in buckets of small grain, such as wheat or oats, aids the ripening process and helps ward off insects.

Growing up in Nebraska, I had little opportunity to experiment with pawpaws, but when I was in graduate school in Kentucky, I learned that the woods were full of them. When October came, I placed a note on the department bulletin board that read, "I would appreciate receiving pawpaws and will share the resulting baked goods," and I signed my name. In a few days I became rich beyond my dreams—sacks of pawpaws, boxes of pawpaws, a half-bushel of pawpaws. It was wonderful. I baked them and froze them, I made pawpaw cookies and pudding and ice cream and bread. My fellow students ate it all and gave me serious feedback. The consensus was that the bread was marvelous and that the rest were good, except the pudding, which they thought was a waste of good pawpaws that could have been made into bread. Here is the recipe for pawpaw bread. (It takes on a pale rosy tint as it bakes.)

Pawpaw bread

350 degree oven
2 cups all-purpose flour
1 teaspoon soda
½ teaspoon salt

½ cup margarine or butter
1 cup granulated sugar
2 eggs
1 cup mashed pawpaw pulp
½ cup nutmeats (hickories if you have them)

Grease a 9 x 5 x 3–inch loaf pan with margarine or butter and set it aside. Sift the flour, soda, and salt together onto a piece of waxed paper. With an electric mixer, cream the margarine or butter until fluffy. Gradually add the sugar and continue beating until thick and light. Add the eggs, one at a time, and beat well. Add about half of the dry ingredients and stir only until the batter is blended (don't beat), then add half of the pawpaw pulp, again stirring only enough to mix. Add the remaining dry ingredients and the remaining pawpaw pulp in the same way. Fold in the nutmeats. Bake for about 1 hour or until the surface springs back when lightly touched at the center.

Remove from the oven and allow to cool for about 10 minutes, then loosen the sides with a table knife and turn the loaf out onto a plate. Cover with a cloth and allow it to cool completely (hot bread crumbles when cut). Pawpaw bread freezes well—simply store it in a tightly covered container.

Buffaloberry, bullberry, deerberry

Shepherdia argentea (Pursh) Nutt.

Oleaster family: Elaeagnaceae

Description: The buffaloberry is a much-branched native shrub, silvery gray in color, and formidably armed with sharp twigs. The shrubs usually grow in groups of several and, although they may reach 20 feet in height, typically stand no more than 14 feet tall. The leaves are opposite, rather small, and elongated in shape; the leaf margins are entire. Both the upper and lower surfaces of the leaves as well as the branches are covered with minute silver-gray plates, which account for the overall silvery appearance. The flowers are small and inconspicuous and mostly clustered around the spines, with male and female flowers occurring on separate shrubs. The fruits, which are small, red orange, and round to oval, contain a single seed.

Distribution: Northwestern and north-central United States and into Canada, also reported in the southwest; scattered throughout the northern and west-central Great Plains.

Habitat: Prairies, hillsides, ravines, along fence rows, roadsides, and edges of pastures; in full sun and often in dry, rocky soils.

Edible parts: Ripe fruits, fresh or dried, cooked or uncooked, but uncooked fruits are usually considered undesirable.

Season to collect: Autumn, usually after the first frost.

Cautions: It is unwise to harvest buffaloberries by hand because the fruits are mostly clustered around the sharp spines—better to use the tarp-and-stick method described below. Caution children to watch out for spines, especially those on branches that occur at eye height.

Additional information and recipes: Buffaloberries become glossy and red orange and look ripe before they really are. If used too soon, they have a raw, unpleasant taste even when cooked. Truly ripe fruits not only are glossy and red orange, but will loosen and fall when the branch is given a sharp jolt. Traditionally, everyone waited until after the first hard frost to harvest buffaloberries, but now opinions differ about whether it is the frost that sweetens the fruits or simply that by remaining on the shrub so late into the autumn, they have time to become fully ripe. (I still seem to have better luck after frost.)

The method for harvesting buffaloberries remains the same. Spread a tarp or blanket under the bush, then use a stick to strike and shake the branches. If ripe, the fruit will fall easily onto the tarp or blanket. But so will a considerable amount of leaves and other debris, which must be picked out before the fruit can be used or stored. Also, much of the fruit may fall with the small stems attached. For jelly, a few of these stems will not be noticeable, but to use buffaloberries for pie or as dried fruit to add to baked goods, these stems must be removed. I think it is easier to pick out the debris and remove the stems before washing, but some persons wash first. After these tasks have been performed, the fruit is ready to use or to store. To store, buffaloberries may be frozen in tightly covered containers or dried.

To dry buffaloberries
Remove any stems or debris. Place the fruit in a colander and wash under running water. Allow the fruit to drain well, then blot up extra moisture with a kitchen towel. Shake the fruit out into a shallow pan lined with a kitchen towel or onto a clean window screen. Protect the fruit from insects by covering it with 1 or 2 layers of cheesecloth, then place the pan or screen in a light, airy place for several days or until the fruit is shriveled but still slightly chewy—the consistency should be a little drier than currants or raisins. Freeze or store in a cool place in a tightly covered container.

To extract buffaloberry juice
5 cups buffaloberries
1½ cups water
   Put the buffaloberries and water into a large, heavy kettle and bring them to a boil over high heat. Reduce the heat, cover the kettle with a lid, and allow to boil gently for 10 minutes. Crush the berries with a potato masher, then pour them into a damp jelly cloth and squeeze to extract the juice. Makes about 4 cups of juice.

Buffaloberry jelly without added pectin
buffaloberry juice
granulated sugar
   Read about jelly making, Appendix A.
   Measure the juice and put it into a large, heavy kettle. Stir in an equal amount of sugar and bring to a boil over high heat. Reduce the heat and allow the liquid to boil gently until it reaches the jelling point. Typically, the boiling time will be 15 to 20 minutes. Test for doneness with a jelly thermometer or use the spoon or cold saucer method. When done, remove the kettle from the heat and quickly skim off the foam. Pour the jelly into hot,

sterile jars, leaving ¼ inch headspace. Cap the jars with two-piece screwband lids and process for 5 minutes in a boiling water bath. Makes a little less jelly than the amount of juice you began with.

Buffaloberry jelly with added pectin
4 cups buffaloberry juice
¼ cup lemon juice
1 package powdered pectin
4 cups granulated sugar
   Read about jelly making, Appendix A.
   Measure the sugar and set it aside. Stir the juices and pectin together in a large, heavy kettle and bring to a boil over high heat. Add the sugar all at one time. Stir and again bring to a full boil. Begin timing and allow to boil for 2 minutes. Remove the kettle from the heat and quickly skim off the foam. Pour the jelly into hot, sterile jars, leaving ¼ inch headspace. Cap the jars with two-piece screwband lids and process for 5 minutes in a boiling water bath. Makes about 5 cups of jelly.

Buffaloberry pie
pastry for a one-crust 8-inch pie
2 cups fresh or frozen buffaloberries
1 package strawberry-flavored gelatin
1 ½ cups water
¾ cup granulated sugar
2 tablespoons cornstarch
¼ cup light corn syrup
   Make the crust and bake it as directed in Appendix B. Put the buffaloberries into a medium-sized bowl and set it aside.
   Combine the water, gelatin, sugar, cornstarch, and syrup in a saucepan over medium heat. Stir and cook until the mixture thickens slightly. Add this to the buffaloberries and stir gently to combine. Pour the mixture into the baked pie shell, smoothing it out with the back of a spoon. Allow the pie to cool. Makes 6 servings.

Wild persimmon
Diospyros virginiana L.

Ebony family: Ebenaceae

Description: The wild persimmon is a tall native tree growing to a height of 70 feet; it may occur singly or in groups. The bark is dark gray and usually furrowed, with flat, blocky ridges, but the texture varies considerably from tree to tree. The leaves are alternate, simple, and entire; the upper surface is green and smooth, the lower surface, pale and either smooth or with hairs. The flowers are pale yellow and urn-shaped, with male and female flowers occurring on separate trees. (An occasional tree will bear flowers that have both male and female parts.) The fruits are rounded and smooth. Hard and green at first, they become soft and orange to purple brown as they ripen. Underripe fruits are quite plump; fully ripe fruits are slightly shriveled and have soft, orange, very sweet flesh. Each fruit has several flat brown seeds.

Distribution: Eastern and southeastern United States; southeastern Great Plains (from western Missouri into Kansas and Oklahoma).

Habitat: Open woods, hillsides, along roadsides, and edges of pastures and fields.

Edible parts: Fully ripe fruits, cooked or uncooked.

Season to collect: Late autumn, usually after a frost.

Caution: Make certain that the fruits are truly ripe. Less than fully ripe persimmons are very astringent—even a single bite can be extremely unpleasant.

Additional information and recipes: Although the flavor of the fruit varies from tree to tree (with some superior to others year after year), wild persimmons generally are smaller, sweeter, and more perishable than the kind sold in grocery stores.

As with several other wild fruits, opinions differ about whether a frost is needed to ripen persimmons. I have had better results by allowing the fruits to remain on the tree until after frost, but some authorities claim that slightly underripe fruits may be taken from the tree, placed in a covered container, and allowed to ripen at home. Perhaps like the flavor, the ability to ripen off of the branch varies from tree to tree.

Some persons use a broom or long stick to shake the branches and let the fruits fall, but because I usually wait until the fruits are so ripe that falling would smash them, I use a ladder and pick them by hand. Because persimmons are so soft, a shallow box works better than a pail to transport the harvest.

Once you are home, the fruit must be sorted. Very ripe persimmons should be used as soon as possible. It is best to remove the seeds from all of the fruit, refrigerating or freezing the pulp until you are ready to use it. Nothing needs to be added to the pulp before it is frozen—simply put it into tightly covered containers and freeze. It keeps so well this way that persimmon treats can be enjoyed all winter.

Although they are good fresh from the tree and chilled, persimmons are more often used in pies, cookies, cakes, breads, and, of course, the best known of all, persimmon pudding. So dark brown it is almost black, this rich, delicate pudding has a flavor like no other. Make it with hickory nuts if you can—the combination is particularly delicious. But before anything can be baked, the persimmon pulp and seeds must be separated.

To extract persimmon pulp

More than one method is used for removing the seeds from persimmons. One way is to cut the fruits open with a knife and remove the seeds by hand, but for large amounts it is more time efficient to use a food mill or a cone-shaped colander and pestle. It may be helpful to know that it takes a little more than 1 quart of persimmons to make 1 cup of pulp.

Wild persimmon pudding

350 degree oven
¼ cup (½ stick) butter
⅔ cup all-purpose flour
1 teaspoon baking powder
1 teaspoon cinnamon
1 cup persimmon pulp
1 cup granulated sugar
1 egg, beaten
½ cup buttermilk
½ cup light cream or evaporated milk
1 teaspoon vanilla extract

Grease a 9 x 9 x 2–inch baking pan and set it aside. Melt the butter in a saucepan and set it aside also. Sift the flour, baking powder, and cinnamon together into a large bowl. Add the remaining ingredients and mix well. Pour into the baking pan and bake for 1 hour. The pudding will puff up while baking, then fall back as it cools. Cool the pudding in the pan on a rack.

Serve cold, with whipped cream or vanilla ice cream. Makes 9 to 12 servings. The recipe may be doubled.

Wild persimmon pudding without egg
350 degree oven
1 cup all-purpose flour
1 cup granulated sugar
2 teaspoons baking soda
½ teaspoon salt
1 ½ teaspoons ground cinnamon
½ teaspoon ground nutmeg
1 cup persimmon pulp
1 ½ cups milk
1 teaspoon vanilla extract
1 tablespoon melted margarine
1 cup dried currants (from a grocery store)
½ cup coarsely broken nutmeats (hickory, if possible)

Grease a 7 x 11 x 1 ½–inch cake pan with margarine. Have ready a larger, shallow pan filled with about 1 inch of hot water. Set both aside.

Sift the flour, sugar, soda, salt, and spices together onto a sheet of waxed paper. In a large bowl, stir together the persimmon pulp, milk, vanilla, and margarine. Add the sifted ingredients and stir until well blended, then add the currants and nutmeats and stir again. Pour into the prepared pan, then place it into the pan of water. Bake for 1 hour. Remove from the oven and carefully take the cake pan out of the pan of water. Cool the pudding in the pan on a wire rack, then cut it into squares. Serve plain or with whipped cream. Makes 12 servings.

Wild persimmon bars
350 degree oven
BARS
1 cup persimmon pulp
1 teaspoon baking soda
1 ½ cups all-purpose flour
1 teaspoon ground cinnamon
½ teaspoon ground nutmeg
¼ teaspoon ground cloves
1 egg
1 cup granulated sugar

½ teaspoon salt
½ cup cooking oil
1 teaspoon vanilla extract
1 cup dried currants (or ½ cup raisins)
½ cup coarsely broken nutmeats (hickory, if possible)

Grease a 10 x 15 x 1–inch jelly-roll pan with margarine and set it aside. In a medium-sized bowl, stir the soda into the persimmon pulp. Set this aside for about 5 minutes. Meanwhile, sift the flour and spices together onto a sheet of waxed paper. Put the egg, sugar, salt, and oil into a large bowl and beat them with an electric mixer until blended. Add the persimmon pulp and beat well, then add the sifted dry ingredients and beat only until well mixed. Stir in the vanilla, currants, and nutmeats. Pour the batter into the prepared pan and spread it out to the edges. Using a spatula dipped in water, lightly smooth the surface of the batter to make it as even as possible. Bake for 20 minutes. Remove the pan from the oven and allow it to cool on a wire rack for 5 to 10 minutes, then frost the bars with glaze.

GLAZE

1 cup powdered sugar
2 tablespoons lemon juice

Stir the sugar and juice together and spread this over the sheet of uncut persimmon bars. When cool, cut into 1½ x 2–inch bars. Makes 50 bars. These are better the next day, after they have had time to mellow.

florets

Jerusalem artichoke
Helianthus tuberosa L.

Sunflower family: Asteraceae

Description: The Jerusalem artichoke is a perennial sunflower, not an artichoke, and is native to North America, not Jerusalem. Under good conditions the plants may grow to a height of 12 feet or more, but ordinarily they reach no more than 8 feet. They can reproduce from seed but more commonly spread by underground tuber-bearing rootstocks. The tubers resemble small sweet potatoes and are usually fairly smooth, with light tan or brown skin—sometimes with a reddish purple tinge; the flesh is white or yellowish. The leaves of the mature plant are medium to large, dark green, and rough to the touch. The leaf margins are usually serrate and the leaf blade extends at least part way down on either side of the petiole. The leaves may be all opposite or opposite on the lower portion of the plant and alternate above. As in all sunflowers and other members of the sunflower family, what appears to be a single flower is actually a composite of many small flowers (florets), each usually having but a single petal. The outer ones that form a ring are called ray florets and the ones forming the center are called disk florets. Although in the common sunflower the ray florets are yellow and the disk florets are brown, in the Jerusalem artichoke both ray and disk florets are yellow.

Distribution: Eastern and central United States and into Canada, with scattered populations west and wherever introduced; in the Great Plains, North Dakota, south and east to central Oklahoma.

Habitat: Moist to nearly dry soil along ditches, roadsides, fence rows, and streams; sometimes planted in yards and gardens; plants do best in full sun but will tolerate partial shade.

Seasons to collect: Tubers may be found on the rootstocks in late autumn, winter, and early spring, but are absent during the warmer months of the year when the plant is making its greatest growth aboveground.

Edible parts: Cooked or uncooked tubers.

Cautions: It is *extremely important* to remember that the tubers of Jerusalem artichoke closely resemble the tuberlike roots of the deadly poisonous plant water hemlock (*Cicuta maculata* L.), a member of the parsley family that grows along streams and in moist areas throughout much of the Great Plains as well as in other areas of the United States and Canada. All parts of the water hemlock are poisonous if eaten, but it is the roots that have most often caused death for both humans and livestock. A single bite of water hemlock can be fatal, and even the dried roots of dead plants may retain a considerable amount of toxin.

During the growing season, the aboveground portions of water hemlock and Jerusalem artichoke are easy to tell apart. The leaves of the water hemlock are divided into leaflets; the flowers are small and white and are borne in flat clusters. But because Jerusalem artichoke tubers are usually dug after frost has withered the aboveground portions of the plant, it is best not to seek them in moist areas, such as stream banks, where water hemlock might grow. For maximum safety, grow your own Jerusalem artichokes or find plants while they are in bloom in late summer or autumn and mark each with a stake so that you can return later in the year and dig the tubers. Having a patch of Jerusalem artichokes in your own backyard is handy and ensures safe harvests, but remember that this plant spreads rapidly—you will need to give thought to where you plant it or it may come up in neighbors' yards.

One more caution: although most persons can eat Jerusalem artichokes perfectly well, some experience flatulence and mild to acute abdominal distress, regardless of whether the tubers are raw or cooked. This is because the tubers contain inulin, a carbohydrate that not everyone digests easily. Many grocery stores now carry cultivated forms of Jerusalem artichoke or a hybrid under the name of sunchoke, but I have yet to find a warning on a single package. To be safe, try only a small portion of Jerusalem artichoke the first time to determine whether you can or cannot eat these tubers—and certainly, do not serve them to unadvised guests.

Additional information and recipes: The use of Jerusalem artichoke tubers for food by Indian people living near the Missouri River was noted by the botanist Melvin Gilmore in the early 1900s. The Jerusalem artichoke was also eaten by settlers during colonial times and introduced into Europe by the early 1600s, where for a while it became a popular novelty vegetable, receiving, not surprisingly, both high praise and outright condemnation. But just where or when along the way the larger, more rounded, cultivated forms evolved is not known.

Although the wild tubers are smaller than the garden forms, their more streamlined shape makes them easier to scrub and peel. The taste and other characteristics of the tubers are about the same. The aboveground portions are similar, but wild plants are usually shorter than cultivated forms. Wild, cultivated, and hybrid forms are all prolific and will grow nearly anywhere.

To lay in a store of tubers for winter, it is necessary to dig them before the ground freezes. Digging is usually an easy task because the tubers rarely occur very far belowground. Most of the soil falls away with the digging—a simple washing will get the rest and you are ready to proceed. Once dug, however, the tubers often lose their crispness, even when refrigerated. If they were not nearly impossible to remove from frozen ground, it would be best simply to leave them there until needed. The method described by Kelly Kindscher in *Edible Wild Plants of the Prairies* is probably the best way to ensure having good-quality Jerusalem artichokes in winter: "In the fall, after a hard freeze, I dig up my tuberous sunflowers and bury them in a leaf-insulated pit about one and one-half to two feet deep. . . . I cover these tightly with more leaves, place a large board on top of the entire pit, and then place some plastic sacks full of leaves on top of the board." Kindscher further advises readers to locate the pit away from areas likely to be frequented by mice or other small mammals.

Any season they can be found, Jerusalem artichoke tubers are good plain, added to vegetable or fruit salads, or cooked in a variety of ways. Even if they lose some of their crispness, they can still be used. The raw tubers have a crunchy consistency something like that of water chestnuts; the cooked texture resembles that of white potatoes, though a little more moist.

Braised Jerusalem artichokes

1 pound Jerusalem artichoke tubers
3 tablespoons butter
3 tablespoons water
salt and freshly ground black pepper to taste

Scrub but do not peel the tubers; cut them into slices about ¼ inch thick. Place the butter, water, and sliced tubers into a skillet over medium heat. Add salt and pepper and stir until the butter has melted. Cover with a lid and cook for about 5 minutes, shaking the skillet often so that none of the slices stick to the bottom and burn. Serve hot, either plain or with a little catsup. Makes 4 to 6 servings.

Boiled Jerusalem artichokes

Peel the tubers and place them in a pot, using about 1 cup water for each pound. Cover the pot with a lid and cook over medium heat until tender— about 10 to 15 minutes. Serve hot, as is, or mash with a little butter, milk, and seasonings. Save any leftovers for use in making the patties or puffs below.

Jerusalem artichoke patties or puffs

1 cup boiled, mashed tubers

1 egg

⅓ cup all-purpose flour (or use part flour, part cornmeal)

¼ teaspoon baking powder

salt and freshly ground black pepper to taste

3 tablespoons cooking oil (if making patties)

or

3 to 4 cups peanut oil for deep-frying (if making puffs)

Mix together the mashed tubers and egg, stirring well to combine. Add remaining ingredients and again stir well. If desired, bacon, sauteed green onion slices, grated cheese, or seasonings such as garlic powder or grated Parmesan cheese may be added.

To make patties, heat the oil in a skillet over medium-high heat. Spoon portions of batter the size of hamburger patties into the skillet. Flatten the patties and cook them until browned on each side. Makes 4 patties.

To make puffs, use a deep-fat fryer or heat about 3 inches of oil in a saucepan. The temperature is right when a small amount of batter dropped into the hot oil quickly rises to the top and turns brown. If you use a deep-fat thermometer, the temperature should be 375 degrees. Drop the batter by tablespoonsful into the hot oil. Use tongs to turn the puffs so that they brown on all sides. Remove and drain the puffs on paper towels. Serve hot. Makes about 12 puffs.

Jerusalem artichoke chips

⅓ cup very thinly sliced Jerusalem artichoke tubers

1 cup water

3 tablespoons lemon juice (about ½ lemon)

3 to 4 cups peanut oil (for deep-frying)

Refrigerate the slices in water and lemon juice for at least 1 hour. Drain and pat dry with a paper towel, then fry in hot oil until light brown. (See recipe above for checking the temperature of the oil.) Use tongs to remove the chips from the oil and allow the chips to drain on paper towels. Add salt or other seasonings. These are especially good with hot cheese dips. Makes about 1 cup of loosely packed chips.

The following recipe calls for commercial mustard and celery seed, the kind available in grocery stores. Some wild seeds resembling them are extremely poisonous.

Jerusalem artichoke pickles

2½ cups peeled, thinly sliced Jerusalem artichoke tubers
4 teaspoons pickling salt
1½ cups cold water
½ cup chopped onion
¾ cup granulated sugar
½ cup apple cider vinegar
½ teaspoon commercial mustard seed
½ teaspoon commercial celery seed

Combine the water and pickling salt, pour over the sliced tubers, and refrigerate for 2 hours. Drain the slices and place them with the other ingredients in a medium-sized pot. Heat until the liquid reaches a gentle boil. Allow to boil uncovered for 3 minutes. Remove from the heat.

If the pickles are to be used within 2 weeks, allow them to cool, then refrigerate them in a covered container. If the pickles are to be preserved for later use, do not cool; instead, pour them immediately into hot scalded jars, filling to ½ inch from the rim so that the top layer of slices is covered by the hot liquid. Cap the jars with two-piece screwband lids and process in a boiling water bath for 15 minutes. Makes about 2 cups of pickles. The recipe may be doubled or more.

Jerusalem artichokes with tomatoes

2 tablespoons butter
2 tablespoons olive oil
1 cup canned tomatoes, chopped
salt and freshly ground pepper to taste
1 teaspoon crumbled dried basil
2 cups peeled, sliced, and cooked Jerusalem artichoke tubers

Heat the butter and olive oil; add the tomatoes, salt, and pepper. Stir in the basil and cook over low heat, stirring constantly, until the mixture begins to boil. Add the sliced tubers and reheat. Makes 4 servings.

Canning, Freezing, and Drying

The original people of the Great Plains often preserved food by drying. The settlers who came to the plains also dried foods, but used pickling, salting, and canning as well. In winter, meat could be preserved by allowing it to freeze, but it was not until much later that freezing could be used as a method for preserving fruits and vegetables. Essentially, all methods of food preservation are aimed at accomplishing the same thing—protecting food from spoiling.

Food spoilage is caused primarily by microorganisms such as bacteria, molds, and yeasts, and by enzymes that are natural substances present in all fruits and vegetables. Exposure to sunlight and air also contributes to deterioration.

At present, although there is renewed interest in drying, the methods most commonly used to preserve food are canning and freezing, and with either of these processes, *the importance of knowing and practicing safe procedures cannot be emphasized too strongly*. Some kinds of spoilage are difficult to detect, yet can result in severe sickness and even death. Botulism, caused by a toxin produced by the bacterium *Clostridium botulinum,* is often fatal. In addition to reading the information below, consult one or more good books on canning and freezing and, except for the books recommended on page 303, choose from those published no later than 1990. Certain procedures commonly used before 1990 have been found to be unsafe.

As these books will tell you, it is extremely important to select fresh, good-quality fruits and vegetables and to use proper equipment and supplies. Fruits and vegetables must be washed thoroughly. Equipment must be clean; pots and kettles must be of the appropriate size and shape. Supplies such as lids and freezer bags must be new. (Jars and screwbands may be used again and again, but never reuse canning lids.) Check all containers and lids for defects and discard any that are not perfect.

If at any time a jar of canned food looks discolored or has mold, doesn't smell right, shows signs of leaking, isn't sealed, or in any other way seems unusual, throw it out, jar and all. The same goes for containers of frozen food. Frozen food that has been allowed to thaw but wasn't used or cooked right away should be discarded. Dried food must be kept dry. Any sign of mold or mildew or anything else unusual means it can't be used. *Never, never taste food to determine whether or not it is spoiled.*

Canning

Canning involves high heat and large quantities of hot food and water, so take precautions to avoid burning yourself, and make certain that others, particularly children, are not in danger. (When my children were young, I canned at night when they were asleep.)

Vegetables, such as pokeweed, must be processed in a pressure canner. Jams, jellies, syrups, and fruit juices must be processed in a boiling water canner by the method called the boiling water bath. Other methods are no longer considered safe.

Although nearly everyone has heard that boiling water kills microorganisms, not everyone knows that it takes a specific length of time and that the temperature at which water boils varies with the altitude—the higher the altitude, the lower the boiling temperature. For example, at 1,000 feet above sea level, water boils at approximately 212 degrees Fahrenheit, whereas at 7,000 it boils at about 199 degrees. Therefore, because boiling water is not as hot at high altitudes, food processed in a boiling water canner must be processed longer at higher elevations; similarly, food processed in a pressure canner must be processed under greater pressure. More information about adjusting for altitude appears in the sections that follow.

PRESSURE CANNING

The recipe for canning pokeweed shoots is the only one in this book requiring pressure canning. Two types of pressure canners, the dial gauge and the weighted gauge, are available and either type may be used. Follow the manufacturer's instructions carefully. Know the altitude of your area (call your county agent) and use the correct pressure.

BOILING WATER BATH CANNING

To process food by the boiling water bath method, it is advisable to buy a canning kettle designed for that purpose, but be aware that some are better than others. Some canners are too shallow, so take a measuring tape with you when you shop. The depth should allow for 1 inch of water (2 is better) above the top of the jar as it sits on the rack, plus at least another inch of space (again 2 is better) above that to prevent the water from boiling over. A canner measuring 10 inches from the bottom to the rim will be deep enough to process pints, but for quarts, a depth of 12 inches is needed. Also, examine the rack inside the canner. It should be constructed in such a way that jars will not fall through the spaces between the wires, which should be heavy enough to adequately support jars of food. Canner lids fit loosely, but they should fit.

Also important (and inexpensive) is a jar lifter. If you don't have one, purchase it along with the canner. A cone-shaped colander with a wooden pestle is handy to have, and necessary for some recipes. These come as a set and are usually available where canning kettles are sold. A jelly bag or cloth is used in extracting fruit juice for jelly making—a clean white dishtowel will work. Canning jars and two-piece screwband lids are available in most grocery stores. These lids are made to self-seal during the canning process. Other types of lids are no longer recommended. Once you have the necessary equipment and supplies and the food you want to preserve, the process can begin.

Assemble all supplies such as sugar and pectin. Wash the fruit and do whatever basic preparation is necessary (such as extracting the juice for making jelly). Now give your attention to preparing the jars and lids.

There is a difference between canning jam, jelly, or syrup and canning fruit juice. Jars for jam, jelly, and syrup must be sterilized before being filled, but because fruit juices are processed longer in the boiling-water canner, the jars for canning elderberry-rhubarb, wild plum, or chokecherry juice need only to be thoroughly washed, rinsed, and scalded.

The boiling water canner can be used to sterilize jars. Simply place the jars right side up in the rack, then pour very hot water into and around them until the water is at least 1 inch above their rims. Bring the water to a boil and begin timing. For altitudes of less than 1,000 feet, boil for 10 minutes. Add 1 minute for each additional 1,000 feet of elevation.

At the end of the boiling time, turn the heat to low and allow the jars to remain in the hot water until they are to be filled. Follow the manufacturer's directions for preparing the canning lids—most recommend putting the lids into a saucepan and pouring in enough boiling water to cover, then allowing them to remain for at least 3 minutes. When putting the lids in the pan, stand tongs and a metal teaspoon in also. The spoon will be used for skimming off foam, and the tongs are a considerable help in retrieving the lids from the hot water. Both need to be scalded.

Next, prepare the food according to the recipe. Remove the sterilized jars with the jar lifter, pouring the water from each back into the canner. Pour or ladle the hot food into the hot jars. Remove the foam with the scalded spoon and use a fresh tissue moistened with boiled water to remove any drips around the rim. Cap each jar with a two-piece screwband lid. Note that the lids should be screwed on firmly but not tightened excessively.

Use the jar lifter to set the filled jars one by one, into the rack in the canner. If necessary, add more hot water so that there is from 1 to 2 inches of water above the lids of the jars. Place the lid on the canner and turn up the heat so that the water boils briskly.

When the filled jars have boiled for the recommended amount of time, turn off the heat and remove the canner lid. Set out a large wire cake rack or lay several kitchen towels on a heat-resistant surface. Using the jar lifter, remove each jar and carefully place it on the rack or towels to cool. Leave at least 2 inches between jars.

As the food cools, a vacuum is created inside the jar and pulls the lid down tightly onto the rim. When this pull is sufficient to cause the slight dome of the lid to snap downward, the lid is said to have sealed. When this happens, the sound is a soft snap or pop—a happy sound to the cook. Even so, when the jars are thoroughly cooled, all lids must be checked to make sure that they did seal. Usually an unsealed lid can easily be spotted because it will still retain its slightly domed shape, but to make certain, press the center of the lid—if it springs back, it did not seal. Refrigerate and use up any jars of food that didn't seal; store the others in a cool, dry place away from light. For best quality, use canned food within a year of canning.

Finally, label each jar with the name of the contents and the date of canning, but put the label on the lid, not on the jar. Self-stick labels leave a gummy film on jars that is unsanitary and hard to remove when you want to reuse the jar.

Jam, Jelly, and Syrup Making: For over a hundred years cooks have canned jams, jellies, and syrups by simply pouring the cooked ingredients, boiling hot, into sterilized jars, sealing them with paraffin or various kinds of lids, and storing them away. But things have changed. Paraffin is no longer considered safe, and the only lids recommended are the two-piece screwband lids that self-seal during processing.

The biggest change of all is that new guidelines from the United States Department of Agriculture require jams, jellies, and syrups (unless frozen or refrigerated) to be processed by the boiling water bath method. Up to 1,000 feet above sea level, the recommended processing time is 5 minutes, with an additional minute for every 1,000 feet of elevation. To use older methods, they warn, is dangerous.

The new procedure is difficult for long-time cooks like myself, because many of the old tried-and-true jam and jelly recipes don't jell properly after being processed in this manner. And they don't taste quite the same. But safety is more important, so for jam, jelly, and syrup recipes, I have given the processing time for altitudes of up to 1,000 feet above sea level, and persons at higher altitudes will need to make appropriate adjustments.

Some cooks refrigerate their jams, jellies, and syrups rather than subjecting them to the added processing of the boiling water bath. If refrigerated, these products should be used within a month because some microorganisms, such as molds, will grow even under refrigeration. Frozen jams, jellies, and syrups may be kept for up to a year. Because foods containing moisture expand when frozen, it is important to leave adequate headspace—at least 1 inch for most containers.

In years past, when a spot of mold was discovered on the surface of jam or jelly, it was common practice to simply scoop it out and serve what was left. But there is more to mold than meets the eye. The spot on the surface is only a small part of the mold. Tiny, invisible threads similar to roots may have grown into the food below, where they may have produced harmful toxins. So if mold is found, discard the entire contents of the jar.

Although this all sounds grim, these dangers must be made known. Once they are understood and the appropriate steps taken, the cook can get down to the more pleasurable aspects of jam, jelly, and syrup making.

A large, heavy kettle is essential—one having a capacity of 8 quarts is ideal. The timing in some recipes requires a clock or watch with a second hand. A cone-shaped colander is required to prepare some fruits. Other necessary equipment will be found in most kitchens.

The basic components of jam and jelly are fruit, water, sugar, acid, and pectin. Pectin is also used in making some syrups. Actually, pectin is a substance that occurs naturally in fruit. When present in proper proportions to the sugar and acid, it causes jams and jellies to jell. Some fruits, however, do not contain enough pectin, so more must be added. Pectin can be purchased in both powdered and liquid form at most grocery stores.

For jams and jellies, use ½ pint (1 cup) jars; for syrups, use ½ pint or pint jars. Juices may be canned in ½ pint, pint, or quart jars. For processing by boiling water bath leave ¼ inch headspace for jams and jellies, and ½ inch headspace for syrup and juices.

Jam

Unlike jellies and syrups, which are made primarily with juices, jams contain pulp or chunks of fruit as well. Because of this, they are quite thick even as they cook and should be stirred often to prevent burning.

For jams *with added pectin,* the sugar is added after the fruit and pectin have come to a boil. When the mixture again reaches a boil, it is allowed to boil rapidly for only 1 minute before it is removed from the heat. For jams *without added pectin,* the cooking time varies, usually in the range of 10 to 30 minutes.

An easy test is to scoop some jam up with a spoon—when it holds a slightly rounded shape, it is done. (Remember that jam will become thicker as it cools.)

Another way is to put a small amount of hot jam (about ½ teaspoonful) on a saucer and set it into the freezing compartment of your refrigerator for a few minutes. (Take the kettle off of the burner while you do this so that the jam won't burn.) Remove the saucer and check the jam's consistency. If it seems thick enough, it is done.

Jelly

There is an old saying that "if jelly doesn't jell, it isn't a failure, it's syrup." And that is really the only difference between the two: both are made of fruit juice, but jelly is jelled and has form, whereas syrup, although sometimes quite thick, is a liquid that pours. So never discard jelly that didn't set—simply use it as a dip for toast or pour it on pancakes.

When making jelly, don't double the recipe. Cooking times are worked out for a specific amount of fruit, and boiling over and spilling are more likely with large quantities.

The first step, after the fruit has cooked, is to extract the juice. The method most often suggested in cookbooks is to pour the cooked fruit into a damp jelly bag suspended over a large kettle and let the juice drip through.

The bag is usually hung from a broomstick supported by two chairs and the juice is allowed to drip through on its own.

Another common method is to poke a damp cotton dishtowel into a cone-shaped colander in such a way that the center of the towel is in the tip of the colander and its corners hang out over the rim. A large kettle is placed below, and the fruit is poured into the cloth. When most of the juice has dripped through, the cloth is drawn up and squeezed. A large spoon can be used to press the lump of fruit in the cloth against the inside of the colander.

It is true that to have sparkling clear jelly, the juice must not be squeezed through a bag or cloth because very small particles of pulp are pushed through the mesh of the cloth. But wild fruit juices are too precious—I squeeze out as much as I can and overlook a little cloudiness.

For jellies *with added pectin,* the sugar is added after the juice and pectin have come to a boil. When the mixture again reaches a boil, it is allowed to boil rapidly for only 1 minute before it is removed from the heat. Cooking times vary for jellies *without added pectin,* and a test is necessary to tell when they are done. As with jam, the time will usually be between 10 and 30 minutes.

Doneness can be determined by using a jelly-jam thermometer. At any elevation, jelly is considered done at 8 degrees above the boiling point of water (using Fahrenheit). By boiling a pan of water, measuring the temperature with the thermometer, and adding 8 degrees, you can determine the jelling point for your particular location. (For example, at 1,000 feet above sea level, jelly would be done at 220 degrees Fahrenheit; at higher altitudes, it would be done at lower temperatures.) For accuracy, remember to bend down and read the thermometer straight on.

Perhaps the test most often used is to dip up some of the jelly in a cool metal spoon, raise the spoon up out of the steam, and slowly turn it over on its side so that the jelly spills back into the kettle. If two or more drops run together and the remainder slides off in something of a sheet, the jelly is done.

A third way is to use the cold saucer method described for jam. When done, the sample of jelly on the plate will be soft but hold its shape and, when pushed from the side, will wrinkle slightly.

Be aware that when you use a boiling water bath, jellies that would ordinarily jell within 24 hours may take days or weeks.

Syrups

Syrups are processed in a boiling water bath like jams and jellies, except that the processing time at altitudes of up to 1,000 feet above sea level must be 10 minutes, with 1 minute processing time added for every 1,000-foot increase in elevation.

Juices

Not all juices can be preserved by canning, but elderberry-rhubarb, wild plum, and chokecherry juices may be canned in ½-pint, pint, or quart jars. Bring the juice to a boil and pour it into the hot jars, leaving ½ inch headspace. The processing time in a boiling water bath for altitudes of up to 1,000 feet above sea level is 10 minutes; add 1 minute for each additional 1,000 feet.

Freezing

Proper freezing procedures inhibit the growth of microorganisms and the action of enzymes, but do not destroy them as canning does. For this reason, frozen food must be kept at a temperature of 0 degrees Fahrenheit or lower and must be used as soon as it is taken from the freezer. Both the flavor and texture of the food will be better if the initial freezing is quick and at an even lower temperature. The authors of *Putting Food By* call this "the initial sharp freeze" and suggest a temperature of minus 20 degrees Fahrenheit.

Freezing food requires the same attention to details as canning does— start with firm, fresh fruits or vegetables, follow recommended procedures, and buy the proper supplies. Sandwich bags, aluminum foil, and waxed paper are not recommended as coverings because they allow foods to dry out, a condition called freezer burn. The same goes for cottage cheese tubs and milk cartons. Plastic garbage bags are not designed to hold things that will be eaten and may contain harmful chemicals that, over time, can penetrate food within or around them. In short, it is important to use containers designed for freezing food. Such containers include glass canning jars with two-piece screwband lids, rigid plastic containers, and freezer-grade plastic bags. Plastic bags should be discarded after use; glass and plastic containers may be reused but must be washed in soapy water, rinsed, and scalded with boiling water.

Most wild fruits may be frozen fresh and whole, with or without sugar, in tightly closed containers. Simply look them over and discard any imperfect fruits, wash and drain well, and package. Wild fruit juices may be frozen in glass or plastic containers, but leave at least 1-inch headspace to allow for expansion as the liquid freezes. Juices, such as elderberry-rhubarb, which make good coloring agents can be frozen in ice-cube trays and the cubes put into bags for easy retrieval. Jams, jellies, and syrups also freeze nicely.

Wild vegetables, however, require another step. After washing, sorting, and trimming, they must be blanched with boiling water, then cooled quickly in ice water before they can be frozen. (An exception is watercress that has been treated with water-purifying tablets and will be kept for only a few weeks.) The blanching is done quickly, but it is an important step because it decreases the number of microorganisms on the surface of the vegetables and reduces the action of the enzymes, thus preventing spoilage.

For blanching, you will need a large kettle, a wire basket like that used in deep-fat frying, and a watch or clock with a second hand. The other necessary equipment will be found in most kitchens. Usually, the amount of water needed is much greater than the amount of prepared vegetables. For most greens, figure on 4 quarts of water for 2 quarts of greens. For pokeweed or other vegetables, use 4 quarts of water for each pound of vegetables. Special directions for freezing dock and purslane are given in their sections.

To begin the freezing process, turn the temperature control to minus 20 degrees Fahrenheit or, if the freezer does not have a numerically graduated control, to the lowest setting, then prepare a large bowl or pan of ice water. Next, bring the water in the kettle to a vigorous boil. Place the vegetables in the basket and carefully lower it into the boiling water. Use a long-handled spoon to push leafy greens into the water. Begin timing. (Because the time varies with the kind of vegetable, this information is given in the individual recipes.) When the time is up, remove the basket and quickly put it into the container of ice water. When the vegetables are cold, remove the basket and let the water drain off. Ladle the vegetables into containers. Expel as much air as possible from plastic bags, but when using glass or plastic containers, leave 1 to 1½ inches headspace to allow for expansion.

Label each container with the name of the food and the date it was frozen. Use freezer tape and waterproof markers—regular tapes come loose and regular markers smear. Place the containers on the freezer shelf in a single layer until they have frozen. After that, they may be stacked. (Remember to readjust the temperature control.)

Drying
Moisture, warm temperatures, dust, and microorganisms combine to cause dried material to spoil. Dried plants such as stinging nettle and leaves used for tea must be brittle dry before being stored or they will mold.

Because certain plants dry better by one method than another, directions for drying appear in individual recipes. Microwaving is always a temptation, but it destroys the flavor of some leaves—you may want to experiment.

However plants are dried, store them in tightly covered containers away from heat and sunlight. Even when stored under the best of conditions, dried leaves lose flavor and color with time and should not be kept longer than a year.

Basic Recipes

Berry Milk

For each cup of milk, add 1 teaspoon sugar and 1 teaspoon vanilla. Stir well. If desired, add a dash of nutmeg or cinnamon. Serve very cold over berries or other fruit.

Rhubarb Juice

A common garden plant throughout the Great Plains, rhubarb is often mixed with wild fruits and juices to add needed acid. However, be aware that only the stalks (petioles) of rhubarb are edible. *Never eat rhubarb leaves.* Although not harmful to touch, rhubarb leaves are poisonous if eaten, even if they have been cooked.

To prepare the stalks, cut off and discard the leafy portion and bottom end of each stalk. Wash well, then cut the stalks into 1-inch pieces.

To extract the juice, use:
1 cup cut-up rhubarb
1 cup water

Put rhubarb and water into a saucepan but do not cover with a lid. Bring to a boil and allow to boil gently for 5 minutes. (When doubling this recipe, boil for 7 to 8 minutes.)

Pour off the juice. Makes about ½ cup juice. (Save the pulp also—sweetened with sugar or honey, it makes an excellent sauce that is particularly good served with rye bread and butter.) To keep for later use, freeze the juice in a container having a tightly fitting lid—allow 1 inch headspace.

Fresh rhubarb may be frozen and cooked later. Simply wash and trim the stalks, cut them into 1-inch pieces, and freeze in a tightly covered container. (One cup portions, frozen in freezer-weight plastic bags are handy.) To use, bring the required amount of water to a boil, then add the frozen rhubarb and stir until the chunks have separated. Proceed as with fresh rhubarb.

Pie Crusts

Easy never-fail pie crust
450 degree oven
1 1/3 cups all-purpose flour*
1/2 cup corn oil margarine (1 stick)
3 tablespoons cold water

Put the flour into a large mixing bowl. Add the margarine and cut it in with a pastry blender or two knives, then, using your hands, work the flour and margarine together until the mixture is coarsely blended. Add the water and stir until the dough holds together. Makes enough dough for two 8- or 9-inch single-crust pies or one 8- or 9-inch double-crust pie.

Divide the dough and form each half into a ball, then flatten each into a circle about 1/2 inch thick. Place each half between two sheets of waxed paper. With a rolling pin, roll out each piece of dough to make a circular shape at least 12 inches across. The pastry will be thin and delicate.

To transfer the pastry to the pie pan without tearing it, carefully peel off the top paper, but for support, lay it back onto the pastry and then turn the pastry and both papers over together. Peel away the other paper (which is now on top) and discard it. Lift the remaining paper and pastry and turn both over into the pie pan. Discard this paper also. Arrange the pastry in the pan.

For a two-crust pie, add the filling, then lift the top crust in the same manner as the bottom crust, adjusting as necessary to center it. Using a fork, press the back of the tines into the pastry all around the edge to seal the two crusts together. Trim away excess dough. Make a slash in the top crust to allow steam to escape.

If only one crust is needed, the remaining half of the pastry may be frozen as a ball, or a single crust may be rolled out and arranged in a pie pan, and frozen—either way, store it in a tightly closed container.

Single crusts are often baked before filling. To prepare, put the pastry into the pan as described above, press the edge of the pastry to the rim of the pan with the tines of a fork, then trim away the excess. Prick the bottom and sides of the crust with the fork. Bake for about 10 minutes or until the crust is lightly browned. Allow to cool before filling.

*Or use 1¼ cups whole-wheat pastry flour. Whole wheat makes a more fragile crust. If you find that the dough crumbles once it has been rolled out, simply piece it together in the pan, gently pressing it together to seal the seams. Also note that when baking a whole-wheat crust, it is especially important to watch the baking time because browning is more difficult to detect.

Cream cheese pie crust

300 degree oven

3-ounce package of cream cheese
½ cup (1 stick) margarine or butter
1 cup all-purpose flour
⅛ teaspoon salt

Remove the cream cheese and margarine or butter from the refrigerator. Unwrap both and place them in a medium-sized bowl. When softened to room temperature, stir them together, then add the flour and stir until the dough is well blended. Cover the bowl and refrigerate the dough for at least 1 hour. Makes dough for 12 individual single-crust pies.

To form the individual crusts, use a 12-hole muffin pan or two 6-hole pans. Shape the dough into 12 balls. (An easy way: divide the dough into 3 equal parts, cut each part in half, then cut each of these in half.) Place a ball of dough in each muffin hole and press it around the bottom and up the side to form a small pie shell.

Crumb crust

14 graham crackers 2½ inches square
1 tablespoon sugar
¼ cup melted margarine or butter

Grease an 8- or 9-inch pie pan with margarine or butter and set it aside.

Put the graham crackers into a large, heavy plastic bag and, using a rolling pin or pop bottle, roll them until they are finely crushed. Measure the crumbs—if less than 1½ cups, add more crumbs to make that amount.

In a medium-sized bowl, stir the crumbs, sugar, and margarine or butter until well blended, then pour the mixture into the greased pan. With your fingers, press the mixture firmly against the bottom and side of the pan to form a crust. Chill for about 1 hour before adding the filling.

Additional Sources of Information

Canning and Freezing
Ball Corporation. *Ball Blue Book: The Guide to Home Canning and Freezing.* 32d ed. Muncie, IN: Ball Corporation, 1989.
Greene, Janet, Ruth Hertzberb, and Beatrice Vaughan. *Putting Food By.* 4th ed. Lexington, MA: Stephen Greene Press, 1988.
Kerr Glass Manufacturing Corporation. *Kerr Kitchen Cookbook: Home Canning and Freezing Guide.* Los Angeles: Kerr Glass Manufacturing Corp., 1990.
U.S. Department of Agriculture Extension Service. *Complete Guide to Home Canning.* Agriculture Information Bulletin no. 539. Washington, D.C.: Government Printing Office, 1989.

Edible Wild Plants
Angier, Brandford. *Field Guide to Edible Wild Plants.* Harrisburg, PA: Stackpole Books, 1974.
Gibbons, Euell. *Stalking the Healthful Herbs.* New York: David McKay Co., 1973.
———. *Stalking the Wild Asparagus.* New York: David McKay Co., 1973.
Harrington, H. D. *Edible Native Plants of the Rocky Mountains.* Albuquerque: University of New Mexico Press, 1967.
Kindscher, Kelly. *Edible Wild Plants of the Prairie.* Lawrence: University Press of Kansas, 1987.

Peterson, Lee. *A Field Guide to Eastern Edible Wild Plants.* Boston: Houghton Mifflin Co., 1982.

Phillips, Roger. *Wild Food.* Boston: Little Brown and Co., 1986.

Tatum, Billy Jo. *Billy Jo Tatum's Wild Foods Cookbook and Plant Guide.* New York: Workman Publishing Co., 1976.

Plants of the Great Plains

Bare, Janet. *Wild Flowers and Weeds of Kansas.* Lawrence: Regents Press of Kansas, 1979.

Farrar, Jon. *Wild Flowers of Nebraska and the Great Plains.* Lincoln: *Nebraskaland Magazine,* Nebraska Game and Parks Commission, 1990.

Gilmore, Melvin. *Uses of Plants by the Indians of the Missouri River Region.* In *Thirty-third Annual Report of the Bureau of American Ethnology.* Washington, D.C.: Government Printing Office, 1919; enlarged reprint ed., Lincoln: University of Nebraska Press, 1991.

Great Plains Flora Association. *Flora of the Great Plains.* Lawrence: University Press of Kansas, 1986.

Stephens, Homer A. *Woody Plants of the North Central Plains.* Lawrence: University Press of Kansas, 1973.

Stevens, Orin Alva. *Handbook of North Dakota Plants.* Fargo: North Dakota Institute for Regional Studies, 1963.

Poisonous Plants

Lampe, Dr. Kenneth F., and Mary Ann McCann. *AMA Handbook of Poisonous and Injurious Plants.* Chicago: American Medical Association, 1985.

Hardin, James, and J. M. Arena, M.D. *Human Poisoning from Native and Cultivated Plants.* 2d ed. Durham, NC: Duke University Press, 1974.

Contributors

I am indebted to the following persons for the recipes listed opposite their names. In some instances, recipes that originally called for cultivated plants were adapted for their wild counterparts. In two cases, the same recipe was contributed by two different people.

Sarah Ellen Bailey — Poke sallet
Rowena Boykin — Rowena's dressing
Edith Burd — Potato and nettle casserole
Thelma Chard — Old-fashioned horehound lozenges
Arretta Clingingsmith Doremus — Lambs-quarters greens
Patsy Crooke — Before-frost highbush cranberry jelly
W. Earl Dyer, Jr. — Sandcherries jubilee
Sue Engle — Wild persimmon pudding
Margery Fisher — Buffaloberry instructions
A. Tyrone and Judy Harrison — Milkweed pod pickles
Bite-size popper pies
Black walnut toffee
Chokecherry fizz
Ella M. Guenther — Buffaloberry pie
Marg Heeney — Black walnut caramels

Goldie Hill — Jerusalem artichokes with tomatoes
Nam Sook Hinkley — Cooked woodnettle salad
Helen M. Huntley — Traditional gooseberry pie
Lois Jefferson — Sandcherry pie
Jean Johnson — Cattail spike information
Judy Johnson — Buffalo currant pie
Mary E. Lambrecht — Chokecherry jelly
Ruth N. Larson — Juneberry-rhubarb sauce
Florence Lueninghoener — Mother's favorite hickory cake
Rich Littleton — Scrambled eggs with wild onions
Loma McIlvaine — Butterscotch pecan pie
Cattail pollen bread

North Dakota State University
Extension Service — After-frost highbush cranberry jelly
Celia Sandoz Ostrander — Buffaloberry jelly with pectin
Virginia Priefert — Wild strawberry leather
Mary C. Reitan — Celebration cake
Mary Gayle Roberts — Not-too-sweet pecan pie
Eileen Schofield — Black walnut loaf cake
Maxine Smith — Buffalo currant pie
Doris Swanson — Chokecherry jelly
Viola Trewatha — To freeze pokeweed shoots
Sharon Vandenack — Milkweed hors d'oeuvres
Emma A. Wall — Half-hour pie
Emma Jean Warren — Wild strawberry and rhubarb jam
Carl Wolfe — Blackberry cake
Myrtle M. Young — Mulberry-zucchini pie
Mulberry filled cookies

Index

of Plants

Allium stellatum. *See* Wild onions
Allium textile. *See* Wild onions
Amelanchier alnifolia. *See* Juneberries
Amelanchier arborea. *See* Juneberries
Amelanchier humilis. *See* Juneberries
American hazelnut. *See* Hazelnuts
Amorpha canadensis. *See* Leadplant
Apocynum cannabidum (poisonous). *See*
  Dogbane
Asclepias speciosa. *See* Milkweed
Asclepias syriaca. *See* Milkweed
Asimina triloba. *See* Pawpaw
Asparagus, 36–40
Asparagus officinale. *See* Asparagus

Beaked hazelnut. *See* Hazelnuts
Bigroot prickly-pear. *See* Prickly-pear cactus
Big shagbark hickory. *See* Hickory nuts
Blackberries, 168–74
Blackcherries. *See* Chokecherries and wild
  blackcherries
Black currant. *See* Buffalo currant
Black elderberry. *See* Elderberries
Black mulberry. *See* Mulberries
Black raspberry. *See* Raspberries
Black walnuts, 248–57
Blue prairie violet. *See* Wild violets
Broad-leaved cattail. *See* Cattails
Buffaloberries, 273–76
Buffalo currant, 137–41
Bullberry. *See* Buffaloberries

Carya illinoensis. *See* Pecans
Carya laciniosa. *See* Hickory nuts
Carya ovata. *See* Hickory nuts
Catnip, 41–43
Cattails, 86–94
Chenopodium album. *See* Lambs-quarters
Chenopodium berlandieri. *See* Lambs-quarters
Chokecherries and wild blackcherries, 175–
  85
Cicuta maculata (poisonous). *See* Water
  hemlock
Clammy groundcherry. *See* Groundcherries
Common milkweed. *See* Milkweed
Corylus americana. *See* Hazelnuts

Corylus cornuta. See Hazelnuts
Curly dock. *See* Dock
Custard apple. *See* Pawpaws

Deerberry. *See* Buffaloberries
Death camas (poisonous), 118
Dandelions, 16–22
Day-lilies, 100–103
Diospyros virginiana. See Wild persimmons
Dock, 23–29
Dogbane (poisonous), 55
Downy blue violet. *See* Wild violets

Elderberries, 104–8, 223–28

Field mint. *See* Mint
Filbert. *See* Hazelnuts
Fragaria vesca. See Wild strawberries
Fragaria virginiana. See Wild strawberries

Gooseberries. *See* Missouri Gooseberries
Grapes. *See* Wild grapes
Groundcherries, 229–36

Hazelnuts, 237–41
Helianthus tuberosa. See Jerusalem artichoke
Hemerocallis fulva. See Day-lilies
Hickory nuts, 242–47
Highbush blackberry. *See* Blackberries
Highbush cranberries, 219–22
Horehound, 109–12

Inkberry. *See* Pokeweed

Jerusalem artichoke, 282–87
Juglans nigra. See Black walnuts
Juneberries, 150–56

Lambs-quarters, 49–52
Laportea canadensis. See Wood nettles
Leadplant, 190–93
Low juneberry. *See* Juneberries

Marrubium vulgare. See Horehound
Matricaria matricarioides. See Pineapple-weed

May-apple, 186–89
Meadow violet. *See* Wild violets
Mentha arvensis. See Mint
Mentha piperita. See Mint
Mentha spicata. See Mint
Milkweed, 53–57, 113–16, 157–60
Mint, 95–99
Missouri gooseberries, 75–80
Morus alba. See Mulberries
Morus rubra. See Mulberries
Mulberries, 121–32

Narrow-leaved cattail. *See* Cattails
Nasturtium officinale. See Watercress
Nepeta cateria. See Catnip
Nettles. *See* Stinging nettles; Wood nettles

Onions. *See* Wild onions
Opuntia macrorhiza. See Prickly-pear cactus
Oxalis stricta. See Yellow wood sorrel

Patience dock. *See* Dock
Pawpaws, 269–72
Pecans, 258–68
Peppermint. *See* Mint
Persimmon. *See* Wild persimmons
Physalis heterophylla. See Groundcherries
Phytolacca americana. See Pokeweed
Pigweed. *See* Lambs-quarters
Pineapple-weed, 60–62
Pink wild onion. *See* Wild onions
Pitseed goosefoot. *See* Lambs-quarters
Plains prickly-pear. *See* Prickly-pear cactus
Plum. *See* Wild plums
Podophyllum peltatum. See May-apple
Pokeberry. *See* Pokeweed
Pokeweed, 44–48
Poison sumac (poisonous), 216–17
Portulaca oleracea. See Purslane
Prairie onion. *See* Wild onions
Prickly-pear cactus, 81–85, 211–14
Prunus americana. See Wild plums
Prunus pumila var. *besseyi. See* Sandcherries
Prunus serotina. See Chokecherries and wild
    blackcherries
Prunus virginiana. See Chokecherries and

wild blackcherries
Purslane, 133–36
Pusley. *See* Purslane

Raspberries, 161–68
Red mulberry. *See* Mulberries
Red raspberry. *See* Raspberries
Red-seeded dandelion. *See* Dandelions
Rhus glabra. See Smooth sumac
Ribes missouriense. See Missouri gooseberries
Ribes odoratum. See Buffalo currant
Riverbank grape. *See* Wild grapes
Rosa species. *See* Wild roses
Rose. *See* Wild roses
Rubus allegheniensis. See Blackberries
Rubus ideaus. See Raspberries
Rubus occidentalis. See Raspberries
Rubus ostryifolius. See Blackberries
Rubus pensilvanicus. See Blackberries
Rumcherry. *See* Chokecherries and wild blackcherries
Rumex crispus. See Dock
Rumex patientia. See Dock

Sambucus canadensis. See Elderberries
Sandcherries, 142–49
Sarvisberry. *See* Juneberries
Saskatoonberry. *See* Juneberries
Serviceberry. *See* Juneberries
Shagbark hickory. *See* Hickory nuts
Sheep shower. *See* Yellow wood sorrel
Shellbark hickory. *See* Hickory nuts
Shepherdia argentea. See Buffaloberries
Showy milkweed. *See* Milkweed
Shumac. *See* Smooth sumac
Smooth sumac, 215–18
Sour dock. *See* Dock
Spinach dock. *See* Dock
Spearmint. *See* Mint
Strawberry. *See* Wild strawberries
Stinging nettles, 6–12
Sumac. *See* Smooth sumac

Sumach. *See* Smooth sumac

Taraxacum officinale. See Dandelions
Taraxacum laevigatum. See Dandelions
Textile onion. *See* Wild onions
Toxicodendron vernix (poisonous). *See* Poison sumac
Tree juneberry. *See* Juneberries
Typha angustifolia. See Cattails
Typha domingensis. See Cattails
Typha latifolia. See Cattails

Urtica dioica. See Stinging nettles

Viburnum opulus. See Highbush cranberries
Viola pratincola. See Wild violets
Viola sororia. See Wild violets
Vitis riparia. See Wild grapes

Watercress, 2–5
Water hemlock (poisonous), 105–6, 283–84
White mulberry. *See* Mulberries
White wild onion. *See* Wild onions
Wild blackcherries. *See* Chokecherries and wild blackcherries
Wild chamomile. *See* Pineapple-weed
Wild grapes, 201–6
Wild onions, 117–20
Wild persimmons, 277–81
Wild plums, 194–200
Wild roses, 63–67, 207–10
Wild strawberries, 68–74
Wild violets, 30–35
Woodland strawberry. *See* Wild strawberries
Wood nettles, 13–15
Wood sorrel. *See* Yellow wood sorrel

Yellow dock. *See* Dock
Yellow wood sorrel, 58–59

Zigadenus species (poisonous). *See* Death camas

Index

of Recipes by Plant

Asparagus
  cooked asparagus, 38–39
  cream of asparagus soup, 39–40
  stir-fried asparagus slices, 39

Blackberries
  blackberry cake, 173–74
  blackberry dumplings, 174
  blackberry jam without pectin, 170
  blackberry jam with pectin, 172
  blackberry jelly without pectin, 170–71
  blackberry jelly with pectin, 171
  blackberry pie, 172–73
  chunky blackberry syrup, 172
  to extract blackberry juice, 170
  to freeze blackberries, 170
Black walnuts
  black walnut and yogurt dressing, 257
  black walnut caramels, 251–52
  black walnut fudge, 252–53
  black walnut loaf cake, 256–57
  black walnut toffee, 253–54
  black walnut wafers, 256
  Mom's black walnut bread pudding, 254
  threshermen's cookies, 255–56
Buffaloberries
  buffaloberry jelly without pectin, 275–76
  buffaloberry jelly with pectin, 276
  buffaloberry pie, 276
  to dry buffaloberries, 275
  to extract buffaloberry juice, 275
Buffalo currants
  buffalo currant jam, 140
  buffalo currant jelly, 139
  buffalo currant pie, 140–41
  buffalo currant syrup, 139
  chunky currant topping, 139–40
  to extract currant juice, 139

Catnip
  catnip tea, 43
  to dry catnip, 43
Cattails
  cattail pollen bread, 93–94
  cattail pollen pancakes, 90–91
  cattail pollen pound cake, 92–93

cattail root starch, 88
cattail shoot buds, 89
cattail shoots, 89
cattail spike casserole, 89–90
gold nugget cream puffs, 91–92
green cattail spikes, 89
sunshine muffins, 91
Chokecherries and wild blackcherries
chocolate-covered chokecherry jells, 184–85
chokecherry fizz, 180
chokecherry-glazed apples, 185
chokecherry gumdrops, 183–84
chokecherry jam without pectin, 181
chokecherry jam with pectin, 181
chokecherry jelly, 179
chokecherry syrup, 180
chokecherry–wild plum jam, 182
chokecherry–wild plum jelly, 179–80
chokecherry-yogurt dessert, 182
half-hour pie, 182–83
to can chokecherry juice, 179
to extract chokecherry juice, 178–79
to freeze chokecherries, 178
to make chokecherry puree, 180–81

Dandelions
dandelion brew, 21–22
dandelion greens with new potatoes, 20
dandelion quiche, 20–21
scrambled eggs with dandelion, 20
traditional dandelion greens, 19
Day-lilies
stuffed day-lily flower hors d'oeuvres, 102–3
to cook day-lily buds, 102
Dock
crockpot pork with dock, 26–27
dock greens, 25
dock roll-ups, 27–28
roast pork with dock dressing, 28–29
to freeze dock greens, 26

Elderberry flowers (elderblow)
elderblow pancakes, 107–8
elderblow tea, 107

to dry elderblow, 106–7
Elderberry fruit
elderberry-grape jelly, 205–6
elderberry pie, 227–28
elderberry-plum jelly, 226
elderberry-rhubarb juice, 225
elderberry syrup, 226
purple passion pie, 226–27
to can elderberry-rhubarb juice, 225
to extract elderberry juice, 225
to freeze elderberry-rhubarb juice, 225–26
wild grape and elderberry jelly without pectin, 205
wild grape and elderberry jelly with pectin, 205–6

Groundcherries
bite-size popper pies, 235–36
groundcherry drizzle, 233
groundcherry jam, 233–34
groundcherry and lettuce salad with rosy cactus dressing, 232–33
groundcherry marmalade, 234
groundcherry pie, 235
groundcherry sauce, 233
groundcherry soup, 232

Hazelnuts
hazelnut cake, 241
spiced chicken with hazelnuts, 239–41
to toast hazelnuts, 239
Hickory nuts
hickory-apple cake, 247
hickory-carrot cake, 246–47
Mother's favorite hickory cake, 244–45
Highbush cranberries
after-frost highbush cranberry jelly, 222
before-frost highbush cranberry jelly, 222
highbush cranberry sauce, 221
to extract highbush cranberry juice, 221–22
Horehound
old-fashioned horehound lozenges, 111–12

Jerusalem artichokes
boiled Jerusalem artichokes, 285

Jerusalem artichokes (*cont.*)
  braised Jerusalem artichokes, 285
  Jerusalem artichoke chips, 286
  Jerusalem artichoke patties or puffs, 286
  Jerusalem artichoke pickles, 287
  Jerusalem artichokes with tomatoes, 287
Juneberries
  frosted juneberry puffs, 155–56
  juneberry jam, 154
  juneberry pie, 153–54
  juneberry-rhubarb sauce, 152–53
  juneberry topping, 153
  to dry juneberries, 154–55

Lambs-quarters
  creamed lambs-quarters with mushrooms,
    52
  lambs-quarters greens, 51–52
  to freeze lambs-quarters greens, 52
Leadplant
  leadplant tea, 192–93
  to dry leadplant leaflets, 192

May-apple
  may-apple jam, 188–89
  may-apple jelly, 188
  to extract may-apple juice, 187–88
Milkweed buds and flowers
  milkweed flower fritters, 115–16
  to cook milkweed flower buds, 114
Milkweed pods
  milkweed hors d'oeuvres, 159
  milkweed pod pickles, 159–60
  stuffed milkweed pod casserole, 158
  to cook milkweed pods, 158
Milkweed shoots
  hearty milkweed sandwich, 56–57
  to cook milkweed shoots, 56
Mint
  fresh mint cooler, 98
  hot mint tea, 98
  mint and apple jelly, 99
  mint jelly, 98–99
  to dry mint, 97
Missouri gooseberries
  gooseberry custard pie, 77–78

ripe gooseberry jam, 79–80
ripe gooseberry jelly, 79
to freeze gooseberries, 77
traditional gooseberry pie, 78
underripe gooseberry jam, 79–80
underripe gooseberry jelly, 78–79
Mulberries
  chilled mulberry-lemon dessert, 128
  chunky mulberry syrup, 127
  Mom's mulberry-zucchini pie, 130
  mulberry-filled cookies, 130–32
  mulberry gelatin, 127–28
  mulberry jam, 126
  mulberry jelly, 125
  mulberry pie, 129
  mulberry-rhubarb jelly, 126
  mulberry-rhubarb pie, 129–30
  mulberry-rhubarb syrup, 126–27
  to extract mulberry juice, 125
  to freeze mulberries, 125

Pawpaws
  pawpaw bread, 271
Pecans
  butterscotch pie with pecans, 263–64
  celebration cake, 265–68
  coleslaw with toasted pecans and dates,
    261
  crispy oatmeal-pecan cookies, 261–62
  individual pecan pies, 262–63
  not-too-sweet pecan pie, 262
  rice medley with toasted pecans, 260–61
  to toast pecan meats, 260
Pineapple-weed
  pineapple-weed tea, 62
  to dry pineapple-weed, 62
Pokeweed
  poke sallet, 47–48
  to can pokeweed shoots, 48
  to freeze pokeweed shoots, 48
Prickly-pear cactus fruit
  prickly-pear jelly, 213
  prickly-pear syrup, 214
  rosy cactus dressing, 214, 232–33
  to extract juice from prickly-pear fruit, 213
Prickly-pear cactus pads

cactus tartar sauce, 85
pickled cactus relish, 84–85
to prepare cactus pads, 84
Purslane
  purslane and oxtail soup, 135–36
  to freeze purslane, 135

Raspberries
  basic raspberry puree, 163–64
  black raspberry jelly, 165
  raspberry-honey topping, 166
  raspberry ice, 164
  raspberry jam, 166
  raspberry leaf tea, 167
  raspberry sherbet, 164
  raspberry syrup, 165
  red raspberry jelly, 165
  to dry raspberry leaves, 167
  to extract raspberry juice, 164–65
  to freeze raspberries, 164

Sandcherries
  Ainsworth sandcherry pie, 147–48
  sandcherries jubilee, 148–49
  sandcherry jam, 146
  sandcherry jelly, 145–46
  sandcherry topping, 146–47
  sandcherry–wild plum jelly, 146
  to extract sandcherry juice, 145
  to freeze sandcherries, 145
  traditional sandcherry pie, 147
Smooth sumac
  sumacade, 218
Stinging nettles
  hot nettle greens, 11–12
  nettle noodles, 10–11
  potato and nettle casserole, 12
  to dry stinging nettles, 9–10
  to freeze nettle greens, 12
  to make nettle powder, 10

Watercress
  cream of watercress soup, 3–4
  Rowena's salad dressing, 5
  spring greens with leftover potatoes, 4
  spring medley salad, 4

to freeze watercress, 3
watercress sandwiches, 4
watercress-tomato soup, 4
Wild grapes
  wild grape and elderberry jelly without
    pectin, 205
  wild grape and elderberry jelly with pectin,
    205–6
  wild grape jam, 206
  wild grape jelly without pectin, 204
  wild grape jelly with pectin, 204
  to extract wild grape juice, 204
Wild onions
  scrambled eggs with wild onions and
    cheese, 119–20
Wild persimmons
  to extract persimmon pulp, 279
  wild persimmon bars, 280–81
  wild persimmon pudding, 279–80
  wild persimmon pudding without egg,
    280
Wild plums
  chokecherry–wild plum jam, 182
  chokecherry–wild plum jelly, 179–80
  spiced wild plum sauce, 199
  to can wild plum juice, 198
  to extract wild plum juice and pulp, 197
  wild plum combination jelly, 198–99
  wild plum jam, 198
  wild plum jelly, 198
  wild plum upside-down cake, 199–200
Wild roses
  rose petal syrup, 66–67
Wild rose hips
  cream of rose hip soup, 209
  fresh rose hip puree, 209
  rose hip dip, 210
  rose hip honey, 209–10
  rose hip tea, 208–9
  to dry rose hips, 208
Wild strawberries
  wild strawberry and rhubarb jam, 71
  wild strawberry jam, 70–71
  wild strawberry leaf tea, 70
  wild strawberry leather, 74
  wild strawberry shortcake, 73–74

Wild strawberries (*cont.*)
  wild strawberry sunshine topping, 72–73
  wild strawberry syrup, 71–72
Wild violets
  chicken dumplings with wild violets, 34–35
  crystallized violet flowers, 33
  to make violet liquid, 32
  wild violet and lettuce salad with cream
    dressing, 33–34
  wild violet and noodle soup, 35
  wild violet jelly, 33
  wild violet syrup, 32
Wood nettle
  cooked wood nettle salad, 15

Yellow wood sorrel, 58–59
  nibble or garnish, 59

Index

of Recipes by
Food Category

Breads and pancakes
  cattail pollen bread, 93–94
  cattail pollen pancakes, 90–91
  elderblow pancakes, 107–8
  frosted juneberry puffs, 115–16
  gold nugget cream puffs, 91–92
  milkweed flower fritters, 114–15
  pawpaw bread, 271–72
  sunshine muffins, 91

Cakes
  blackberry cake, 173–74
  black walnut loaf cake, 256–57
  cattail pollen pound cake, 92–93
  celebration cake, 265–68
  hazelnut cake, 241
  hickory-apple cake, 247
  hickory-carrot cake, 246
  Mother's favorite hickory cake, 244
  wild plum upside-down cake, 199–200
Candies
  black walnut caramels, 251–52
  black walnut fudge, 252–53
  black walnut toffee, 253–54
  chocolate-covered chokecherry jells, 184–85
  chokecherry gumdrops, 183–84
  old-fashioned horehound lozenges, 111–12
Canning, 289–96
  chokecherry juice, 179
  elderberry-rhubarb juice, 225
  pokeweed shoots, 48
  wild plum juice, 198
Cookies
  bite-size popper pies, 235–36
  black walnut wafers, 256
  crispy oatmeal-pecan cookies, 261
  mulberry-filled cookies, 130–32
  threshermen's cookies, 255–56
  wild persimmon bars, 280–81

Desserts
  berry milk, 299
  blackberry dumplings, 174
  chilled mulberry-lemon dessert, 128–29
  chokecherry-glazed apples, 185

Desserts (*cont.*)
chokecherry-yogurt dessert, 182
gold nugget cream puffs (cream or pudding filling), 91–92
mulberry gelatin, 127
persimmon pudding, 279–80
persimmon pudding without egg, 280
raspberry ice, 164
raspberry sherbet, 164
wild strawberry shortcake, 73–74
Dressings, sauces, and dips
black walnut and yogurt dressing, 257
cactus tartar sauce, 85
groundcherry sauce, 233
highbush cranberry sauce, 221
juneberry-rhubarb sauce, 152–53
rose hip dip, 210
rosy cactus dressing, 214
Rowena's salad dressing, 5
spiced wild plum sauce, 199
Drying, 289–90, 297–98
buffaloberries, 275
catnip, 43
elderblow, 106–7
juneberries, 154–55
leadplant leaflets, 192
mint, 97
nettles, 9
pineapple-weed, 62
raspberry leaves, 167
rose hips, 207

Entrees
cattail spike casserole, 89–90
chicken dumplings with wild violets, 34
creamed lambs-quarters with mushrooms, 52
crockpot pork and dock, 26–27
dandelion quiche, 20–21
dandelion scrambled eggs, 20
dock roll-ups, 27–28
gold nugget cream puffs (meat or vegetable filling), 91–92
nettle noodles, 10–11
potato and nettle casserole, 12
rice medley with toasted pecans, 260–61

roast pork and dock dressing, 28–29
scrambled eggs with wild onions and cheese, 119
spiced chicken with hazelnuts, 239–41
stuffed milkweed pod casserole, 158

Freezing, 289–90, 296–97
blackberries, 170
chokecherries, 178
dock, 26
elderberry-rhubarb juice, 225–26
lambs-quarters, 52
mulberries, 125
pokeweed, 48
purslane, 135
raspberries, 164
sandcherries, 145
stinging nettles, 12
watercress, 2

Garnishes
crystallized wild violet flowers, 33
yellow wood sorrel, 59–60

Hors d'oeuvres
Jerusalem artichoke chips, 286
milkweed hors d'oeuvres, 159
stuffed day-lily hors d'oeuvres, 102

Jam and marmalade
blackberry jam without pectin, 171
blackberry jam with pectin, 172
buffalo currant jam, 140
chokecherry jam without pectin, 181
chokecherry jam with pectin, 181
chokecherry–wild plum, 182
groundcherry jam, 233–34
groundcherry marmalade, 234
juneberry jam, 154
may-apple jam, 188–89
mulberry jam, 126
raspberry jam, 166
ripe gooseberry jam, 80
sandcherry jam, 146
underripe gooseberry jam, 80
wild grape jam, 233–34

wild plum jam, 198
wild strawberry jam, 70–71
wild strawberry and rhubarb jam, 71–72
Jelly
    after-frost highbush cranberry jelly, 222
    before-frost highbush cranberry jelly, 222
    blackberry jelly without pectin, 170–71
    blackberry jelly with pectin, 171
    black raspberry jelly, 165
    buffaloberry jelly without pectin, 275–76
    buffaloberry jelly with pectin, 276
    buffalo currant jelly, 139
    chokecherry jelly, 179
    chokecherry–wild plum jelly, 179–80
    elderberry-plum jelly, 226
    may-apple jelly, 188
    mulberry jelly, 125–26
    mulberry-rhubarb jelly, 126
    prickly-pear jelly, 213
    red raspberry jelly, 165
    ripe gooseberry jelly, 79–80
    sandcherry jelly, 145–46
    sandcherry–wild plum jelly, 146
    underripe gooseberry jelly, 78–79
    wild grape and elderberry jelly without
        pectin, 205
    wild grape and elderberry jelly with pectin,
        205–6
    wild grape jelly without pectin, 204
    wild grape jelly with pectin, 204
    wild plum combination jelly, 188–89
    wild plum jelly, 188
    wild violet jelly, 33
Juice
    buffaloberry, 275
    buffalo currant, 139
    chokecherry, 179
    elderberry, 225
    elderberry-rhubarb, 225
    highbush cranberry, 221–22
    may-apple, 187–88
    mulberry, 139
    prickly-pear, 213
    raspberry, 164–65
    rhubarb, 299–300
    wild grape, 204

wild plum, 197
Pickles and relishes
    Jerusalem artichoke pickles, 287
    milkweed pod pickles, 159–60
    pickled cactus relish, 84–85
Pies
    Ainsworth sandcherry pie, 147–48
    blackberry pie, 172–73
    buffaloberry pie, 276
    buffalo currant pie, 140–41
    butterscotch pie with pecans, 263–64
    cream cheese crust, 301
    crumb crust, 301
    easy, never-fail crust, 300–301
    elderberry pie, 227
    gooseberry custard pie, 77–78
    groundcherry pie, 235
    individual pecan pies, 262–63
    juneberry pie, 153–54
    Mom's mulberry-zucchini pie, 130
    mulberry pie, 129
    mulberry-rhubarb pie, 129–30
    not-too-sweet pecan pie, 262
    purple passion pie, 226–27
    traditional gooseberry pie, 78
Purees and pulp
    basic raspberry puree, 163–64
    chokecherry puree, 180–81
    persimmon pulp, 279
    rose hip puree, 209
    wild plum pulp, 197

Salads
    coleslaw with toasted pecans and dates,
        261
    cooked wood nettle salad, 15
    groundcherry-lettuce salad with rosy
        cactus dressing, 232
    spring medley salad, 4
    wild violet and lettuce salad with cream
        dressing, 33–34
Sandwiches
    hearty milkweed, 56–57
    watercress, 4
Soups
    cream of asparagus, 39–40

Soups (*cont.*)
  cream of rose hip, 209
  cream of watercress, 3
  groundcherry, 232
  purslane and oxtail, 135–36
  watercress-tomato, 4
  wild violet and noodle, 35
Syrups and toppings
  buffalo currant syrup, 139
  chokecherry syrup, 180
  chunky blackberry syrup, 172
  chunky currant topping, 139–40
  chunky mulberry syrup, 127
  groundcherry drizzle, 233
  juneberry topping, 153
  mulberry-rhubarb syrup, 126–27
  prickly-pear syrup, 214
  raspberry-honey topping, 166
  raspberry syrup, 165
  rose hip honey, 209–10
  sandcherry topping, 146–47
  wild rose petal syrup, 66–67
  wild strawberry sunshine topping, 72–73
  wild strawberry syrup, 71–72
  wild violet syrup, 32

Teas and other drinks
  catnip tea, 43
  chokecherry fizz, 180
  dandelion brew, 21–22
  elderblow tea, 107

  fresh mint cooler, 98
  hot mint tea, 98
  leadplant tea, 192–93
  pineapple-weed tea, 62
  raspberry leaf tea, 167
  rose hip tea, 207
  sumacade, 218
  wild strawberry leaf tea, 70

Vegetables
  boiled Jerusalem artichokes, 285
  braised Jerusalem artichokes, 285
  cattail shoot buds, 89
  cattail shoots, 89
  cattail spikes, 89
  cooked asparagus, 38–39
  dandelion greens and new potatoes, 20
  day-lily buds, 102
  dock greens, 25–26
  hot nettle greens, 11–12
  Jerusalem artichokes with tomatoes, 287
  lambs-quarters greens, 51
  milkweed buds, 114
  milkweed pods, 158
  milkweed shoots, 56
  poke sallet, 47
  purslane, 135
  spring greens with leftover potatoes, 4
  stir-fried asparagus slices, 39
  traditional dandelion greens, 19
  wild violet greens, 31